Praise for *Dying for an iPhone*

"*Dying for an iPhone* is far and away the most comprehensive account of the lives and working conditions of the people who produce what is perhaps the iconic commodity of the twenty-first century—the iPhone. But it is much more than that. We also see how Apple and Foxconn, working within a neoliberal trade regime promoted by the US, Taiwanese, and Chinese governments alike, transcended national boundaries to develop a brutally exploitative system of labor discipline. It is an incisive account of the social dislocation, but also the resistance, wrought when capitalists of many nations unite against workers. Global in outlook while still presenting fine-grained and highly engaging accounts of workers' lived experiences, this book is a shining example of public scholarship."

—Eli Friedman, coeditor of *China on Strike*

"Critical, accessible, and rigorously researched, this book offers the most comprehensive analysis of Foxconn, the world's largest electronics factory: its bleak landscape, dire consequences, and inspiring efforts to change it for the better."

—Jack Linchuan Qiu, author of *Goodbye iSlave: A Manifesto for Digital Abolition*

"Holding a sleek new iPhone in our hands it is difficult to imagine the brutal work lives of the people who assemble our smartphones. In *Dying for an iPhone* Jenny Chan, Mark Selden, and Pun Ngai make this reality visible. Drawing on in-depth field work and a deep knowledge of the global electronics industry, the authors demonstrate not only the steep human cost of our love affair with smartphones, but also the fierce struggles by Chinese workers to improve their working conditions."

—Nicole Aschoff, author of *The Smartphone Society: Technology, Power, and Resistance in the New Gilded Age*

T0037799

"*Dying for an iPhone* takes readers deep inside the dark Satanic mills of Foxconn's industrial empire. Drawing on the words of the workers themselves, the book offers an invaluable portrait of the Chinese working class as it pumps blood (sometimes literally) into the productive heart of world capitalism."
—Ben Tarnoff, cofounder of *Logic Magazine*

"A deep dive into exploitation and labor struggle in the world of high-tech electronics manufacturing in China during the past decade. *Dying for an iPhone* is an exposé of the human suffering behind the brands. Everyone should read this."
—Hsiao-Hung Pai, Taiwanese journalist

"*Dying for an iPhone* is an absolutely necessary read for anyone seeking to understand the realities of modern-day capitalism. Contrary to the mythology of Silicon Valley, this carefully researched book explains why companies like Apple owe their success more to exploitation than to innovation."
—Wendy Liu, author of *Abolish Silicon Valley:*
How to Liberate Technology from Capitalism

"A sobering investigation into the human, social, and environmental costs of producing the devices we have come to rely on, a process in which both corporations and we, the consumers, are complicit."
—Nick Holdstock, author of *Chasing the Chinese Dream*

"When reading chapters describing the assembly line experience of workers, and the scientific management system, I could only compare it to the chapter in Marx's *Capital*, when we are taken into the hidden abode of production. *Dying for an iPhone* is truly a great achievement to present such incisive description and analysis in a highly readable and accessible form."
—Jeffery Hermanson, International
Union Educational League

Dying for
an
iPhone

APPLE, FOXCONN, AND THE
LIVES OF CHINA'S WORKERS

Jenny Chan, Mark Selden, and Pun Ngai

Haymarket Books
Chicago, Illinois

© 2020 Jenny Chan, Mark Selden, and Pun Ngai

Published in 2020 by
Haymarket Books
P.O. Box 180165
Chicago, IL 60618
773-583-7884
www.haymarketbooks.org
info@haymarketbooks.org

ISBN: 978-1-64259-124-8

Distributed to the trade in the US through Consortium Book Sales and
Distribution (www.cbsd.com) and internationally through Ingram Publisher Services International (www.ingramcontent.com).

This book was published with the generous support of Lannan Foundation
and Wallace Action Fund.

Special discounts are available for bulk purchases by organizations and
institutions. Please call 773-583-7884 or email info@haymarketbooks.
org for more information.

Cover design by David Gee.

Printed in the United Kingdom.

Library of Congress Cataloging-in-Publication data is available.

10 9 8 7 6 5 4 3 2 1

Contents

For workers in China and globally

List of Tables and Figures

Tables

Figures

Preface

To die is the only way to testify that we ever lived.
Perhaps for the Foxconn employees and employees like
us, the use of death is to testify that we were ever alive
at all, and that while we lived, we had only despair.

—A Chinese worker's blog, May 27, 2010[1]

It was in January 2010 that we first heard about the suicides of workers at the Foxconn electronics plant in the Chinese city of Shenzhen, adjacent to Hong Kong. In subsequent months, we closely followed reports—dubbed the "suicide express" in the media. After "the 9th Foxconn jumper" committed suicide on May 11, several university researchers and students, including the authors, discussed what might be done to prevent more suicides. One week later, we joined others to issue a public statement calling on Foxconn, the Chinese government, and the All-China Federation of Trade Unions to act decisively to end the "chain of suicides." The statement read:

> From the moment the new generation of rural migrant workers step beyond the doors of their houses, they never think of going back to farming like their parents. The moment they see there is little possibility of building a home in the city through hard work, the very meaning of their work collapses. The path ahead is blocked, and the road to retreat is closed. Trapped in this situation, the workers face a serious identity crisis and this magnifies psychological and emotional problems. Digging into this deeper level of societal and structural conditions, we come

closer to understanding the "no way back" mentality of these Foxconn employees.[2]

By December 2010, eighteen workers were known to have attempted suicide at Foxconn facilities. Fourteen were dead. Four survived with crippling injuries. They ranged in age from seventeen to twenty-five— all were rural migrants in the prime of youth, emblematic of the new Chinese working class.[3]

The large banner on the ground reads, "What is the price of flesh and blood?" The banner on the top right says, "Dreams shattered." Demonstrators in Taipei placed flowers to commemorate the Foxconn worker victims on May 28, 2010.

Foxconn's parent company, the Hon Hai Precision Industry Company, was established by Terry Gou in Taiwan in February 1974. The trade name Foxconn alludes to the corporation's claim to produce connectors at fox-like speed. Within four decades, Foxconn would evolve from a small processing factory to become the world leader in high-end electronics manufacturing with plants extending throughout China and, subsequently, throughout the world. Foxconn has more than two hundred subsidiaries and branch offices in Asia, the Americas, and Europe.

As Foxconn strives to dominate global electronics manufacturing and advanced technology, its aspirations align with China's goal to become the world's economic and technological superpower. Foxconn has achieved stunning growth through a combination of shrewd business practices, mergers and acquisitions, patent acquisition, and astute cultivation of relations with the Chinese government.

The company's claims go beyond its technology: "Hon Hai / Foxconn's commitment to continual education, investing in its people long term and localization globally not only leads to the deep collaborating relationships with leading institutions of higher learning, but also helps to make Hon Hai / Foxconn the largest exporter in Greater China and the second-largest exporter in the Czech Republic."[4] Foxconn, with nearly one million workers—the vast majority of them in mainland China—is the world's largest industrial employer.[5] But what precisely are Foxconn's priorities, and is a "commitment to continual education, investing in its people long term" among them?

China remains the heart of Foxconn's global corporate empire and its profitability. In 2018, Foxconn accounted for 4.1 percent of China's total imports and exports,[6] with revenues topping US$175 billion—or, in the currency of the New Taiwan dollar, TWD 5.2 trillion.[7] The company's claims are grandiose: "Foxconn is a global industry-leading manufacturer of Computer, Communications and Consumer Electronics (3C) components." Focusing on "Cloud Computing, Mobile Devices, Internet of Things, Big Data, Artificial Intelligence, Smart Networks, Robotics/Automation, Foxconn has built sophisticated capabilities around key Industrial Internet technologies."[8] Indeed, Foxconn has striven to move from low value-added processing and manufacturing to more profitable businesses and services, harnessing the power of intellectual property and technical invention. Where others have focused on these issues, we repeatedly return to gauging the corporation's rise as it affects its one million employees, the great majority of them rural migrant workers.

Apple, Foxconn, and Chinese Workers

Foxconn's largest customer by far is Apple. But its clients are a Who's Who of global electronics corporations, among them Alphabet (formerly Google), Amazon, BlackBerry, Cisco, Dell, Fujitsu, GE, HP, IBM, Intel, LG, Microsoft, Nintendo, Panasonic, Philips, Samsung, Sony, and Toshiba, as well as such leading Chinese firms as Lenovo, Huawei, ZTE, and Xiaomi. Foxconn assembles iPhones, iPads, iPods, Macs, TVs, Xboxes, PlayStations, Wii U's, Kindles, printers, and myriad digital devices. While primarily contracting for global electronics firms, Foxconn also produces a variety of products under its own name. The company looks to a future in which its major growth areas center on Foxconn brands operating at cutting-edge technological frontiers led by robotics and artificial intelligence. It is a future with profound implications for its labor force, the world economy, and geopolitics.

Apple and Foxconn are independent companies, but they are inextricably linked in product development, engineering research, manufacturing processes, logistics, sales, and after-sales services. By the end of the 1990s, Apple had exported all of its US-based manufacturing jobs and some of its research facilities overseas.[9] Apple only retained a small number of workers and staff at its Macintosh computer factory in Ireland. This outsourcing means that Apple's success is inseparable from the contributions of its international suppliers and their workers, above all Foxconn and its Chinese employees.

The Apple mystique has centered on its rapid rise to a hegemonic position in the design and marketing of a range of electronics products led in recent years by the iPhone, and the aura surrounding Steve Jobs (1955–2011), its cofounder and for decades its dominant presence. Tim Cook, who succeeded the late Steve Jobs as Apple CEO in August 2011, is hailed by journalist Leander Kahney as "the genius who took Apple to the next level."[10] Overshadowed in that American success story are the lives and welfare of the mainly Chinese workers who produce the products of the global megabrand that so many long to possess, and the relationship between Apple and Foxconn that sets the parameters of factory life.

Dying for an iPhone

Dying for an iPhone has a double meaning. A new generation of workers is struggling to meet corporate requirements for speed and precision in producing iPhones and other high-tech products precisely at a time when consumers around the globe are queuing up to buy the newest models. Apple's success is intimately bound up with the production of quality products at high speed. Given its control of the commanding heights of hardware, software, and design, Apple has remained in the driver's seat in setting the terms and conditions for Foxconn and, in turn, for its workers. As of 2010, Foxconn was the exclusive final manufacturer not only of iPhones for Apple, but also a major contractor of a wide array of electronics products for many other technology giants.

The suicide-prevention nets strung around Foxconn's China-based facilities and the barred dormitory windows in late May 2010—appearing at the peak of the suicide clusters and remaining ever since—serve to refresh collective memories about the despair that drove young workers to kill themselves, the companies' responsibilities for this tragedy, and collective efforts by workers and their supporters to create a more humane workplace.

A Collective Investigation in China

In summer 2010, we collaborated with researchers from China, Taiwan, and Hong Kong to conduct undercover research at Foxconn's major manufacturing sites in nine Chinese cities, mainly in southern, eastern, and northern regions: Shenzhen, Shanghai, Kunshan, Hangzhou, Nanjing, Tianjin, Langfang, Taiyuan, and Wuhan. Our goal was not just to look into the hidden abode of

Foxconn production on the ground, but also to assess the extent to which the Chinese state and global tech corporations fulfilled their responsibilities to protect workers in the context of transnational production.

In spring 2011, we returned to Foxconn's manufacturing bases in Shenzhen, where half a million employees were toiling day and night to make our smartphones, tablets, and many other electronics products. We also visited two emerging "Apple cities"—Zhengzhou in Henan province and Chengdu in Sichuan province—where Foxconn's new megafactories assembled iPhones and iPads, respectively, at wages well below those in the coastal areas that were the sites of older plants. Following capital movements and through multisited research, we witnessed Foxconn's rapid expansion across provinces with strong support by local governments, thereby creating a 24-hour, high-speed production network with more than forty industrial parks in China alone.

In December 2013, we wrote to Terry Gou, Foxconn founder and CEO, and Tim Cook, the CEO of Apple, describing the conditions our research had uncovered and expressing concerns about the well-being of Foxconn workers. In addition, we contacted the Foxconn Global Social and Environmental Responsibility Committee, the Apple Supplier Responsibility Program, and the Fair Labor Association (Apple was a member from January 2012 to October 2016). Our purpose was to gain corporate perspectives on issues that our research had uncovered: low wages and benefits, compulsory overtime, lack of fundamental health and safety precautions, abusive treatment of teenage student interns, and managerial repression of workers' attempts to press demands for securing rights guaranteed by employment contracts and national labor laws. While Apple and Foxconn paid close attention to the public relations challenges posed by strikes, fires and explosions, and worker suicides, our effort to engage the corporations in discussion of labor responsibility produced only corporate rationalizations and platitudes.[11]

By contrast, workers would be far more responsive to our attempts to understand their lives. Our multiyear fieldwork, which continued to the outbreak of new coronavirus in the end of 2019, is based on interviews with Foxconn workers, student interns, teachers (who monitor the internship programs of their students), managers, and government officials, supplemented with field observations and extensive documentary research. Through interviews, poems, songs, open letters, photos, and videos shared with us, this book presents firsthand portraits of workers and teenage student interns—their hopes, dreams, and struggles to survive.[12]

Challenges to a Global Labor Regime

Foxconn is the king of the "electronics workshop of the world." While the company has achieved enormous wealth, it remains subordinate to the global brands, above all Apple, which sets the price and the volume of the orders placed with Foxconn and rival producers. In this competitive terrain, Foxconn is vulnerable to sweatshop charges as it seeks to meet the demands for quality and speed set by Apple and other brands. Not only Foxconn but also Apple and other brands may be named and shamed through labor strikes and walkouts as well as press criticism, undermining the corporate image with economic and reputational loss. In these circumstances, workers and their supporters may succeed in exploiting corporate social responsibility discourse to win public support for worker rights, at times appealing for consumer support at home and abroad, and force corporate compliance with legal and moral norms.[13] In particular, we recognize that universities—their students and faculties—are open to learning about and acting upon information about corporate abuses as many have taken part in social movements involving sneakers, sweatshirts, and other products that particularly catered to students and universities.

With the reintroduction of capitalist production methods since reform and opening-up, China in recent decades has been the site of high levels of contentious politics with numerous worker strikes and protests. In key nodes of globalized electronics production, particularly in periods in which sales leaps are expected, such as the launch of new models, large-scale labor actions can send important messages to the state, to Foxconn, and to global brands, including Apple, sometimes contributing to worker gains. Officials, in the interest of maintaining social and political stability, serve as brokers to pressure companies into compromising with workers. However, workers who confront management, and, on occasion, the government and police, risk being charged with disrupting the social order and being fired and/or imprisoned.

Chinese labor relations remain unstable, prompting legal reforms that have meant to improve the lot of workers and to preserve the corporate-state nexus of power that demobilizes workers. Aggrieved workers oscillate between legal and extralegal tactics for resolving conflicts in order to draw attention and responses from the government, media, and the concerned public. Under the leadership of Xi Jinping from 2013, defiant workers, including Foxconn employees, have continued to protest abuses and fight to secure fundamental rights. Despite crackdown on nongovernmental organizations and human rights lawyers, they have persisted, at times with support from students and citizens. Should workers at Foxconn and elsewhere succeed in organizing and mobilizing effectively, they would inspire many more to strive to make a better future together.

1

A Suicide Survivor

I was so desperate that my mind went blank.

—Tian Yu, a 17-year-old suicide survivor[1]

At about eight in the morning on March 17, 2010, Tian Yu threw herself from the fourth floor of a Foxconn factory dormitory. Just a little over a month earlier, she had come to Shenzhen city, the fast-rising megalopolis adjacent to Hong Kong that has become the cutting edge of development in China's electronics industry. While still a predominantly rural area when it was designated as China's first Special Economic Zone in 1980, Shenzhen experienced extraordinary economic and population growth in the following decades to become a major metropolis with a population exceeding 10 million by 2010, with nearly 8 million internal migrants from within Guangdong and other provices (who were also known as the "floating" population).[2]

Yu, who hailed from a farming village in the central province of Hubei, landed a job at Foxconn in Shenzhen. At the moment that she attempted to take her life, global consumers were impatiently waiting for the revamped iPhone 4 and the first-generation iPad. Working on an Apple product line of Foxconn's integrated Digital Product Business Group (iDPBG), Yu was responsible for spot inspections of glass screens to see whether they were scratched. An ever-shorter production cycle, accelerated finishing time, and heavy overtime requirements placed intense pressures on Yu and her coworkers.

Miraculously, Yu survived the fall, but suffered three spinal fractures and four hip fractures. She was left paralyzed from the waist down. Her job at the factory, her first, will probably be her last.

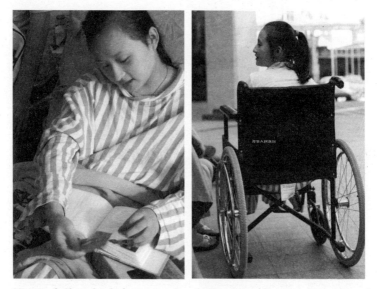

Tian Yu, half-paralyzed after jumping from the Foxconn Longhua factory dormitory, received treatment in the Shenzhen Longhua People's Hospital in Guangdong province.

Surviving Foxconn

Our first meeting with Yu took place in July 2010 at the Shenzhen Longhua People's Hospital, where she was recovering from the injuries sustained in her suicide attempt. Aware of her fragile physical and psychological state, the researchers were fearful that their presence might cause Yu and her family further pain. However, both Yu's parents at her bedside, and Yu herself when she awoke, put them at ease by welcoming their presence.

Over the following weeks, as Yu established bonds of trust with the researchers, she talked about her family background, the circumstances that led to her employment at Foxconn, and her experiences working on the assembly line and living in the factory dormitory. During interviews with Yu and her family, it became clear that her story had much in common with that of many Foxconn employees, comprised predominantly of the new generation of Chinese rural migrant workers.

"I was born into a farming family in February 1993 in a village," Yu related. What was recently a village is now part of Laohekou (Old River Mouth) city, which has a population of 530,000. Located on the Han River close to the Henan provincial border, it was liberated in the course of the anti-Japanese resistance of the 1940s. Following a redistributive land reform, in the mid-1950s, agricultural production was organized along collective lines. During the late 1970s, with the establishment of a household responsibility system in agriculture, followed in 1982 by the dismantling of the people's communes, farmland was contracted to individual households.

"At best my family could earn about 15,000 yuan on the land in a year, hardly enough to sustain six people. Growing corn and wheat on tiny parcels of land and keeping a few pigs and chickens might not leave us hungry," Yu said, "but making a better life is challenging if one seeks to eke out a living on the small family plot."

Yu belonged to the generation of "left-behind children" as both parents joined the early out-migration wave that enveloped China's countryside. Yu's grandmother brought her up while her parents were far from home supporting the family as migrant factory workers. Like many of the 61 million children who were left behind, she spent her early childhood playing with other neighborhood children.[3] There was little parental guidance. Eventually, her parents returned home to resume farming having earned just enough money to renovate the house. Yu, the eldest child, has a sister and a brother. She hoped, in the future, to be able to help look after her brother, who was born deaf.[4]

From Farm to Factory

China's accession to the World Trade Organization in 2001 brought about great challenges to villagers, who faced a flood of cheap subsidized crops imported from overseas even as export-driven industrialization expanded. Despite gains associated with the elimination of agricultural taxes in 2005 and the subsequent establishment of a social insurance scheme under the new socialist countryside campaign, as most young people departed for the cities and industrial jobs, the prospects for household-based agriculture and rural development generally darkened. Sporadic efforts toward cooperative rural construction and alternative development initiatives aside, opportunities for sustainable farming and lucrative nonfarm work in remote villages remained scarce.

After graduating from junior secondary school and completing a short course at the local vocational school, Yu decided to leave home to find a job. For her cohort of rural youth, the future, the only hope, lay in the cities. By 2010, TV and especially internet technology and mobile communications had opened a window on the real and imagined city lifestyle. "Almost all the young people of my age had gone off to work, and I was excited to see the world outside, too," Yu explained.

Soon after the Spring Festival, the Chinese New Year, in early February 2010, Yu's father gave her 500 yuan to tide her over while searching for work. He also provided a secondhand cell phone so that she could call home. He asked her to stay safe.

In the morning, "my cousin brought me to the long-distance bus station," Yu recalled of her departure for the city. "For the first time in my life I was far away from home. Getting off the bus, my first impression of the industrial town was that Shenzhen was nothing like what I had seen on TV."

On February 8, at the company recruitment center, "I queued up for the whole morning, filled out the job application form, pressed my fingertips onto the electronic reader, scanned my identity card, and took a blood test to complete the health check procedures."

Yu was offered a job and assigned a staff number: F9347140. She also received a color-printed Foxconn Employee Handbook, which was replete with upbeat language for new workers: "Hurry toward your finest dreams, pursue a magnificent life. At Foxconn, you can expand your knowledge and accumulate experience. Your dreams extend from here until tomorrow."

Later, after a quick lunch, a human resources manager at an employee orientation told a group of new recruits, including Yu, "Your potential is only limited by your aspirations! There's no choosing your birth, but here you will reach your destiny. Here you need only dream, and you will soar!"

The manager told stories of entrepreneurs like Apple chief Steve Jobs, Intel chairman Andrew Grove, and Microsoft founder Bill Gates to inspire youthful new Chinese workers. Indeed, no less than Apple, Foxconn executives were masters of painting an idyllic future for workers and consumers.

"Then, I and hundreds of other new workers were taken from Foxconn's recruitment center to the factory, about an hour's ride on the company bus. The setting sun bathed the Foxconn facilities in golden light," Yu recalled.

Inside Foxconn

The gigantic Longhua "campus," as the Foxconn managers like to call it, organizes production and daily living activities in a densely populated environment. The complex includes multistory factories, dormitories, warehouses, two hospitals, two libraries, a bookstore, a kindergarten, an educational institute (grandiosely dubbed Foxconn University), a post office, a fire department with two fire engines, an exclusive television network, banks, soccer fields, basketball courts, tennis courts, track and field, swimming pools, cyber theaters, shops, supermarkets, cafeterias, restaurants, guest houses, and even a wedding dress shop. Container trucks and forklifts rumble nonstop, serving a grid of factories that churn out iPhones and other electronics products for Apple and many global giants.

The factory directory displays a list of ten total zones—eight covering A through H, and two other zones labeled J and L—and they are further subdivided into A1, A2, A3, J20, L6, L7, and so on. It takes almost an hour to walk from the south main gate to the north main gate, and another hour to walk from the east to the west gate. Yu did not know what each building was, nor did she know the meaning of the English acronyms that could be seen written everywhere.

"I arrived late for my first day of work. The factory was so big, and I got lost. I spent a long time looking for the workshop," Yu said. When asked if she was scolded for being late, she answered so quietly that we could not hear her response.

Sisters or Strangers?

"I woke up at 6:30 a.m., attended a morning meeting at 7:20, started work at 7:40, went to lunch at 11:00, and then usually skipped the evening meal to work overtime until 7:40 p.m." On top of the "standard twelve-hour shift" during busy periods, like all other workers, Yu attended compulsory unpaid work meetings every day. "I reported to the line leader twenty minutes before the start of work for roll call. He exhorted us to maintain high productivity, reach daily output targets, and keep discipline."

A long workday of enforced silence, punctuated only by the noise of the machines, is the norm. Yu noted, "Friendly chit-chat among coworkers is not very common even during the break. Everyone rushes to queue up for lunch and eat quickly." In contrast to the corporate image of "a warm family with a loving heart," Foxconn workers frequently experience isolation and loneliness, some of it seemingly deliberately created by managerial staff to prevent the formation of strong social bonds among workers.

Managers, foremen, and line leaders prohibit conversation during working hours in the workshop. The assembly lines run on a 24-hour, nonstop basis, particularly when the production schedule is tight. The well-lit factory floor was visible throughout the night from afar. Yu felt that there was no way to say no to overtime.

New workers, like Yu, are often reprimanded for working "too slowly" on the line, regardless of their efforts to keep up with the "standard work pace." Emphasizing the company's claim to produce the world's best products for global customers, the maximum allowable rate of defective products is set low. Yu several times said that she had made no mistakes on the screens she worked on, but the line leader blamed her repeatedly for mistakes that she did not make.

With only a single day off every second week, or two rest days during the whole month, there was no spare time for Yu to use the Olympic-sized swimming pool or other recreational or educational facilities in "the factory city."

"I was switched to the night shift in March. Checking the screens of the products made my eyes feel intense pain," Yu told us.

Living in the Dormitory

Foxconn houses its employees in dormitories at or close to the factory. The workplace and living space are compressed to facilitate high-speed, round-the-clock production. The dormitory warehouses a massive migrant labor force without the care and love of family. Whether single or married, the worker is assigned a bunk space for one person. The "private space" consists simply of one's own bed behind a self-made curtain with little common living space.

Yu's roommates had jobs in six business groups and seven production departments. With roommates assigned from different departments and different shifts, and many speaking different dialects, it was difficult to socialize. When speaking of her roommates,

Yu said, "We were not close." She then showed us the management
record of her dormitory room.

Table 1.1 A Foxconn dormitory room list, 2010.

	Staff No.	Business Groups*	Production Departments	Dormitory Registration
1.	F9341932	NWInG	FKD	January 29, 2010
2.	F9450222	SHZBG	Mac BU (II)	March 18, 2010
3.	F9422526	CMMSG	AP (V)	March 10, 2010
4.	F9447733	CCPBG	TAMG TEAM	July 27, 2009
5.	F9425127	CMMSG	IPPD LX (I)	March 10, 2010
6.	F9347140 [Tian Yu]	iDPBG	DSPG DSD LCM	February 8, 2010
7.	F9341960	NWInG	FKD	January 29, 2010
8.	F9295026	PCEBG	ABD (II)	December 21, 2009

*NWInG (Net-Work Inter-Connection Business Group)
SHZBG (Super Hong Zhun Business Group, also known as Super Precision
Mechanical Business Group)
CMMSG (Component Module Move Service Group)
CCPBG (Consumer and Computer Products Business Group)
iDPBG (integrated Digital Product Business Group)
PCEBG (Personal Computing Electronics Business Group)
Note: Workers receive no explanation of the English acronyms of business
groups or production departments.

Although eight young girls were housed in the same room, Yu
explained, "We were strangers to each other. Some of us had just
moved in as others moved out. None of the roommates was from
Hubei." None spoke her dialect. Yu's father explained the significance of this: "When she first came to Shenzhen, sometimes when
others spoke, she couldn't understand much."

"At Foxconn, when I felt lonely, I would sometimes chat online,"
Yu told us. But those chatting on the QQ instant messaging community often remain far apart in time and space.[5] For factory new-
comers from distant provinces, it takes a long time to develop a
virtual friendship with mutual trust and shared understanding.

The Accumulation of Despair

"After I had worked a month, when it was time to distribute wages, everyone else got their wage debit cards, but I did not." Yu was deeply troubled.

At Foxconn, the cash flow required for workers' wages is large and payment is done by a banking system through the provision of wage debit cards rather than paying cash to individual workers. A debit card is a bank card with which a worker can deposit, withdraw, and transfer money from 24-hour ATM machines that are accessible from within the Longhua complex and other Foxconn facilities.

Yu asked the line leader what had happened. Although she worked at Longhua, she was told that there was no record of her personal information at Longhua.

Unbeknownst to Yu, the Human Resources Department at Foxconn Guanlan had kept her personnel file and failed to transfer the documents to Longhua where she actually worked. She had been interviewed at the recruitment center in Guanlan before being sent to the Longhua facility. The result was that her debit card account at Foxconn Longhua had never been set up.

"I had no choice but to take a bus to Foxconn Guanlan on my own," Yu recounted.

The Foxconn factory in Guanlan subdistrict, which began production in 2007, employed 130,000 workers in early 2010. Entering an unfamiliar factory compound, Yu remembered, "I went to Block C10, B1, B2, and from floor to floor of building after building to inquire about my wage card." After a fruitless day of searching for the right office, with managers and administrators deflecting responsibility, Yu was unable to learn what had happened to her wage card or how to solve the problem. "I went from office to office by myself but no one would point me in the right direction. They all brushed me off, telling me to ask someone else."

Yu had not been paid for a month of work, approximately 1,400 yuan consisting of basic pay of 900 yuan plus overtime premiums.

By then it was the middle of March, and after more than one month in Shenzhen, she had spent all of the money her parents had given her. "Where could I borrow money? At this moment of crisis my cell phone broke, and I was unable to get in touch with my cousin in Shenzhen."

Yu had reached the breaking point. The exhausting assembly line, harsh factory discipline, and friendless dormitory, together with the difficulty she faced contacting her family, were compounded by the exhaustion of her funds and the company's failure to pay her. She felt overwhelmed.

One Life to Live

"I was so desperate that my mind went blank." In the early morning on March 17, Yu jumped from her dormitory building. After twelve days in a coma, she awoke to find that she had become paralyzed from the waist down.

Yu was hospitalized for more than six months. Finally Foxconn disbursed a one-off "humanitarian payment" to "help the Tian family to go home." It was a bid to end its responsibility over employee suicide and to remove the problem from the eyes of the Chinese and international press.

In the words of Yu's father, "It was as if they were buying and selling a thing."

When Yu left the hospital, she also left us with some troubling questions about the lives of one million Foxconn workers and the responsibilities of corporations and the Chinese government to protect workers.

2

Foxconn: The World's Largest Electronics Manufacturer

Leadership is being decisive. Leadership is a righteous dictatorship. Leadership is a battle between experimentation and practicality.

—Terry Gou, founder and CEO of
Foxconn Technology Group[1]

If Steve Jobs was Apple's creative soul, Terry Gou is Foxconn's self-proclaimed "decisive and righteous dictator." Since 1974, Gou has led his company to win each battle "between experimentation and practicality" to become the world's top electronics manufacturer.[2] In 2018, the *Harvard Business Review* ranked Gou among the "best-performing CEOs" around the globe, 18th out of 100.[3] Perhaps emboldened by corporate success, Gou provisionally resigned in 2019 as company chairman to run for Taiwan's 2020 presidency, but lost to Daniel Han Kuo-yu, the Kaohsiung mayor and Nationalist Party candidate, in the presidential primary in July.

The challenges that Foxconn initially faced taught Gou, an ambitious businessman, to maximize every opportunity to compete. One piece of advice that Apple's Steve Jobs regularly provided to college graduates and potential employees was, "Stay hungry. Stay foolish."[4] Gou's version of this slogan is: "Hungry people have especially clear minds."[5] His ambitions extend beyond low-margin manufacturing in the service of global brands to robot-driven production of smart electric cars, semiconductors, big data technology, medical and health-care electronics, and retail e-businesses.

"In twenty years," a business executive suggested in 2010, "there will be only two companies—everything will be made by Foxconn and sold by Wal-Mart."[6] An exaggeration. But it does underlie the impressive growth of Foxconn. The future of Foxconn in Taiwan, China, and elsewhere will shape the lives of its employees and many more workers and consumers in the global economy.

Terry Gou's Foxconn

Terry Gou, whose parents had fled from Shanxi province in North China to Taiwan during the Chinese civil war in the late 1940s, was born in Taipei in October 1950. At age twenty-three, he set up a plastic and metal processing company in Tucheng Industrial Zone, Taipei. The self-made entrepreneur was quick to seize the new opportunities created by a Taiwan industrialization policy that took advantage of China's reintegration into the world economy. China's emergence to become a pillar of international trade and a major site of overseas investment followed the US-China opening of the early 1970s and the China-Taiwan opening of the 1980s, paving the way for the accelerated relocation of capital from the West to East Asia and the rapid transformation of global production networks.[7]

The 1985 Plaza Accord,[8] resulting in the appreciation of Taiwan's currency relative to the US dollar (up about 40 percent at the peak), led Taiwanese business leaders to expand investments, primarily in China and other low-wage countries in Southeast Asia.[9] Taiwan and Hong Kong enterprises invested US$107 billion between 1982 and 1994, that is, more than 70 percent of the foreign direct investment inflow to mainland China during this period to create a new Greater China industrial-exporting entity.[10]

Foxconn's rise occurred in the context of a global industrial transformation and outsourcing as corporate giants in the US, Europe, and East Asia shifted major production sites abroad. IBM, the world leader in business computing, was a pioneer in moving its assembly offshore in the 1960s. The microelectronic components of IBM System 360 computers were then assembled by workers in Japan and Taiwan, because "the cost of labor there was so low" that it was far cheaper to produce in East Asia than in New York or even the American South.[11] Radio Corporation of America (RCA), the consumer electronics firm, likewise took advantage of cheap labor and a loose regulatory environment in Taiwan's export-processing zones in the 1970s.[12]

By 1978, China's wage levels were approximately 3 percent of those in the US and far lower than wages in neighboring areas and countries including Taiwan, Hong Kong, and Singapore.[13] The Chinese manufacturing wage advantage would be maintained for the next quarter century as the virtually unlimited supply of rural migrants became the primary source of industrial labor in general and electronics in particular. Indeed, the incomes of Chinese workers throughout the 1980s and 1990s remained far below the level of earlier East Asian industrializers during their periods of highest growth.[14] In addition to the labor cost factor, many foreign electronics firms pressured their Taiwanese suppliers to move to China to be better positioned to sell their products to Chinese consumers and the world.

At the same time, China's technological level advanced in step with a dramatic expansion of education, training, and production for the world market. Investment in China by the Chinese diaspora in Taiwan, Hong Kong, and beyond provided the main source of capital and technology to China's burgeoning industries. Initially, this centered on textiles, apparel, and shoes, but by the mid-1980s it had extended to electronics and other more technologically sophisticated realms. By 1985, prior to the arrival of Foxconn, Shenzhen's electronics industry had grown "from one company with 300 employees to sixty firms employing 13,000 people."[15]

Foxconn: From Taipei to Shenzhen

In Shenzhen, in 1988, Foxconn began with a workforce of 150 Chinese rural migrants, approximately 100 of whom were young women, who were perceived as having such desirable attributes as dexterity and docility, making them ideally suited to assembly work. According to one estimate, during the 1980s, approximately 70 percent of the initial factory labor force in the Shenzhen Special Economic Zone was female, typical of the gendered division of labor in export-oriented industries.[16]

Over the past four decades, mobility of Chinese labor has vastly increased. In retrospect, China's household registration system, established in 1958, had erected a sharp divide between city and countryside, with villagers prohibited from leaving their collectives to seek work in the cities. Deng Xiaoping (1904–1997), the paramount reform-minded leader of post-Mao China, opened the way for rural migrants to take up jobs in coastal factories and development zones during the 1980s. Indeed, as hundreds of millions of rural migrants gained access to urban jobs, they would become the core of the new working class.

Yet, a generation later, Chinese rural migrants are still denied equal citizenship rights, such as access to urban apartments, health benefits, pensions, and welfare rights as well as access to public schools, all of which are guaranteed to residents who possess urban household registration. It is also important to note that entitlements to housing and social services for local residents were, however, largely diminished in the course of commercialization during the late 1990s and early 2000s.

In the midst of bankruptcy, privatization, and reorganization of firms at the turn of the century, by 2002, over 60 million urban workers were laid off from state sector jobs. That is, there was "a 44 percent reduction of the 1993 state sector workforce within a 10-year period."[17] With the rise of the private sector, including international capital, state and collective sector jobs as a share of urban employment fell sharply from "76 percent in 1995 to 41 percent in 2000 to only 27 percent in 2005."[18] The "iron rice bowl" tenure enjoyed by the older cohort of workers with urban household registrations was dismantled. Laid-off workers, whose numbers would soar again in the 2008 world recession, competed for jobs at Foxconn and other workplaces.

Foxconn, with its production of personal computers, mobile phones, video game consoles, and other consumer electronics products for global brands, quickly outstripped most other manufacturers in providing low-cost, efficient services to Apple and other leading international brands. Job fliers posted on lampposts, footbridges, and display boards around factory areas encouraged young people to work at Foxconn. Male and female youth, age sixteen and above, who were in good physical and mental health, were recruited for assembly jobs.

Foxconn Employees and Revenues

In 1991, founder and chairman Terry Gou listed shares on the Taiwan Stock Exchange following the company's investment in China three years earlier. By the end of 1996, Foxconn employed 9,000 workers and staff globally, the majority based in China. After reaching 100,000 employees in 2003, Foxconn expanded by leaps and bounds to more than 700,000 in 2008. Its resilience during the global economic downturn of 2008 was shown in the continuous growth of revenues and employees in 2009. Foxconn's rapid expansion of its global labor force reached a peak of 1,300,000 in 2012. By 2018, Foxconn's total labor force dropped to 863,000 as the company turned to outsourced workers for a significant share of its labor force (see figure 2.1 and table 2.1).

Figure 2.1. Foxconn employees and revenues, 1996–2018.

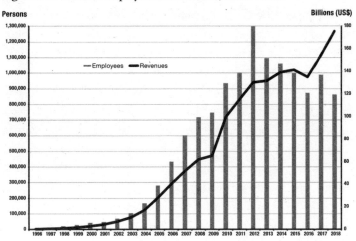

Note: The earliest publicly accessible company data on employees and revenues is from 1996. *Sources:* Foxconn Technology Group, various years.[19]

As recently as 1996, according to the earliest publicly accessible company data, Foxconn's revenue was only half a billion US dollars. A critical factor in Foxconn's subsequent expansion was China's accession to the World Trade Organization in 2001. From that time, with wider access to international markets, exporters, including Foxconn and others, grew rapidly. Between 2003 and 2004, Foxconn acquired handset assembly plants owned by Motorola in Mexico and by Eimo Oyj in Finland, and merged with Ambit Microsystems Corporation in Taiwan, enabling it to branch out from computer production to mobile communications equipment manufacturing.[20] As *CommonWealth Magazine* breathlessly reported, "Gou presided over successive lightning quick acquisitions across Scandinavia, South America and Asia, becoming Taiwan's first business chief to complete mergers on three different continents within a single year."[21] Still, the mainland Chinese production base of Foxconn remains by far the most important to its enormous growth and profitability. By 2005, Tse-Kang Leng estimated that

"90 percent of Hon Hai's net profit" was generated from "its business in China," and the integration of Hon Hai Precision Industry in China and the world has since deepened.[22]

Table 2.1. Foxconn employees and revenues, 1996–2018.

Year	Foxconn employees	Revenues (US$ billions)
1996	9,000	0.5
1997	14,000	0.7
1998	20,000	1.2
1999	29,000	1.8
2000	44,000	2.8
2001	47,000	4.4
2002	69,000	7.1
2003	104,000	10.7
2004	168,000	17.2
2005	280,000	28.0
2006	433,000	40.5
2007	603,000	51.8
2008	717,000	61.8
2009	748,000	65.3
2010	935,000	99.9
2011	1,001,000	115.0
2012	1,300,000	130.1
2013	1,097,000	131.7
2014	1,061,000	139.0
2015	1,000,000	141.2
2016	873,000	135.1
2017	988,000	154.7
2018	863,000	175.6

Note: The earliest publicly accessible company data on employees and revenues is from 1996. *Source:* Foxconn Technology Group, various years.[23]

By 2010, a year notable for the spate of worker suicides, Foxconn achieved US$100 billion in sales for the first time. A 2012 industry survey revealed that Foxconn had become the largest contract manufacturer "by a factor of nearly four compared to its closest competitor." Foxconn's expansion was so great that the growth of the industry was highly correlated with the growth of the company, and its largest customers, led by Apple.[24]

Measured by total annual revenues, despite a slight fall in 2016 (US$135.1 billion) in part due to the acquisition of Japan's Sharp Corporation and its investment in robotics—its first fall in revenues since 1996—in 2018, Foxconn reached an unprecedented US$175.6 billion in revenues. The success of Foxconn, as analyzed by Charlie Chiang (a chief of the Industrial Development Division in the Economic Bureau of Taichung City Government of Taiwan) and Ho-Don Yan (a professor in the Department of Economics of Feng Chia University, Taiwan), is derived from its embeddedness in industrial innovation and globalized production networks.[25] What remains understudied is Foxconn's utilization and control of labor in China and the world.

Profits in Comparative Perspective

From raw material extraction to processing to final assembly, Foxconn has built a network predicated on vertical integration and flexible coordination across multiple facilities and 24-hour continuous assembly. In terms of profits, the remarkable fact is that in fiscal year 2018, Foxconn recorded *higher* profits than many of its most powerful clients, including Panasonic (US$2.6 billion)[26] and Xiaomi (US$2 billion).[27] However, Foxconn's US$4.3 billion (TWD 129 billion) in profit pales beside those of Apple, the world's most valuable tech company.[28] In 2018, Apple generated super profits of US$59.5 billion, more than thirteen times greater than Foxconn's[29] (see table 2.2 and figure 2.2).

Table 2.2. Profits and revenues in the world's seventeen largest tech firms, 2018.

	Revenues (US$ billions)	Profits (US$ billions)
Apple	265.6	59.5
Samsung Electronics	221.6	39.9
Alphabet (Google)	136.8	30.7
Facebook	55.8	22.1
Intel	70.8	21.1
Microsoft	110.4	16.6
Micron Technology	30.4	14.1
SK Hynix	36.8	14.1
Taiwan Semiconductor Manufacturing	34.2	12.0
Tencent Holdings	47.3	11.9
Toshiba	33.3	9.1
Huawei Investment & Holding	109.0	9.0
IBM (International Business Machines)	79.6	8.7
Sony	78.2	8.3
HP	58.5	5.3
SAP	29.2	4.8
Hon Hai Precision Industry (Foxconn)	175.6	4.3

Source: Fortune Global 2019.[30]

Examining Foxconn's thin profit margins, a number of Chinese analysts have expressed skepticism over the advances of Foxconn's research and development. Wu Kan, a fund manager at Shanghai-based Shanshan Finance, commented that "the market has doubts over how much real hi-tech the company has on hand." Likewise, Dai Ming, a Hengsheng Asset fund manager in Shanghai, noted that "the company has low profit margins and its plan to develop smart manufacturing is still in the storytelling stage."[31]

Figure 2.2. Profits and revenues in the world's seventeen largest tech firms, 2018.

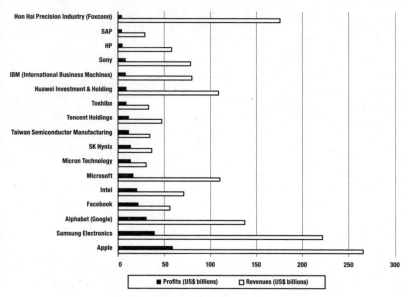

Source: Fortune Global 2019.[32]

To increase efficiency and profits, Foxconn has steadily climbed the value chain through research, patent acquisition, automation, and digitization. The Tsinghua-Foxconn Nanotechnology Research Center is located at Tsinghua University, one of China's leading universities in Beijing. Scientists there study materials at the nano-scale (the preface "nano" means one-billionth) to take advantage of such properties as greater strength and lighter weight. As early as 2010 Foxconn had acquired 39,870 patents worldwide in nano-technology, heat transfer, optical coating, electrical machinery, semiconductor equipment, and wireless networking. The number doubled to 79,600 patents in 2016.[33] It further rose to 86,600 in 2018, demonstrating Foxconn's successful technopreneurship.[34] That year, Foxconn Industrial Internet Company, a subsidiary that makes industrial robots and cloud services equipment, was listed on Shanghai's stock exchange.[35]

Workers and "Foxbots"

For some years, Terry Gou has been preoccupied with the dream of fielding a comprehensive fleet of robots he dubs "Foxbots." Styled as the "harmonious men" in the company's lingo, Foxbots are automatons capable of spraying, welding, pressing, polishing, quality testing, and assembling printed circuit boards. In January 2012, during a weeklong planning workshop at Foxconn's Taipei headquarters, Gou screened the Hollywood film *Real Steel*, about boxing gone high-tech, with human boxers replaced by steel robots, for senior executives. He was excited by this glimpse of the robotic future. "In the past when I went to watch movies with my wife," he said, "we always saw films she liked and I would just fall asleep. But [*Real Steel*] was very innovative and I think there are lots of ideas about robots and automation there that are worth referencing."[36]

Foxconn's transformational vision is in sync with the technological upgrading policy promoted by China's leaders. In 2014, in an interview with *Bloomberg*, Terry Gou elaborated the company's strategy:

> We don't want to go back to traditional, labor-intensive jobs. Simple and boring.... We want to rely on high technology. We want to depend on efficiency. Technology and efficiency are the new future and business strategy.[37]

Chia-Peng Day, former director of GM-Fanuc Robotics and general manager of Foxconn's Automation Technology Department Committee, reported that as of July 2016, Foxconn had "installed about 40,000 fully operational industrial robots," in addition to "hundreds of thousands of other pieces of automated equipment."[38]

Over the past decade, however, the major changes inside Foxconn were *not* the replacement of workers with robots but the replacement of full-time employees with growing numbers of student interns and contingent subcontracted laborers. To date, robotics still plays a relatively small part in Foxconn's production regime.

So far, it merely complements the human role in assembly that remains at the heart of Foxconn's manufacturing base.

Foxconn's Production Sites in China

Foxconn is China's biggest private sector employer. In 2018, Foxconn celebrated its thirtieth anniversary of investment in the mainland. While centered in Shenzhen close to Hong Kong, the wholly owned Taiwanese company moved to geographic clusters of the Pearl River Delta in South China, the Yangzi River Delta (concentrated around Shanghai and extending across the eastern provinces of Jiangsu and Zhejiang), and the Bohai Rim (including Beijing, Tianjin, and surrounding provinces of Hebei, Shandong, and Liaoning), where preferential policies, previously limited to southern coastal areas, expanded to encourage new investment. Tapping the state fund for a more balanced growth, Foxconn has further constructed new facilities in central and western regions as well as northeast Jilin province to develop a nationwide industrial supply base.

Today, Foxconn operates more than forty manufacturing complexes in nineteen provinces and in all four leading cities with provincial status: Beijing, Tianjin, Shanghai, and Chongqing (see figure 2.3).[39] In several provinces, the company has multiple manufacturing facilities. For example, in Guangdong, China's most populous and prosperous province, Foxconn operates in Shenzhen, Guangzhou, Dongguan, Huizhou, Foshan, Zhongshan, and Zhuhai.

In South China, Foxconn has moved ahead with new projects in the Guangdong-Hong Kong-Macao Greater Bay Area, comprising nine fast-developing cities in Guangdong province and China's special administrative regions of Hong Kong and Macao.[40] Entrepreneurs and officials alike are hoping to create a world-class innovative cluster and a trading power. In 2016, Foxconn decided to set up an ultra-high-definition panel facility by transferring technical know-how of newly acquired Japanese electronics veteran Sharp to

Guangzhou, provincial capital of Guangdong. To secure the investment, the Guangzhou municipal government "sold a plot of land covering 1.26 million square meters" to Foxconn "for 989 million yuan—a price that was only a fraction, or about 5 percent, of the price charged to other developers."[41] In Zhuhai, on the border of Macao, in 2018 Foxconn began construction of a semiconductor plant. Foxconn Zhuhai focuses on integrated circuitry and high-performance chips for artificial intelligence and 5G (fifth-generation wireless technology) high-speed networks. The municipal government will "spare no effort to optimize the business environment and provide quality and efficient services for Foxconn development in Zhuhai."[42] With the opening of the fifty-five-kilometer Hong Kong-Zhuhai-Macao Bridge on October 24, 2018, and the strengthening of connections with scientists and technological experts, the development of the Greater Bay Area in the coming years will add to the regional importance of the Foxconn facility.

Figure 2.3. Foxconn locations in Greater China, 1974–2020.

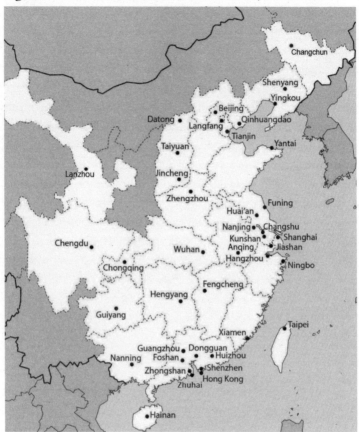

Source: Foxconn Technology Group (2020).[43]

Foxconn has upgraded manufacturing of computers, communication and network equipment, automotive electronics, and precision molds in Zhejiang and Jiangsu provinces in East China, taking advantage of the advanced digital infrastructure and commercial services. It strives to capture greater value in engineering innovations, technology research and development, and branding in the Yangzi River Delta centered on Shanghai. In China's northeast provinces, Foxconn has expanded investment in bioplastics, high-tech products, and artificial intelligence under a revival program. Traditionally a heavy industrial and military base, the regional economy (Liaoning, Jilin, and Heilongjiang) is being restructured with a diverse range of new industries and services, forming clusters of supplier networks.

Also noteworthy is Foxconn's inland expansion. In 2018, most of the new Foxconn employees were "located in South China, Central China and Southwest China," harnessing land and human resources for innovation-driven growth in areas with minimum wages substantially lower than in coastal regions.[44] Foxconn's iPhone plant in Zhengzhou city, in Henan, and its iPad plant in Chengdu city, in Sichuan, both began operations in the latter half of 2010 amidst the suicide tragedy. Apple has exclusive access to the Foxconn production facilities in both areas.

In the southwest, the Guiyang industrial park in Guizhou province is located more than 1,100 kilometers from Shenzhen. Louis Woo, special assistant to Foxconn CEO Terry Gou, commented, "Being close to the pool of workers is one of Foxconn's main reasons for going to Guiyang."[45] Perhaps more to the point, here too Foxconn was drawn by lavish incentives provided by the local government to secure high value-added industries, services, and jobs. This suggests that Guiyang is fast changing from "an unknown city" to "China's big data valley."[46]

Foxconn, along with Huawei and other Chinese tech companies, set up database centers in the Guian New Area on the fringes of Guiyang. The Guian New Area is "one of the five new areas developed under China's Western Development Program and the eighth national-level new area in China."[47] Government officials have greatly promoted the "Go West" program to relocate to areas previously bypassed by the industrial- and export-oriented development of the 1980s and 1990s, removing hurdles for major enterprises to register businesses. In May 2018, Apple also shifted its Chinese iCloud business to Guian in partnership with government-run Guizhou-Cloud Big Data.[48] Meanwhile, Chinese giant enterprises Tencent and Alibaba have similarly collaborated with the government to build data infrastructure in the new area.

In northwest China, Foxconn has tapped the emerging opportunities of the Belt and Road Initiative to expand its output in Lanzhou, the capital and largest city of Gansu province. The production base specializes in information technology industries, along with cloud computing and big data services in an area that is a gateway to Southeast Asia and Middle East markets for shipments of electronics products.[49]

To sum up, Foxconn has expanded its investments from coastal areas to all parts of China. In this way, it has taken advantage both of lower wages and access to markets on China's land borders, thanks to the infrastructural support and numerous incentives provided by the central and local governments. Foxconn's slogan is "China rooted, global footprint."[50] Its ever-expanding "electronics empire" is primarily built on the labor of workers in China (and the world), along with the accumulation of patents and advancement of technology.

3

Apple Meets Foxconn

Here

The foam lining highlights the perfection of Apple
But not our tomorrow
The scanner repeatedly announces "OK"
But not the "FAIL" in our hearts
24 hours a day, the blinding lamps illuminate the iPhones
Scrambling our days and nights
Thousands of repeated movements accomplish impeccable work
Testing the limits of our painful, numb shoulders
Each screw turns diligently
But they can't turn around our future.

—A Foxconn iPhone Worker[1]

Apple meets Foxconn, *here*, on the shop floor where workers assemble iPhones day and night. As early as 2000, Foxconn started to build iMacs for Apple, among other branded consumer electronics. In 2002, with soaring demand for sophisticated electronics components and production services, Foxconn became the number one exporter of Greater China, a position it would consolidate and hold to the present.[2]

In the wake of the spate of suicides at Foxconn's facilities, in 2011 Apple shifted some iPhone and iPad orders to other suppliers, simultaneously diversifying its suppliers and placing Foxconn on notice to guard against adverse publicity. In subsequent years, while Apple has taken a number of steps to reduce its dependence on Foxconn, the two companies' fortunes remain deeply entwined. Apple relies above all on Foxconn, while also contracting with Quanta Computer, Pegatron, and other manufacturers based in China.

Steve Jobs, Apple's Legendary Leader

Apple Computer was founded in 1976 by Steve Jobs, Steve Wozniak, and Ronald Wayne. It was incorporated in California in 1977. In a ranch-style house's attached garage in Los Altos, the two Steves invented the Apple I Computer and upgraded it to the Apple II in 1977.[3] In 1980, with orders from companies and schools, Apple registered as a public company in the US and opened a sixty-employee factory at Hollyhill in Cork, Ireland.[4] In 1981, Apple contracted new facilities in Southeast Asia to ramp up Apple II personal computers, such as those in Singapore. "Our business was designing, educating and marketing. I thought that Apple should do the least amount of work that it could and . . . let the subcontractors have the problems," commented Michael Scott, the first CEO of Apple Computer from 1977 to 1981.[5]

Prioritizing design, streamlined business processes, and core product development plans, in 1984 Apple launched the Macintosh to compete with IBM in the fast-growing personal computer market. The Mac improved on personal computers with a graphical user interface and mouse input. In January 1984 Apple opened the 160,000-square-feet Fremont, California, factory on Warm Springs Boulevard: "At that time, the facility was one of the nation's most automated plants, utilizing manufacturing methods such as robotics, just-in-time materials delivery, and a linear assembly line."[6] Two years later, the assembly of Macs was relocated to Fountain, Colorado, in the US, and Cork, Ireland, to cut costs.

Despite the advances of the Mac, Apple was unable to compete with IBM. In 1985 Jobs lost a power struggle to control the company and resigned. In the late 1980s, the Mac set new design and software standards and carved out a small part of the burgeoning market, but IBM continued to dominate and Apple faced formidable financial problems. By the mid-1990s, Apple stood at the brink of bankruptcy. *Wired* magazine published a 1997 issue with a one-word front cover: "Pray."[7] That year, Michael Dell, the founder and CEO of Dell, when asked what he would do to fix Apple, was reported as saying, "I'd shut it down, and give the money back to the shareholders."[8] But "in its darkest days, when Apple was dangerously close to being irrelevant," Adam Lashinsky writes, "its institutional psyche retained the pride of having pioneered the personal computer."[9]

Designed by Apple in California, Assembled by Foxconn in China

"Think Different" was the tagline of an Apple campaign in 1997, the year that Steve Jobs returned to Apple, which bought NeXT, the company he had founded on leaving Apple. The ad, with characteristic Apple bravado, featured Jobs alongside Albert Einstein, Martin Luther King Jr., Mahatma Gandhi, John Lennon, Maria Callas, Bob Dylan, and other iconic achievers of the twentieth century. "While some may see them as the crazy ones, we see genius," narrates Jobs. "Because the people who are crazy enough to think they can change the world are the ones who do."[10]

All Apple products have to be intuitive, that is, transparent, elegant, and easy to use. Apple CEO Steve Jobs "needed things to be perfect," wrote Malcolm Gladwell in the *New Yorker*, "and it took time to figure out what perfect was."[11] In rebranding Apple, Jobs had tried to lure Richard Sapper, designer of IBM's notebook ThinkPad—"a black cigar box"—to join him, but he did not succeed.[12] Only a while later when he began to work with Jony Ive, who would lead a team of industrial designers as the chief design officer at Apple's design studio, did he gain confidence in the future of the company, whose signature strength lies in its consummate focus on design and the simplicity of its operation.

By 1998, Apple had launched the iMac personal computer with an upgraded operating system that enabled it to compete with IBM and Dell. The iMac, built on the foundations of the original Macintosh computer, wedded contemporary design and advanced technology. Many more *i*-labeled products would follow. But what was the meaning of "*i*"? Jobs explained the lowercase letter *i* using a slide that read: "internet, individual, instruct, inform, inspire."[13] He might have added *imagine, impulse, illuminate, illustrate, intuitive, irresistible,* and *indispensable.*

"Try to imagine a Dell laptop evoking a feeling of any kind," rhetorically mused Adam Lashinsky, "other than frustration."[14] *Fortune* magazine similarly asked, "What makes Apple golden?" and answered: "Apple has demonstrated how to create real, breath-taking growth by dreaming up products so new and ingenious that they have upended one industry after another: consumer electronics, the record industry, the movie industry, video, and music production."[15] As of January 2000, in two years Apple's market capitalization had risen "from less than $2 billion to over $16 billion," demonstrating its resurrection under the leadership of Jobs and the new executive team.[16]

Apple: From Silicon Valley to Shenzhen

Apple cofounder Steve Jobs had once boasted of the Mac "as a machine that is made in America."[17] Indeed it was, in the early years before production and assembly moved abroad, above all to China and East Asia. By outsourcing and collaborating with Foxconn, Apple would soar to a position of strength with the creation and marketing of new products at the turn of the twenty-first century. In Foxconn's mega-production base in Shenzhen city, a complete production process was set up—"from procuring the raw steel for PC casings to putting together the finished product"—winning contracts from Apple, Dell, and other clients.[18]

Two major Apple business groups, namely, iDPBG (integrated Digital Product Business Group) and iDSBG (innovation Digital System Business Group), have become "the superstars at Foxconn," a production manager said in his recounting of the corporate history. More than a dozen "business groups" compete within Foxconn on speed, quality, efficiency, engineering services, and added value to maximize profits. The manager elaborated:

> At the beginning, we had only a small business group handling Apple's contracts. We assembled Macs and shipped them to Apple retail stores in the United States and elsewhere. Later we had more orders for the Mac, the digital music player iPod, and iPhone.

When Apple created the iPod digital music player with a click-wheel user interface and white earphones in 2001, the company embarked on a new direction. Click, click, click. It's music to our fingers and ears! Light, beautiful, and lovable, the iPod changed the way music was personalized, just as the Sony Walkman had decades earlier.

In 2003 Foxconn supplied aluminum-alloy cases for Apple's Power Mac G5 Desktop, which was launched as "the world's fastest personal computer."[19] From Power Mac to MacBook Pro, Foxconn management and workers demonstrated an ability to quickly master product complexity and shorten product cycles while maintaining high-quality precision standards and efficiency. Analyst Thomas Dinges highlighted that "the key factor for success in the current business environment for outsourced manufacturing is speed—delivering reduced time to market." Foxconn executives shared this view: "To win, focus on speed, not just cost," translating it into a precise formula for operations.[20] Actually, the key is efficiency, that is, speed combined with quality craftsmanship. Still, speeding up opens the possibility of slashing cost, oftentimes at the expense of workers.

If the iPod came to define a generation of digital music lovers, and the Mac the state of the art in desktop computers, have

Apple consumers ever wondered where and how they are made? And under what conditions? The tight timelines of electronics production and delivery, and sudden spikes and drops in global consumption, pose a challenge to supplier factory workers throughout the world in the form of harsh demands for high speed and overtime labor.

"Clean Up Your Computer"

With the global shift of manufacturing jobs, researchers, journalists, and activists have begun to throw light on labor conditions in the export-led Chinese electronics industry. In 2004, the Catholic Agency for Overseas Development (CAFOD), the overseas development and relief agency of the Catholic Church in England and Wales and part of Caritas Internationalis, released a report entitled "Clean Up Your Computer." CAFOD focused attention on the working conditions of electronics workers in China, Thailand, and Mexico. "The 138,468,000 personal computers that left the computer factories in 2003 were not produced in some Silicon Valley utopia," the researchers concluded.[21] In fact, Chinese, Thai, and Mexican factory workers, many of them rural migrants who enjoyed little social protection, faced long shifts for low pay.

In July 2004, Foxconn workers informed the Shenzhen-based labor rights group the Institute of Contemporary Observation that they had "only one day off every three weeks" to keep up with the production schedule. The day and night shifts were rotated every three weeks. A 22-year-old female worker shared the consequences of the intense work pressure with the researchers: "I had a nightmare about being wrapped up in a cable; the more I tried to free myself, the tighter it became."[22] For many, particularly in periods of corporate duress, life is reduced to becoming a cog on the production line "wrapped up in a cable." Between the borderline of consciousness and subconsciousness, this worker desperately sought to find her way. She was hardly alone.

Foxconn's "iPod City"

Buyers' scheduling and purchasing practices were closely linked to suppliers' imposition of draconian compulsory overtime and harsh discipline on workers. In June 2006, the British newspaper *Mail on Sunday* exposed the "iPod sweatshop" in the Foxconn Longhua factory that produced the Apple music players. At "iPod City," workers clocked in twelve- to fifteen-hour shifts, six to seven days a week, during peak production seasons.[23]

China's national labor law stipulates a forty-hour regular workweek, which can be extended by a maximum of three hours a day or thirty-six hours a month, but only when workers consent. While Apple requires its suppliers to meet the working hour standards stipulated by applicable laws, in reality, it fails to monitor working conditions.

Apple, which initially attempted to distance itself from "Foxconn's problems," was soon compelled to look into its supplier's labor conditions following a provocative *BBC* news feature proclaiming, "iPod 'slave' claims investigated."[24] Concerning working hours, Apple stated: "Except in emergency or unusual situations, a work week should be restricted to 60 hours, including overtime, and workers should be allowed at least one day off per seven-day week. Under no circumstances may working hours exceed the maximum set by applicable laws. Suppliers must offer vacation time, leave periods and holidays consistent with applicable laws."[25] How did Apple confront the fact that provisions of both China's labor laws and its own supplier code of conduct were violated, including provisions barring excessive overtime?

Following a "1,200 person-hours" investigation, on August 17, 2006, Apple released its "Report on iPod Manufacturing":

> We found no instances of forced overtime. . . . We did, however, find that employees worked longer hours than permitted by our Code of Conduct, which limits normal workweeks to 60 hours and requires at least one day off each week. We reviewed seven

months of records [January to July 2006] from multiple shifts
of different production lines and found that the weekly limit
was exceeded 35% of the time and employees worked more than
six consecutive days 25% of the time.[26]

Workers at Foxconn repeatedly informed journalists that overtime
work was "compulsory."[27] In the buyer-dominated supply chain,
Foxconn executives well understood that failure to meet Apple production targets in the run-up to new models and the holiday rush
could mean loss of contracts. The result was that Foxconn's coercive
management repeatedly forced overtime, often to illegal levels.

The Shenzhen municipal government likewise turned a blind
eye to abusive workplace conditions. As early as July 2006, Foxconn
took aim at *China Business News* editor Weng Bao and journalist
Wang You, who filed follow-up reports about labor violations at
the iPod assembly factories in Longhua. Even before Foxconn's libel
case was heard, the Shenzhen People's Court stepped in to freeze
the two reporters' personal bank accounts and assets at a time when
they faced a prospective fine of 30,000,000 yuan (US$3.7 million)
for damaging Foxconn's reputation. The corporate defamation
claims and the libel case that targeted the two journalists, rather
than the news agency, were the first of their kind in China. But in
August, following public outcry led by the Paris-based Reporters
Without Borders (*Reporters Sans Frontières*), Foxconn dropped the
lawsuit and accepted a symbolic one yuan (12 US cents) payment.[28]

Joel Simon, executive director of the New York City–based
Committee to Protect Journalists, commented, "We are pleased
that Foxconn backed away from its suit. . . . But the court's decision
to inflict such draconian punishments as the freezing of personal
assets even before a trial, reflects the government's willingness to
serve powerful vested interests in China at the expense of a free
media."[29] The suit sent an ominous signal to already embattled
investigative journalists.

Despite, or perhaps in part because of, the court action, the
exposé of "the iPod slaves" at Foxconn caused a stir. IBM, Dell,

HP, and other tech giants reviewed their respective supplier codes of conduct to ensure ethical practices in their transnational production networks. Collectively, the firms sought to strengthen the Electronic Industry Citizenship Coalition (now the Responsible Business Alliance) to safeguard their common interests.[30] In December 2006, Apple also overhauled its supplier code of conduct that was published just a year earlier. The opening statement of the updated Apple Supplier Code of Conduct reads: "Apple is committed to ensuring that working conditions in Apple's supply chain are safe, that workers are treated with respect and dignity, and that manufacturing processes are environmentally responsible."[31] How then would Apple fulfill its commitment?

2007: Birth of the iPhone

In January 2007, Apple Computer changed its name to Apple Inc. The elimination of the word "Computer" reflected the company's aspirations and burgeoning noncomputer product lines as well as its penchant for simplification. Speaking at Macworld Expo in San Francisco, Apple CEO Steve Jobs announced, "The Mac, iPod, Apple TV and iPhone. Only one of those is a computer. So we're changing the name."[32] Jobs then introduced the iPhone as three products in one, combining a widescreen iPod, a mobile phone, and an internet communications device. He stated that the "iPhone is a revolutionary and magical product that is literally five years ahead of any other mobile phone." And he could not hide his pride: "We are all born with the ultimate pointing device—our fingers—and iPhone uses them to create the most revolutionary user interface since the mouse."[33]

With the iPhone, Apple upstaged Nokia and Motorola, which until 2007 were among the world leaders in mobile phones. We slide our finger across the screen to unlock the phone's buttons. We do a lot of tapping on the iPhone's on-screen buttons. We zoom in on a photo by placing two fingers on the glass and spreading them. For many, a smartphone became a "fifth limb" that extends the functionality of arms, legs, and minds to make wide-ranging contacts that are redefining many elements of everyday life.

Jony Ive, Apple's chief designer, recalled the original iPhone launch in January 2007:

> We were very nervous—we were concerned how people would make a transition from touching physical buttons that moved, that made a noise . . . to glass that didn't move. [But] it's terribly important that you constantly question the assumptions you've made.[34]

Long-held assumptions about the phone user interface were shattered overnight. With its unparalleled design edge, Apple would continue to excite many people about its products. Its claims were, as ever, expansive:

> There were ideas about the way computers worked. We changed them. There were ideas about how music could be played. We changed them. There were ideas about what a phone was. We changed them.[35]

"Microsoft foresaw a computer on every person's desk, a radical idea when IBM mainframes took up entire rooms," the *New York Times*'s James Stewart commented. "But Apple went a big step further: Its vision was a computer in every pocket."[36] That computer was designed, and functioned, as a phone—the iPhone.

iPhone Workers

In June 2008, Apple launched the iPhone 3G (third generation) model, which allowed mobile phones to access the Internet at high speed. The company announced, "Just one year after launching the iPhone, we're launching the new iPhone 3G that is twice as fast at half the price."[37] Mark Zuckerberg, founder and CEO of Facebook, inaugurated a lucrative partnership with Apple that dates from that time:

Facebook is even cooler on the iPhone 3G, with the ability to discover friends nearby, or to effortlessly take pictures and upload them instantly to their Facebook account. . . . iPhone is one of the most popular ways for people to enjoy Facebook on-the-go.[38]

Less known to the world is how the iPhones were made by Foxconn workers in China. A Foxconn human resources manager, in our interview, assessed the impact of Apple's purchasing policies on the company:

During the 2008 Global Financial Crisis, Foxconn cut prices to Apple on components, such as connectors and printed circuit boards, and assembly, to retain high-volume orders. Margins were cut. Still, the rock bottom line was kept, that is, Foxconn did not report a loss on the iPhone contract. We were able to stay in the black while cutting margins by charging a premium on customized engineering services and quality assurance. The upgrading of the iPhones in part relied on our senior product engineers' research analyses and constructive suggestions.

The manager also revealed the crucial point about Apple's price squeeze. Foxconn was forced to slash the price charged to Apple to maintain its iPhone contracts. For its part, Apple recognized Foxconn's ability to guarantee quality and speed of delivery.

In fiscal year 2009, Apple sold 20,731,000 iPhones, and sales increased by 93 percent to 39,989,000 units in fiscal year 2010.[39] With a sudden influx of rush orders from Apple, among other firms, Foxconn workers—including the suicidal workers—were toiling day and night.

Figure 3.1 shows Apple's iPhone units sold from the first quarter of fiscal year 2010 to the fourth quarter of fiscal year 2018 (see also table 3.1). Clearly, the iPhone has gained increasing global popularity over time, even when Apple faced mounting pressure in the global smartphone market. Less noted is the fact that iPhone shipments experienced extreme spikes during the holiday seasons and close to the new year. Foxconn, the largest Apple supplier, needs to periodically extend working hours and adapt its workforces to the boom-and-bust trends of Apple products. As we will see in later chapters, the company is incentivized to shun longer-term commitments to employees and to expand flexible employment.

Figure 3.1. iPhone units sold, 2009–2018.

Millions (units)

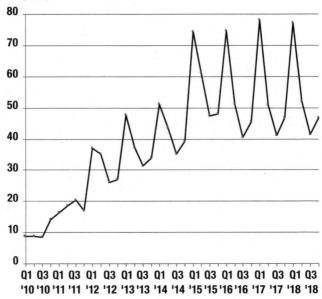

Note: Apple had stopped releasing unit sales of iPhones as of fiscal year 2019 (ended September 28).
Sources: Apple's quarterly earnings reports (Form 10-Q), various years.[40]

Table 3.1. iPhone units sold, 2009–2018.

Apple	iPhone unit sales (Millions)				Total
Fiscal Year	Q1 (Sep–Dec)	Q2 (Dec–Mar)	Q3 (Mar–Jun)	Q4 (Jun–Sep)	
2010	8.74	8.75	8.40	14.10	39.99
2011	16.24	18.65	20.34	17.07	72.30
2012	37.04	35.06	26.03	26.91	125.04
2013	47.79	37.43	31.24	33.80	150.26
2014	51.03	43.72	35.20	39.27	169.22
2015	74.47	61.17	47.53	48.05	231.22
2016	74.78	51.19	40.40	45.51	211.88
2017	78.29	50.76	41.03	46.68	216.76
2018	77.32	52.22	41.30	46.89	217.73

Note: Apple had stopped releasing unit sales of iPhones as of fiscal year 2019 (ended September 28).

Sources: Apple's quarterly earnings reports (Form 10-Q), various years.[41]

Whose Value? Value Appropriation of the iPhone

In 2010, Apple demonstrated its corporate prowess by capturing an extraordinary 58.5 percent of the sales price of the iPhone, a virtually unparalleled achievement in world manufacturing (see figure 3.2). Particularly notable is that labor costs in China accounted for the smallest share of the "made in China" iPhone, a mere 1.8 percent or nearly US$10 of the US$549 retail price of the iPhone 4. American, Japanese, and South Korean firms that produced the most sophisticated electronics components, such as the touchscreen display, memory chips, and microprocessors, captured slightly over 14 percent of the value of the iPhone. The cost of raw materials was just over one-fifth of the total value (21.9 percent). In short, while Foxconn carved out a niche as the exclusive final assembler of the iPhone, the lion's share of the profits was captured by Apple. In this international division of labor, Foxconn captured only a small portion of the value while its workers in electronics processing and assembly received a pittance.

Figure 3.2. Distribution of value for the iPhone, 2010.

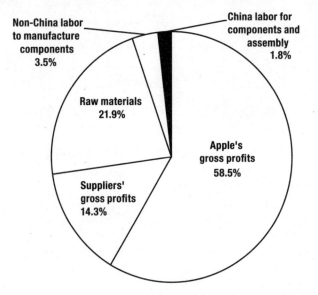

Note: The percentage is calculated on the iPhone 4's retail price of US$549 in 2010. No amount for "distribution and retail" is shown because Apple is paid directly by a cellular company, such as AT&T or Verizon, which handles the final stage of the sale. *Source:* Adapted from Kraemer, Linden, and Dedrick (2011).[42]

Global technology brands generally prefer to "use fewer contractors and engage in long-term relationships with them" but Jason Dedrick and Kenneth Kraemer observed that they "still shift contracts for specific products amongst suppliers based on cost, quality, or unique capabilities."[43] Subsequently, Apple—following the common practice of pitting suppliers against each other to maximize profit—shifted some of its iPhone production to Pegatron, another Taiwan-owned supplier where labor costs were allegedly even lower.[44]

By 2016, when the iPhone 7 debuted, Apple continued to maintain its grip on iPhone profits, despite intense competition from South Korea's Samsung and a number of Chinese firms led by

Huawei and Xiaomi. Apple captured an estimated US$283 of the US$649 retail price of the 32 GB model (nearly 44 percent of the total). By contrast, Chinese workers were estimated to earn just US$8.46 or 1.3 percent of the US$649 retail price.[45]

In July 2016, Apple sold the billionth iPhone. An Apple statement boasted:

> iPhone has become one of the most important, world-changing and successful products in history. It's become more than a constant companion. iPhone is truly an essential part of our daily life and enables much of what we do throughout the day.[46]

It was not an idle boast, though many may wonder whether that new "essential part of our daily life" is to be praised or mourned.

On January 9, 2017, Apple celebrated the tenth anniversary of the iPhone's debut with an event entitled "iPhone at Ten: The Revolution Continues."[47] Apple's super premium iPhone X, with prices starting at US$999, was released in November 2017. Ten years on, over one billion iPhones had been sold worldwide since the original iPhone debut. An executive in a Paris telecommunications conference, observing the company's meteoric rise, commented: "The real reason Apple is successful is because it has one product, in this case the iPhone. It minimizes the decision-making process for the consumer by making things simple."[48]

Apple's Products and Services

In fiscal year 2019, the iPhone generated more than half of Apple's revenues as income from the Mac and iPad dropped precipitously as a percent of income (see table 3.2 and figure 3.3 for the breakdown of Apple's revenues generated from sales of products and services). In total, Apple's revenues (US$260 billion) were primarily driven by growth in services (digital content and customer services) and higher sales in the "wearables, home, and accessories" category.

Table 3.2. Apple's annual revenues by product and service, 2010–2019.

	2010–2011 (ended September 24)	2018–2019 (ended September 28)
	Millions (US$)	
iPhone	45,998	142,381
Mac	21,783	25,740
iPad	19,168	21,280
Wearables, Home, and Accessories	11,927	24,482
Services	9,373	46,291
Total	108,249	260,174

Figure 3.3. Apple's annual revenues by product and service, 2010–2019.

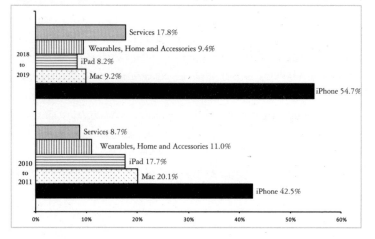

Note: The "iPad," Apple's tablet computer, was launched in 2010. "Wearables, Home, and Accessories" include sales of Apple TV (internet-connected television), Apple Watch (introduced in April 2015), AirPods (wireless Bluetooth earbuds released in December 2016), HomePod (wireless speaker released in February 2018), iPod touch (the seventh-generation model released in May 2019) and other Apple-branded and third-party accessories. "Services" include revenues from the iTunes Store (where consumers can buy music, movies, and TV shows online), the App Store, Apple Pay (a mobile payment service), Apple Music, AppleCare, iCloud, and licensing and other services. *Sources:* Apple's annual financial reports (2013, 2019).[49]

While the iPhone accounted for the greatest part of Apple's profits, the company was quick to supplement that with other lucrative profit streams. Apple introduced the online marketplace App Store with 500 applications (apps) in 2008.[50] Over the next decade, the number of apps grew by leaps and bounds with successive upgrading of the iPhone, Mac, iPad, iPod touch, Apple Watch, and Apple TV. Sales of app downloads, such as games, movies, and songs, all grew rapidly. On January 1, 2017, the online App Store recorded the most impressive single day of business in its history with nearly US$240 million in customer purchases worldwide.[51] It would be surpassed on January 1, 2019, with a total of US$322 million.[52] The top-grossing markets of the App Store included the US, China, Japan, and the UK.

Apple's China Market

In China, Apple has increased its investment in procurement of electronics parts and components, assembly, and data storage as well as processing. Since 2017, the company has further deepened its "connections with customers, government and businesses in China to advance innovation and sustainability," spearheaded by Isabel Ge Mahe, Apple's vice president and managing director for Greater China.[53] The growth of a multidimensional Chinese market would be critical for Apple and many others.

During fiscal year 2019 (ended September 28), Apple's fastest growth occurred in the Americas, reaching 45 percent. Europe's market remained stable (surpassing 23 percent), while Greater China generated 16.8 percent of revenues (see table 3.3 and figure 3.4). A slowing Chinese economy would matter not only to Apple but also to the global economy.

Table 3.3. Apple's annual revenues by region, 2013–2019.

Apple's fiscal year	2014	2015	2016	2017	2018	2019
	Millions (US$)					
Americas	80,095	93,864	86,613	96,600	112,093	116,914
Europe	44,285	50,337	49,952	54,938	62,420	60,288
Greater China	31,853	58,715	48,492	44,764	51,942	43,678
Japan	15,314	15,706	16,928	17,733	21,733	21,506
Rest of Asia Pacific	11,248	15,093	13,654	15,199	17,407	17,788
Total	182,795	233,715	215,639	229,234	265,595	260,174

Note: The Americas includes both North and South America. Europe includes European countries, as well as India, the Middle East, and Africa. Greater China includes China, Hong Kong, and Taiwan. Rest of Asia Pacific includes Australia and those Asian countries not included in Apple's other reportable segments. *Sources:* Apple's annual financial reports (2016, 2019).[54]

Figure 3.4. Apple's annual revenues by region, 2013–2019.

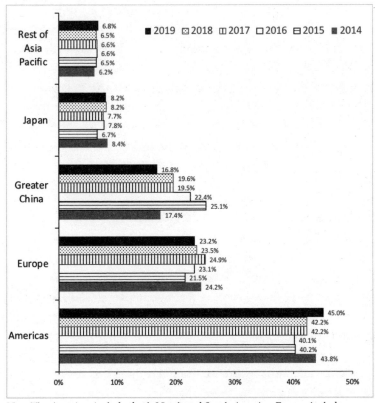

Note: The Americas includes both North and South America. Europe includes
European countries, as well as India, the Middle East, and Africa. Greater
China includes China, Hong Kong, and Taiwan. Rest of Asia Pacific includes
Australia and those Asian countries not included in Apple's other reportable
segments. Sources: Apple's annual financial reports (2016, 2019).[55]

Apple, not unlike its major competitors, has striven to expand globally. The sheer size of China's national economy is undeniably huge, but its gross domestic product (GDP) growth was 6.6 percent in 2018, the lowest rate since 1990.[56] Even when China has continued to deepen its market reform by opening to Apple and other multinationals, and by speeding up industrial upgrading, the downward pressure on growth remains strong. Still, international sales, in which the Greater China market (comprised of China, Hong Kong, and Taiwan) is a significant part, have accounted for 55 to 60 percent of Apple's revenues in recent years.

Apple, Tim Cook, and Chinese Workers

As early as March 2012, Tim Cook—in his new role as Apple's CEO—visited Beijing to meet with then vice premier Li Keqiang, who urged Apple to "expand cooperation with China, actively participate in the development of the western part of China, pay more attention to caring for workers and share development opportunities with the Chinese side."[57] Lead businesses like Apple have actively shed employment through global outsourcing and subcontracting while registering enormous profits in multiple fields. Whether corporate executives like Cook have showed greater care for Chinese workers is highly debatable.

Trained in engineering and business administration at Alabama's Auburn University, Cook earned an MBA from Duke University in 1988. After working for IBM, Intelligent Electronics, and Compaq Computer for a decade, he accepted Steve Jobs's invitation to join Apple in 1998, and has stayed ever since.[58]

Cook climbed Apple's career ladder, serving as senior vice president of operations and executive vice president of worldwide sales and operations. In 2005, he became chief operating officer.[59] Over the next six years, he served as acting chief executive each time that Jobs's health deteriorated.

On October 5, 2011, Steve Jobs died at age fifty-six after a pro-tracted battle with pancreatic cancer. As Apple's new CEO, Cook pledged the company's loyalty to the vision of the founder: "Steve leaves behind a company that only he could have built, and his spirit will forever be the foundation of Apple."[60] Later that month, Apple released its next generation iPhone, the iPhone 4S, dubbed "for Steve."

Since 2013, Apple has contracted with Flex (formerly Flextron-ics) to manufacture the Mac Pro desktop computer in Austin, Texas, taking advantage of tariff exemption from importing some Mac Pro parts and leveraging "the power of American innovation."[61] For manufacturing in America, even when it amounts to just a token gesture when compared with the enormous production base in China, Cook has earned glowing praise.

In 2015 when *Time* magazine crowned Cook one of the world's one hundred most influential people, Democratic congressman John Lewis, invited to write Cook's profile, hailed the CEO's ability to push Apple to "unimaginable profitability—and greater social responsibility."[62] By early August 2018, Apple had transformed itself from a tiny producer of computers in a garage beginning in 1976 to the world's most valuable publicly traded company with a market capitalization (market value of the company's outstanding shares) that surpassed US$1 trillion.[63] "Unimaginable profitability," indeed. But, the company's hype aside, is there credible evidence of "greater social responsibility" on the part of Apple? How do Fox-conn workers, who in recent years have become both producers and consumers of Apple products, view Apple and Foxconn?

4

Managing Foxconn

Growth, thy name is suffering.
A harsh environment is a good thing.
Achieve goals or the sun will no longer rise.
Value efficiency every minute, every second.
Execution is the integration of speed, accuracy, and precision.

—*Gou's Quotations*, Terry Gou, Foxconn
founder and chief executive[1]

Gou's Quotations is a collection of slogans published by Foxconn's Terry Gou that cumulatively constitute the company's work ethos. Quotations adorn the Foxconn factory walls, together with Gou's portrait, underlining the behavior prescribed to drive workers and staff. "Outside the lab," Gou intones, "there is no high-tech, only implementation of discipline." If a primary theme in the *Quotations from Chairman Mao Tse-tung* was the call to rebel, Chairman Gou's collection, ostensibly modeled on the "Little Red Book," substitutes that call with "Obey, obey, absolutely obey!"[2]

Mao Zedong's call for rebellions, disturbances, and even revolutions continued throughout his lifetime, resulting in the purge of the "old elites," "bad elements," "counterrevolutionaries," "rightists," and others. In the aftermath of the Cultural Revolution (1966–1976), reformists rejected the Maoist concepts of uninterrupted revolution and class struggle. But this rejection could not hide the problems of rising inequality in the workplace and in the post-Mao Chinese society.

At Foxconn new hires are trained to obey company rules and are inculcated in an organizational culture stressing the supremacy of corporate interests and the individualistic model of success. Those who heed Chairman Gou and endure the most will be rewarded with performance bonuses and promotions. Or so it is proclaimed. But does hard work pay off for workers? Has Foxconn softened its stance toward workers and employees in the aftermath of the wave of suicides? In the buyer-dominated global production chain, how much room do suppliers have to maneuver in order to make management more fair and humane?

The Aftermath of Employee Suicides

As of May 2010, Liu Kun, the Foxconn public communications director, pointed out that the company had more than one million employees in China alone, and that the reasons for suicides are invariably multiple. "Given its size, the rate of self-killing at Foxconn is not necessarily far from China's relatively high average," reported the *Guardian* newspaper, quoting the cavalier comment of company officials.[3]

But suicide is *not* evenly distributed in any population. Studies suggest elderly suicides represent over 40 percent of Chinese suicides.[4] It is important to note that the Foxconn suicide cluster was carried out by young employees working for a single company, most of them in factories in or near Shenzhen. Why would suicides by these young employees living in the cities spike when Beijing-based medical professionals found that 88 percent of suicides by Chinese youth occurred in the countryside?[5] The concentration of the suicide cases points to something new and important, which begs for an explanation in the context of the company, the industry, and the wider society.

Foxconn's responses were defensive ones, in the same vein as the erection of bars and nets to prevent those bent on suicide from leaping. Instead of investigating the reasons that drove youthful workers to suicide, in mid-May 2010, CEO Terry Gou invited Buddhist monks to dispel evil spirits at Shenzhen factory sites. At the same time, Foxconn required all job applicants to complete a 36-question psychological test. As the company saw it, responsibility for the suicides lay exclusively with its workers. Those employees lacking the capability to handle "personal problems" were the source of the problem.

Foxconn's human resources department also devised a singularly demeaning solution requiring all employees to sign a "no-suicide pledge" containing a disclaimer clause:

> Should any injury or death arise for which Foxconn cannot be held accountable (including suicide and self-mutilation), I hereby agree to hand over the case to the company's legal and regulatory procedures. I myself and my family members will not seek extra compensation above that required by the law so that the company's reputation would not be ruined and its operations would remain stable.[6]

The no-suicide "consent letter" sought not only to insulate Foxconn from all liability but to place responsibility for all future suicides on the individual worker. After intense criticism from workers, Foxconn dropped the no-suicide pledge.

On June 1, 2010, at D8 (the eighth annual "D: All Things Digital" conference hosted by the *Wall Street Journal*) in Rancho Palos Verdes, California, CEO Steve Jobs responded to the Foxconn suicide tragedy by insisting that Apple was "all over" it. He then defended Foxconn, saying:

> Foxconn is not a sweatshop. You go in this place and it's a factory, but, my gosh, they've got restaurants and movie theaters and hospitals and swimming pools. For a factory, it's pretty nice.[7]

My gosh . . . but where in Jobs's breathless account are the workers who clock long compulsory overtime hours for a pittance to produce Apple products? And where is the recognition of Apple's corporate responsibility as well as that of Foxconn?

A Foxconn worker dormitory with anti-suicide nets.

A Foxconn worker dormitory with windows wired and locked to prevent suicide. The safety devices were installed to stop workers from throwing themselves out of the windows. Whatever the consequences for suicide prevention, this means that the windows are tightly locked at all times. In the event of a fire, workers would be trapped inside.

Foxconn's "Care and Love" Program

The Foxconn human resources department, in a bid to create stronger bonds and a sense of belonging, set up a "Care and Love Hotline," first at Shenzhen and then at all forty-plus company factories across China. In addition to the 24-hour hotline, social workers, counselors, and trade union staff members maintained walk-in services to help needy workers at the newly built Employee Care Center in the summer of 2010. "Foxconn renewed its commitment to 'respect employees, ensure continuous improvement, contribute to the well-being of society, and achieve sustainability,'" the company trumpeted in announcing its new labor policy.[8]

A Foxconn poster about the Employee Care Center and the Care and Love Hotline 78585. The name of the hotline, in Mandarin, translates roughly to "Please help me, help me!" The company staff promises to "listen to your heart, solve your problems—anytime, anywhere."

"Hand in hand, heart to heart, Foxconn and I grow together," reads a bright-red Foxconn banner above the production line. It suggests that workers and the company share a common destiny. Foxconn management had not been notable for its light-handed touch, still less for its humor. Well, managers also piped in music to soothe workers in production workshops and set up a stress-release fitness room with punching bags adorned with pictures of supervisors!

In June 2010, a team of suicide prevention experts assembled by Apple recommended a series of quick Foxconn actions, "including hiring a large number of psychological counselors, establishing a 24-hour care center, and even attaching large nets to the factory buildings to prevent impulsive suicides."[9] Two experts, accompanied by then Apple chief operating officer Tim Cook and other Apple executives, also "met with Foxconn CEO Terry Gou and members of his senior staff to better understand the conditions at the site and to assess the emergency measures Foxconn was putting in place to prevent more suicides."[10]

Furthermore, Apple commissioned an independent survey of "more than 1,000 workers about their quality of life, sources of stress, psychological health, and other work-related factors." The researchers also "interviewed workers face to face, met separately with their managers, and evaluated working and living conditions firsthand." But neither Apple nor Foxconn released the quantitative and qualitative findings to the public. Instead, Apple made recommendations to Foxconn "for supporting workers' mental health," as well as for "better training of hotline staff and care center counselors and better monitoring to ensure effectiveness." Finally, they assessed Foxconn's response to the suicides positively, concluding that "Foxconn's response had definitely saved lives."[11]

Three things stand out in Apple's appraisal of the suicides and their implications. First, it distanced itself from all responsibility, focusing exclusively on Foxconn. Second, like Foxconn, it confined the issues to the realm of psychology and mental health, ignoring company policies on contentious issues, including wages and excessive compulsory overtime that might relate not only to Foxconn but also to the pressures imposed by Apple. Third, it positively assessed Foxconn's response to the suicides (singling out the use of nets to save lives) with no reference to company practices that may have led to the suicides.

Immediately after the seventeenth suicide case of the year on August 18, 2010, Foxconn organized a "morale-boosting rally" at its Shenzhen Longhua sports stadium. Twenty thousand workers took part in a company parade. Many held up colorful posters that said, "Love me, Love you, Love Terry," referring to CEO Terry Gou. Would the cold, suicide-plagued workplace be filled with corporate love?

Foxconn's Militarized Management System

At nearly 7:00 a.m. each day, hundreds of thousands of Foxconn workers pour in and out of the main factory gates. The human flow continues for more than an hour. Night-shift workers cross the footbridge and pour into the shopping malls and street markets that have sprung up around the factory. Day-shift workers cross the same footbridge, in the opposite direction, heading to work.

From the moment they enter the factory gate, workers are monitored by a security system more intrusive than any that we found in the neighboring smaller electronics-processing factories. "Foxconn has its own security force, just as a country has an army," a stern-faced, broad-shouldered security officer stated as a matter of fact. Workers pass through successive electronic gates and Special Security Zones before arriving at their workshops to start work. Foxconn's tight security preoccupation is reinforced by Apple's concern with secrecy to protect its copyrights, prevent loss of its products, and assure that its high-volume goals are met. With technological advancement, Foxconn has installed a facial recognition system at the main entrances to its Longhua campus to improve identity checks.

A female assembly-line worker elaborated, "We're not allowed to bring cell phones, digital recording devices or any metallic objects into the workshop." This security measure is to protect intellectual property and business data of Foxconn and its clients. She went on to express her dissatisfaction: "If there's a metal button on my clothes, it has to be removed, otherwise I won't be allowed in. Security officers would simply cut the metal button off."

Foxconn workers must wear non-metallic belts to pass through company metal-detector gates for security purposes.

Within the assembly workshop, workers and student interns face multiple layers of management, including assistant line leaders, line leaders, team leaders, and supervisors. Figure 4.1 shows the thirteen-level Foxconn organizational hierarchy. Under CEO Terry Gou's command, an elaborate production system has been built to cope with the ever-shorter product cycle and seasonal fluctuation in global demand for consumer electronics. Senior managers formulate the corporate development strategy and set annual revenue and profit goals, while middle management devises implementation plans and delegates responsibility to assure speed and precision.

In a 2007 interview with the *Wall Street Journal*, journalist Jason Dean characterized Foxconn's Terry Gou as a "warlord" and observed that "he wears a beaded bracelet he got from a temple dedicated to Genghis Khan, the thirteenth-century Mongolian conqueror whom he calls a personal hero."[12] The toughest "generals" of the "Foxconn empire"—including supervisors and managers—are rewarded with free travel, big bonuses, luxurious prizes, shares of company stock, and housing allowances. During the Chinese New Year gala, outstanding employees are designated "Foxconn Stars of the Year," a variant of China's "model workers"[13] in the contemporary context of individual success, making it possible for a select few to fly to the Taipei-based corporate headquarters and to visit famous tourist attractions in Taiwan, such as Alishan National Scenic Area, Sun Moon Lake, and the Taipei 101 Tower. On the other hand, workers who are deemed disobedient or rebellious are often punished and publicly humiliated.

Figure 4.1. Foxconn management hierarchy, 2010.

Note: CEO/Chief Executive Officer (Terry Gou). *Source:* Foxconn Technology Group company information.

Foxconn CEO Terry Gou: "Managing One Million Animals"

Foxconn chief Terry Gou once described the challenges of labor management this way: "As human beings are also animals, to manage one million animals gives me a headache."[14] Gou's statement, made on January 15, 2012, circulated like wildfire. He spoke on the occasion of a visit by the director of the Taipei Zoo to lecture senior management on how to control different animals according to their individual temperaments. A 25-year-old Foxconn worker responded by posting an article entitled "My Bitter Life at Foxconn" on his blog:

> Two days ago, Terry Gou said his employees are animals. I believe these are words from the bottom of his heart. . . . He cares only about his profits, his customers, and his iPhones. He of course cannot feel the bitterness of our lives, the lives of more than one million people.[15]

Eventually the public relations department issued a clarification. "Mr. Gou did say that, since all humans are members of the animal kingdom, it might be possible to learn from [zoo director] Mr. Chin's experience as his team looks for lessons that can be applied to business. Mr. Gou's comments were directed at all humans and not at any specific group."[16] The clarification was hardly less offensive than the original statement.

Discipline and Punish

As workers prepare to begin a shift, managers call out: "How are you?" Workers must respond by shouting in unison, "Good! Very good! Very, very good!" This drill is said to foster disciplined workers. A laser-soldering worker reported, "Before shift-time, a whistle sounds three times. At the first whistle we must rise and put our stools in order. At the second whistle we prepare to work and put on special gloves or equipment. At the third whistle we sit and work."

"No talking, no laughing, no eating, no sleeping" during work hours is the number one factory rule. Any behavior that violates discipline is penalized. "Going to the toilet for more than ten minutes incurs an oral warning, and chatting during work time incurs a written warning," a line leader explained.

Foxconn maintains a policy of demerit points to drive workers to work harder. A woman worker reports: "The policy penalizes workers for petty offenses. I can lose points for having long nails. There are so many things. Just one penalty means losing my monthly bonus."

Disciplinary methods include cancellation of performance bonuses, refusing promotion, and dismissal. There are also punishments not spelled out in the Foxconn Employee Handbook, such as verbal abuse and the compulsory copying of passages from *Gou's Quotations*. "Growth, thy name is suffering"—a worker commented on the quotation and its disciplinary enforcement. She recounted a situation: "My friend was responsible for inserting screws into smartphones. Once he missed a screw by mistake which QC [quality control] caught. When the line leader learned this, he yelled at him and forced him to copy a passage from the *Quotations* three hundred times!"

One frequently cited quotation from Chairman Gou is "A harsh environment is a good thing." In a group interview, several women employees described a ritualistic group punishment that they had endured. Their collective experience was articulated most clearly by one worker:

> After work, all of us—more than one hundred people—are sometimes made to stay behind. This happens whenever a worker is to be punished. A girl is forced to stand at attention and recite aloud a statement of self-criticism. Her voice must be loud enough to be heard by everyone. Our line leader would ask if the worker at the far end of the workshop could hear clearly the mistake she had made. Oftentimes a girl feels she is losing face. It's very embarrassing. She starts to cry. Her

voice becomes very small. . . . Then the line leader shouts: "If one worker loses only one minute [failing to keep up with the work pace], then, how much more time will be wasted by one hundred people?"

Foxconn workers must pay meticulous attention to detail while maintaining the pace of a forced march through repetitive tasks carried out throughout workdays that in busy seasons are frequently extended by overtime. Those who receive a "D" grade for "unsatisfactory performance" in staff appraisal, one interviewee told us, "will be fired."

Industrial Engineering

Industrial engineering is at the heart of Foxconn's gigantic production operation. Engineers study the entire manufacturing process in minute detail, simplify procedures, formulate standards, and put them into practice to minimize costs and maximize efficiency in a dazzling display of contemporary Taylorism, the reigning American system of "scientific management" that flourished in the early twentieth century.[17] Frederick Winslow Taylor (1856–1915), an engineer for a steel company, formulated the principles of corporate management and productivity-raising procedures, breaking down labor processes into minute components and pressing workers to maximize intensity in ways that transformed work organization in the US and beyond.

Taylorism was implemented and adapted in Japan and has often been associated with Toyota since the 1970s.[18] Foxconn's "8S" policy is directly modeled on the "5S" Japanese management method to improve organizational performance. This refers to Seiri (tidiness), Seiton (orderliness), Seiso (cleanliness), Seiketsu (standardization), and Shitsuke (discipline), to which are added Safety, Saving, and Security to compose the Foxconn system. Illustrative is the fact that the posture of workers sitting or standing is monitored no less rigorously than the work itself. "We cannot move past a yellow and black 'zebra line' on the floor," was how a worker explained the position her stool must be placed in while working on the assembly line.

Every second counts toward profit. "It seems as if while I operate the machines, the machines also operate me," a worker reported.

> Take a motherboard from the line, scan the logo, put it in an anti-static bag, stick on a label, and place it on the line. Each of these tasks takes two seconds. Every ten seconds I finish five tasks.

The usual time for competing the Standard Operating Procedure (SOP) in assembly is 25–30 seconds, which means that workers are being asked to work very hard in a short window of time. Electronics parts and components move swiftly by, and workers' youth is worn down by the rhythm of the machines.

The ultrathin new iPhones scratch so easily that they must be held in protective cases during assembly. The cases make workers' delicate operations even more difficult, but no extra time is given to complete each task. "We are working even faster than the machines," a worker commented. "Foxconn management values its engineers, but they are our enemies; we hate them," he added.

> When industrial engineers come around with their stopwatches, we intentionally slow our work pace. At best I can screw eight screws in seven seconds. But the faster I work, the higher the production quotas, so my co-workers and I slow the pace. The engineers are compelled to conduct the test again at another time.

Over time, however, management has steadily won the battle over workers. Engineers revamped the operations manual. "Now we must use both hands at work to increase efficiency and productivity. Not a hand is left idle for a moment," the worker responsible for the screwing stage explained. "For example, I hold an electric screwdriver with my right hand, and fix the screws with my left hand. Then, I pick up another printed circuit board. I screw the screws without a break."

Each iPhone has more than one hundred parts. Every worker specializes in one task and performs repetitive motions at high speed, hourly, daily, ten hours or more on many working days, for months on end. The "advanced production system" crushes human feelings of freshness or accomplishment. A worker described herself as a cog in the machine:

> I am a cog in the visual inspection workstation, which is part of the static electricity assembly line. As the adjacent soldering oven delivers smartphone motherboards, both my hands extend to take the motherboard, then my head starts shifting from left to right, my eyes move from the left side of the motherboard to the right side, then stare from the top to the bottom, without interruption, and when something is off, I call out, and another human part similar to myself will run over, ask about the cause of the error, and fix it. I repeat the same task thousands of times a day. My brain rusts.

The assembly-line work slowly dehumanizes the employees. Is climbing the ladder at Foxconn University a possible way out?

Foxconn University

Through part-time studies at Foxconn University, self-motivated staff aim to gain new skills and earn reward points by attending training courses as the basis of salary increases and promotion. The corporate university, founded in the Longhua manufacturing facility in 2001, aspires to promote best business practices and provide technical training for employees who enroll. It offers degrees and provides scholarships to qualified applicants. Globalization, digitization, experimentation, innovation, automation, and diversification are major themes in management classes. The company envisions that "someday, *every one* of our employees will study at Foxconn University" (emphasis added).[19] Turning vision into action, "since 2016, Foxconn has been investing in a RMB1 billion plan to proactively support and train workers from rural backgrounds," underlying the highest goal to retrain and retain the predominantly young migrant employees.[20]

Foxconn University posters: We are "the explorer of knowledge and education" and "the pioneer of service and innovation."

Foxconn University boasts "extensive partnerships" with Stanford University, the University of Houston, Tsinghua University, and Peking University, among others. It also "cooperates with think tanks to conduct scientific research and personnel training and to promote technology and knowledge sharing."[21] Building on this experience, Foxconn has opened new universities at its Chengdu and Zhengzhou production bases, forming an intercity educational network that is oriented to industrial upgrading. Several line leaders, in our interviews, believed that the activation of the "education and training e-learning platform," accessible online through the Foxconn University smartphone app, would make learning more flexible. However, due to the severe limitations of study time and money, and the exhaustion workers face with compulsory overtime, access to higher education and advanced training for the vast majority of assembly-line workers remains at best a distant dream.

A Line Leader's Nightmare

At Foxconn, workers are not the only people who experience dehumanization and stress. Line leaders, the lowest level of management, are also under stress. Often they vent their frustrations at workers. The result is a vicious cycle. Wang Fenghui, a 23-year-old line leader, elaborated, "Senior managers ask why your production quota was not fulfilled, and you must explain the problem. Then they ask you how you plan to resolve the problem. What can't be said is that the quotas are set so high as to be impossible to fulfill." After each workday, the intense production requirements became the focus of Fenghui's nightmares.

Fenghui talked to us over a beer on the street. Workers in small groups of two to three walked out to get late-night snacks. In contrast to the raucousness of the surrounding crowd, our table was subdued. Fenghui shared his ambivalence about being promoted to line leader: "If we listen too much to our superiors, we have to mistreat workers below us. If we take care of the workers' feelings too much, maybe we won't complete our tasks. When work is busy, it's easy to get angry."

"After the company sets production quotas," Fenghui explained, "we must rely on the workers to carry them out, but some workers refuse to accept supervision, which poses a major problem." Line leaders are sandwiched between management and workers.

Fenghui had recently run into trouble. "Several groups of student interns were dispatched to the workshop, including one group with more than one hundred interns. There were only four hundred people in the workshop. Having so many inexperienced student interns arrive at one time creates enormous pressure because the number of defective products soars." The situation was particularly worrying when the deadline was approaching. "On our line, the pass rate is set at 99.65 percent. Before that, there were just three to four defective products per day, but after the student interns arrived, sometimes there were twenty rejected items in an hour. Each day, we have a discard quota, a standard not to be surpassed. There's no way to give the higher-ups these high defect rates," he sighed.

"Line leaders never have a good day. Before the workers arrive, we have to prepare the assembly lines, lay out the tools, and put all reporting forms in order. If an order must go out at 3:00 p.m. today, our managers will come to the line and urge us to speed up." Fenghui, like many line leaders caught between the demands of management and the pressures experienced by workers, was nervous.

In daily management, arguments often erupt at the lowest level. "Sometimes managers visit the workshop. If they find workers performing poorly, rather than communicate directly with workers, they will have the line leader scold them, and afterwards hold the line leader accountable," Fenghui said. "If something bad happens, I get screwed, one level screws another. . . . Higher-level people vent their anger at those below them, but who can workers vent to? Isn't that among the reasons why some workers jumped from those buildings?"

The soft approach of Foxconn's "Care and Love" campaigns aside, hard targets of output and profit must be fulfilled. No pain, no gain. "Suffering is the identical twin of growth," Foxconn founder Terry Gou tirelessly intones. In our final interview, Fenghui bitterly lamented, "After work, if your eyes are glazed over, your head and face are filthy with grime, and there is a lifeless look in your eyes, you are a Foxconn worker!"

Low Wages and Long Working Hours

Following the chain of suicides during the first half of 2010, Foxconn announced a significant wage hike for all of its workers. The company trumpeted its "big wage increase" to 2,000 yuan a month, beginning in October. Compared with Shenzhen's then statutory minimum wage standard of 1,100 yuan a month, if implemented, Foxconn's basic pay would be 81.8 percent higher! The company's press statement reads:

> Effective 1 October [2010], we instituted across-the-board increases in the minimum wage payments in all of our operations in China. This move follows three months of worker evaluations

[July to September 2010] that have resulted in some 85% of our workforce qualifying for this increase with the remaining 15% having another evaluation in the future because they have not yet passed the evaluation process.[22]

If, in the fourth quarter of 2010, up to 85 percent of Foxconn's then 937,000 employees had received the *basic pay* of 2,000 yuan a month, the sharp increase in labor costs would have been clearly shown on the company's financial statements for 2010 and subsequent years. Examining Foxconn's "2010 Social and Environmental Responsibility Report," however, we find no evidence of a large increase in expenditure for wages. That year, despite the suicide tragedy and bad press, Foxconn highlighted the 53 percent increase in revenues over 2009, reaching nearly 3 trillion New Taiwan Dollars.[23] The company's recruitment ad, in fall 2011, moreover, specified that Foxconn's basic monthly pay was 1,550 yuan in Shenzhen, just 230 yuan above the newly adjusted local minimum wage.[24] Obviously, this level fell far short of the 2,000 yuan/month promised a year earlier.

What is the truth of the matter on the Foxconn wage issue? In March 2012, the Fair Labor Association (FLA) published a report on the wages of 35,166 Foxconn workers based on surveys of 10,262 workers from Guanlan and 8,256 workers from Longhua in Shenzhen, and 16,648 workers from Chengdu in Sichuan province in southwestern China.[25] The FLA, headquartered in Washington, DC, is an association of companies and civil society organizations committed to protecting workers' rights. The FLA study, which was commissioned by Apple, revealed that Foxconn workers' average monthly wages, *including* overtime premiums, were 2,687 yuan in Longhua, 2,872 yuan in Guanlan, and 2,257 yuan in Chengdu.[26] Comparing these findings with the wage data compiled by the Chinese government, Foxconn workers' incomes approximated those of average rural migrants at the national level, that is, 2,290 yuan/month (*including* overtime premiums).[27] Importantly, the FLA report concluded:

With respect to satisfaction with wages, 64.3 percent of workers thought that their salary was not sufficient to cover basic needs. The discontent with salaries was more pronounced in Chengdu where the legal minimum wage is lower; 72 percent of workers at Chengdu said their salaries did not cover basic needs.[28]

Despite the company's fanfare boasting of big pay rises since 2010, Foxconn workers—in Shenzhen as well as in Chengdu—similarly reported that they faced difficulties in covering basic needs.

The headline of the Foxconn Weekly *(November 6, 2010) reads, "Happiness appears on the eyebrows as a result of a pay raise." Effective October 1, 2010, the company reported that "Foxconn workers' wages significantly increased to 2,000 yuan/month" in all its facilities across China. Employees would receive their paychecks for October in the first week of November.*

"Pool the whole country's talent, paint splendid prospects"—a Foxconn job ad in autumn 2011. The three sections of the ad provide information on the following: (1) Recruitment criteria; (2) Recruitment time and date; and (3) Wages and benefits. Job applicants, male or female, should be sixteen or above, physically and mentally healthy, with no contagious or latent diseases. Those who have completed middle school are eligible to apply. Foxconn's probationary period lasted for six months. After the probation, the basic wage would increase by 100 yuan to 1,650 yuan per month. Following a satisfactory appraisal required after three more months, an employee should receive 2,000 yuan per month. In total, with overtime premiums and benefits, the employee could receive 2,000 to 3,300 yuan/month.

As of January 2014, workers of iDSBG (innovation Digital System Business Group), the designated iPad assembly group, confirmed that the *base wage* at Foxconn Longhua was just 1,800 yuan.[29] It was not until March 2015 that the Shenzhen municipal government raised the minimum wage by 12 percent to 2,030 yuan a month, surpassing the 2,000 yuan threshold for the very first time.[30] Accordingly, Foxconn adjusted its pay upward. In short, though wages did eventually rise, Foxconn was far from setting the pace in establishing a living wage, even at a time of registering super profits.

Trapped in the Foxconn Empire

Foxconn's management regime, including its wages and hours policy, is in part a response to the high-pressure purchasing practice of global corporations. It is not only conditioned by the competitiveness of the local labor market. The fluctuation of orders, coupled with tight delivery requirements, shifts production pressure from Apple and other corporate brands to Foxconn and smaller suppliers in transnational manufacturing.

The business demand for intense speed and high productivity has contributed to antagonism and conflict between workers and management, generating grievances on the shop floor. In other words, the turn to "humane management" is heavily constrained by the buyer-driven profit-maximizing global production system.

In the Foxconn empire, workers repeatedly scorned the 24-hour consultation hotlines as serving management control functions, dubbing the care center the "supervision center." This is because those who lodged complaints had their caller identities reported to management. Quickly learning of this breach of privacy, many workers stopped using the hotline and counseling service. Student interns, alongside workers, similarly felt the pressure at work, a story to which we now turn.

5

Voices of Student Interns

Come on, what do you think we've learned manning machines on the line for more than ten hours a day? What's an internship? There's no relation to what we study in school. Every day is just a repetition of one or two simple motions, like a robot.

—Zhang Lintong, a 16-year-old student intern at Foxconn

On March 3, 2011, sixty students from the Zhongjiang Vocational School, Zhongjiang County, Sichuan, arrived at the factory gate of Foxconn Chengdu to begin what they had been told would be internships.[1] Some carried only a few articles of clothing in coarse rice bags, having responded on short notice to the school's announcement of the internship. One student explained what had happened: "Our teacher announced that every vocational school in the province had to cooperate with the local government by sending students to Foxconn to take up internships." He added, "Anyone who could not present a medical report certified by the city hospital that he was very ill had to depart immediately." Brought to Chengdu in two buses, the students stood outside the electronic gate for half an hour listening to instructions from a Foxconn staff member before entering the factory. As we later learned, they were hardly the first group of "interns" recruited by Foxconn in China.

Vocational school students, many of them sixteen years of age, arrive at Foxconn Chengdu, the iPad factory, on March 3, 2011, to begin "internships."

Foxconn's New Blood: Student Interns

Vocational schools follow a work-study model that emphasizes the integration of education with production, as stated in China's 1996 Vocational Education Law. They offer employment-oriented courses for eligible applicants who have completed nine years of schooling (comprising six years of primary education and three years of middle school). Throughout the 1990s, approximately equal numbers of students in grades 10 through 12 were enrolled in vocational high schools and academic high schools.[2] At that time, graduates from vocational schools were assigned to urban state-owned enterprises or urban collective enterprises. They enjoyed stable income, job security, and welfare benefits, with opportunities to rise within the factory hierarchy. With privatization, layoffs, and enterprise restructuring in the late 1990s and thereafter, when many small and medium state firms were closed, student interns often worked in joint ventures and wholly foreign-invested enterprises, among which Foxconn was and still is China's largest industrial employer.

In a more competitive environment of work and employment, China's leaders have sought to boost labor productivity through

expanded investment in vocational training. In 2005, after a series
of national conferences on vocational education and training held
over three years, the State Council released a document entitled
"Decision on Accelerating the Development of Vocational Education." Students from disadvantaged families would be exempted
from school fees, and one thousand model secondary vocational
schools would be established to pilot new learning and teaching
approaches.[3] Critical shortages of skilled workers, coupled with
a quick recovery from the global financial crisis of 2008, led to
renewed attention to the pivotal role of technical education in
meeting the national development priorities.[4] The number of vocational high school students doubled from 11.7 million in 2001 to
22.4 million in 2010, making China's vocational education system
the largest in the world.[5]

High school enrollments grew rapidly in the early years of the
new millennium, from 2002 in the case of regular high schools,
and 2003 in the case of vocational schools. Then, between 2011
and 2018, vocational school enrollments dropped sharply from 22
million to 15.6 million (see figure 5.1 and table 5.1). At the time,
the 2010–2020 National Medium and Long-Term Educational
Reform and Development Plan called for increased enrollment by
2020 to the point where *half* of all high school-level students would
be in vocational schools, that is, 23.5 million.[6] It is a goal that will
not be met by December 2020. But why did vocational study lose
its attractiveness despite the new education policy emphasis?[7]

Even when we consider the low birth rates in China, and the
greater opportunities for some to study overseas (including in
Hong Kong and Macao), the declining attractiveness of vocational
education needs to be explained. Apart from the prioritization
of academic achievement over technical training among teachers,
parents, and students,[8] we disclose a hidden problem through the
prism of corporate-government malpractice: the abuse of student
internship programs by Foxconn and other employers in collusion
with local government.

Figure 5.1. Chinese students in high school and vocational high school, 2001–2018.

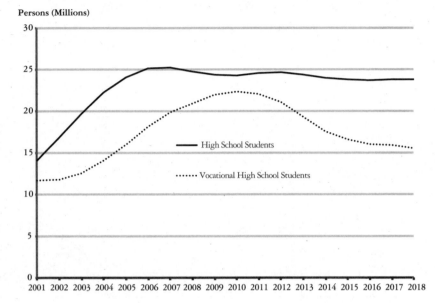

Persons (Millions)

Sources: Ministry of Education of the People's Republic of China (2015, 2019).[9]

Table 5.1. Chinese students in high school and vocational high school, 2001–2018.

	High school students	Vocational high school students
2001	14,050,000	11,703,000
2002	16,838,000	11,725,000
2003	19,648,000	12,546,000
2004	22,204,000	14,092,000
2005	24,091,000	16,000,000
2006	25,145,000	18,099,000
2007	25,224,000	19,870,000
2008	24,763,000	20,857,000
2009	24,343,000	21,941,000
2010	24,273,000	22,374,000
2011	24,548,000	22,043,000
2012	24,672,000	21,127,000
2013	24,359,000	19,230,000
2014	24,005,000	17,553,000
2015	23,744,000	16,567,000
2016	23,666,000	15,990,000
2017	23,745,000	15,925,000
2018	23,754,000	15,553,000

Sources: Ministry of Education of the People's Republic of China (2015, 2019).[10]

Student Internships

In China, internships that are mandatory in vocational education take many different forms. Some are chosen by students on their own initiative, while others are coordinated by educational institutions on behalf of students as partial fulfillment of degree requirements. For students in programs that last three to six years (three years at the senior secondary level and another three years at the tertiary level), a key question is the effectiveness of internship training in internships across a wide range of vocational programs.

A 6,000-student vocational school that trains equipment and machinery technicians proclaims its mission to be:

> Master one skill, create a career;
> Master one skill, make a blue sky.

At a larger school specializing in auto repair and mobile mechanics, Zhumadian Higher Technical School (upgraded to Zhumadian Technical Institute in 2013), the recruitment brochure similarly elaborates on the importance of "studying real skills":

> Our country has a good policy so that families in difficulty pay no tuition!
> To look for a job without learning technical skills is a lifelong mistake!
> Study real skills at Zhumadian Higher Technical School!
> Seeking wealth has limits, but skills and know-how lead to riches!
> Zhumadian Higher Technical School is a cradle of talent!

The school's marketing campaigns focus on its ability to provide prospective students the skills to assure a solid foundation for career building and lifelong security.

Foxconn uses similar marketing strategies. In school-business partnerships, "Foxconn cooperates with vocational schools to provide students with practical skills training that will enable them to find employment after they graduate from these programs," a 2011 company statement claims.[11] But what exactly are the programs providing "practical skills training" all about?

Good internship programs are practice-oriented and participatory, contribute to students' growth and development, and are related to their field of study. But Foxconn said nothing about its workplace training content and skill evaluation methods. Nor did it mention the fact, disclosed to us by fourteen teachers who supervised the Foxconn internship program, that internships were often extended to meet factory production needs, ranging from three months to a full year, in complete disregard for the students' training needs.

Foxconn Internships

During the summer of 2010 alone, Foxconn employed 150,000 student interns nationwide—15 percent of its entire million-strong Chinese workforce,[12] dwarfing Disney's College Program, often cited as being among the world's largest internship programs with more than 50,000 cumulative interns over thirty years.[13]

With continuing demand for the iPhone and iPad, among other best-selling products, Foxconn's labor needs remained strong. In 2010, in the Shenzhen facilities, 28,044 student interns "from over two hundred vocational schools all over China" were assigned to work alongside employees in the integrated Digital Product Business Group (iDPBG), which exclusively serves Apple. This was a six-fold increase from the 4,539 interns who had been assigned to Foxconn's plants in Shenzhen in 2007.[14]

Foxconn student interns were subjected to the same working conditions as regular workers, including alternating day and night shifts, 10- to 12-hour workdays, six to seven days a week during peak seasons. This was despite the fact that the 2007 Administrative Measures for Internships at Secondary Vocational Schools clearly stated that "interns shall not work more than eight hours a day,"[15] and the 2010 Education Circular likewise specified that "interns shall not work overtime beyond the eight-hour workday."[16] Not only must interns' shifts be limited to eight hours, all their training is required to take place during the day to ensure students' safety and physical and mental health, in accordance with the Law on the Protection of Minors. This law aims to protect young people under the age of eighteen and ensure their balanced development and healthy growth. Article 20 stipulates that schools, including vocational schools, should "cooperate with the parents or other guardians of minors to guarantee the students' time for sleeping, recreational activities and physical exercises, and may not increase their burden of study."[17]

Foxconn, with government collusion, systematically violated the letter and the spirit of the law governing interns. In 2010 in Sichuan's Chengdu Hi-Tech Industrial Development Zone, for example, Cao

Wang, age sixteen, who was studying textiles and fashion, learned on arrival that she would be doing nothing but tightening screws throughout her "internship"; Chen Hui, sixteen, a construction student, would polish iPad casings; Yu Yanying, seventeen, studying petro-chemistry, would stick labels on iPad boxes; Huang Ling, seventeen, taking a course in business management, was assigned quality inspection work on the production line. In total, the thirty-eight interviewed interns were studying arts, construction, petro-chemistry, automotive repair, herbal medicine, secretarial services, computer science, business management, accounting, textiles, electronics, and mechanics, among other subjects. Only eight of them, barely one-fifth, were in their third and final year, that is, when internships are mandated to take place. Their average age was 16.5, just above China's statutory minimum working age of 16.

In 2011, student interns and new workers at Foxconn's "iPad city" in Chengdu were paid the same 950 yuan per month as other minimum-wage workers, but unlike their fellow workers, interns were not entitled to a 400-yuan-per-month skills subsidy, regardless of whether they had passed a probationary period.

Moreover, although student interns perform work identical to that of other production workers, Foxconn does not need to enroll them in social security. Under Chinese law, interning students are not classified as employees. Although paid for their labor, their legal status remains that of students. By contrast, for employees, the entitlement to the comprehensive social insurance program paid for by the company and by the workers includes five types of insurance (old age pensions, medical benefits, maternity benefits, work-related injury benefits, and unemployment benefits) and a mandatory housing provident fund.[18]

A quick look at the math reveals that, for 150,000 student interns working in various Foxconn factories during one month in the summer season, the savings from not providing them with social security alone is 30 million yuan—a figure reached by multiplying the number of persons (150,000) and an average per-person payment (200 yuan).[19] While this is a simplified exercise, it conveys a good sense of employer savings; and this is for only one month's insurance expenditure, while many interns work a full year. Moreover, by dispensing with all welfare benefits, and retaining the right to terminate or extend the internships, Foxconn saves large sums at the expense of interns. The government ignores the fact that Foxconn's fraudulent internship program violates a signature state policy to protect the interests of student interns.

Learning to Labor

Liu Siying, who hails from Sichuan's Mianyang city, recalled her internship experience beginning in the 2010 fall semester:

> This is my final year in electronics and mechanical engineering. I really enjoy my studies and have been studying very hard. I even review coursework in the school library during summer vacation. I originally planned to seek an internship at Huawei Technologies, but our teacher persuaded my whole class of forty-two students to intern at Foxconn. He stressed that we'd learn a lot by interning at a large company like Foxconn, which has a worldwide customer base including Huawei and is investing billions in high-tech research.

Huawei has subsequently grown into a leading global information and communications technology solutions provider, a direct challenger to Apple's supremacy in smartphones and the race to 5G technology that promises to lead the way in the international competition to next generation electronics and artificial intelligence applications. In 2014 it was named Chinese Investor of the Year at the British Business Awards.[20] Huawei and Foxconn headquarters are on opposite sides of the Meiguan Expressway in Longhua District, Shenzhen.

From the beginning of her internship, Siying was "tied to the printed circuit board line attaching components to the product back-casing." As student after student explained, from day one, rather than receiving technical training to provide skills and knowledge, they were assigned to the assembly line, performing a single, repetitive task. As Siying told us, the job "requires no skills or prior knowledge." It was a total repudiation of the internship program.

Although we have no information that would indicate whether the internship program offered by Huawei would have been any better than that at Foxconn, Siying regretted her inability to choose her internship site and the loss of the internship experience. Under pressure from the Sichuan government to fulfill a quota for "student interns" at Foxconn, schools enrolled entire classes and suppressed student objections to Foxconn internships that were internships in name only.

"During the night shift, whenever I look out in that direction [pointing to the west], I see the big fluorescent sign of Huawei shining bright red, and at that moment, I feel a pain in my heart," Siying said before sinking into a long silence.

Teachers as Supervisors

Student interns at Foxconn find themselves in a dual managerial system subject to the authority of both schoolteachers and company managers. Teachers play two roles: one is enforcer to ensure that students follow factory rules; the second is counselor to help students deal with feelings of dejection at their work situation and prevent them from returning home. One teacher, Cai Yuan, spoke of students who were reluctant to go to work during the first week after arriving at the Foxconn factory:

> I asked my students to manage their emotions. Calm down. Think carefully if you want to leave; won't your parents be disappointed? I visited my students in the dorm to see if they felt okay on Tuesday night. They answered, "Not too bad." I met them again on Friday night. They said, "Fine." They've gradually gotten used to the work rhythm.

Throughout the internship, the teacher focuses on managing students' emotions because maintaining high morale is a key to assuring a high retention rate of student interns, which is a primary criterion for assessing teacher performance.

Often when interning students fell ill, neither their teachers nor company supervisors seemed to be able to help them. Wang Meiyi, sixteen, suffered from abnormal menstrual pains while assigned to the packaging workshop.

> I used to have relatively regular menstrual periods, but this time my period was delayed until the first week in October. I was frightened. I had such severe cramps that I was covered with sweat on the line, where it's air-conditioned.

In November and December, Meiyi's irregularity and pain persisted. Her line leader was a young man with whom she did not feel comfortable talking about a "girl matter." Further, "I didn't report my sickness to my teacher . . . for the same kind of embarrassment." She went on: "At school, we only have six classes a day, and I got good rest. But here at the factory it's different: We don't have breaks whenever we're behind on production targets. And it's no use complaining to my teacher."

During the day, teachers monitored student attendance. They had access to student attendance records via the company intranet, which listed the students' punch-in time at the start of the work shift and after meals, overtime work, and punch-out time at the end of the shift. Such information allowed teachers to react swiftly to cases of "missing students." In some circumstances, teachers checked students' sick leave applications and decided whether to approve them. In the eyes of interns, the teachers were part of factory management. One respondent explained:

> The real reason our teachers are here to guide us is out of fear that we will quit. So they work with those of us who are moody and advise us to stay. They also come forward to resolve disciplinary problems. We have a troublemaker in our class. He loved to go online, you know twenty-four hours a day on his PlayStation, at the factory dorm. He played video games and didn't go to work for two days. Our teacher thought that he was sick but then he was caught. He received a written warning.

Teachers play a crucial role analogous to that of the company union in pacifying student interns and maintaining the stability of the workforce. Teacher supervisors assure compliance while shielding the company from having to handle many disciplinary problems directly. They also assume the role of parents in regulating the behavior of interning students, thus helping to fulfill the company's production targets.

Employers are acutely aware of how the additional layer of teacher supervisors benefits the company. After the twelve worker suicides at Foxconn's factory-cum-dormitory complexes, in June 2010, the company temporarily halted open recruitment of labor at its two large Shenzhen facilities. A human resources manager dismissively commented, "This was to prevent the entry of those who would jump to their death for company compensation." It did not halt the employment of young student interns, however. The manager explained: "If a student is found to be emotionally unstable or seriously ill, we can ask the responsible teacher to take back the student. In this way we avert the risk of suicide and monitor labor conditions with the assistance of teachers."

School-Business Partnerships

A number of teacher interviewees, we learned, concealed from students and parents the absence of educational value in the internship program because they were being paid not only their regular monthly salary from their schools but also an additional salary from Foxconn for their supervisory service during the internship period. During the school year of 2011–2012, each teacher received 2,000 yuan per month from Foxconn for their role in strengthening labor control. The student interns were therefore pressured not only by the company, but also by their teachers to accept conditions that blatantly violated the educational provisions of their vocational programs and indeed undermined the technical training goals of their school programs.

The mission statement of a technical school says:

Unification of school and business
Unification of theory and practice
Unification of teacher and technician
Unification of student and employee

However, the reality was not a seamless unification, and the discrepancy between promise and the reality faced by interns could scarcely have been greater.

Li Wei, a 17-year-old student, recalled his internship experience: "I enrolled in an automotive repair course in September 2009, and according to the curriculum, the specialized course lasts for three years, with two years at school and a final year of internship." But less than a year into the program, in June 2010, he and his fellow classmates were sent to Foxconn to intern for seven full months. Rather than working on automobiles, he worked on iPhones. "It's exhausting. It's a waste of time," he concluded.

Not long after the students' return to school, the administration began arranging still more internships. Wei was very upset. In his words:

> The school had still not finished planning our specialized classes, but they began setting up internship assignments. We haven't even completed the core classes in our specialization, nor have we grasped the basic skills of automotive repair. How are we going to handle an internship in an auto company? We students have not attained sufficient knowledge in our education, and come time for employment, we'll have no competitive advantage.

Working on the line and living in the factory dormitory, students must comply with the Foxconn "internship program" on pain of not graduating. Throughout the program, several interns signaled their dismay in different ways, such as not going to work on time and slowing down because of a loss of motivation to work. Foxconn's presentation of honorary titles such as the Outstanding

Student Intern Awards—also known as the "hardworking bee" prize—failed to instill stronger commitment and loyalty among interns who found the work demeaning and perceived the internship as one that squandered their education.

One Chinese literature teacher observed that the student intern system was not unlike the abusive "contract labor system" of the 1930s and 1940s. He drew a parallel to the desperate earlier era in which children and teenagers from poverty-stricken villages were sold to labor contractors and dispatched to toil day and night under harsh conditions in Japanese-owned cotton mills in Shanghai.[21] Laughing bitterly, he confided, "I'm a modern day contractor," referring to his role as a coordinator of the internship program. "My daughter is seventeen years old, my only daughter. She's now preparing for the national college entrance exam. No matter what the result is, I won't let her come to intern or work for this company." More importantly, "at Foxconn," he said, "there's no real learning through integration of classroom and workshop. The distortion of vocational education in today's China runs deep."

Student Internship through Government Mobilization

Manager Zhu Wenxiang, a 31-year-old college graduate who joined the human resources department of Foxconn Chengdu on its opening in October 2010 after seven years in a small state-owned factory, was responsible for linking government, vocational schools, and Foxconn. He explained in our interview:

> Over the past year, I held monthly meetings with government leaders, promoting the "Number One Project" tailored to Foxconn. Over a few drinks and shared cigarettes, our colleagues and government officials regularly updated each other on the company's recruitment schedules, thereby establishing a good working relationship.

The Sichuan provincial government prioritized helping Foxconn as its "Number One Project." In the years since the deadly 7.9-scale earthquake that struck Sichuan in May 2008, killing 87,150 people and leaving 4,800,000 homeless, the provincial government redoubled efforts to attract investments to fund reconstruction.[22] New power lines were erected, high-speed rails and airport runways built, and multistory factory dormitories constructed. Not only was there expansion of ground transportation, Foxconn also benefited from upgraded air service, with major airlines offering expanded cargo and passenger capacity that assured quick links to American, European, and Asian markets. Zhuang Hongren, Foxconn's chief investment officer, pledged to "help Chengdu become an unshakeable city" in world electronics.[23]

Regional competition to secure and hold foreign investment across the coastal provinces and among the interior regions is intense. Andrew Ross in his book on global capital flight observes that "it was impossible not to come across evidence of the state's hand in the fostering of high-tech industry."[24] From manufacturing to financial services, Sichuan provincial and Chengdu municipal governments have been actively involved in strategic planning and collaboration.

Officials offered partial funding to construct Foxconn's gigantic production complex and eighteen-story dormitories with twenty-four rooms per floor, and eight workers per room. The first-phase male workers' living zone, located two kilometers from the manufacturing complex, housed twenty thousand people.

Foxconn's economic influence has become so great that CEO Terry Gou is widely known among workers in Chengdu as the "Mayor of 'Foxconn City.'" Local government also subsidizes transportation services for the company. Foxconn employees, interns, and teachers commute to work in public buses dedicated to the company's exclusive use.

"All vocational schools under the jurisdiction of Sichuan province were required to participate in the Foxconn student internship program," a Chengdu Municipal Education Bureau officer told us. Local education bureaus pitched in by identifying vocational schools suitable for linking to Foxconn internship programs. To assure their cooperation, governments disbursed funds to schools that fulfilled company targets for enrolling student interns. Schools that failed to meet human resources requirements lost funds.

Foxconn's iPad assembly facility is located in the Chengdu Hi-Tech Zone, Sichuan province. In February 2011, the State Council joint inspection team carried out an on-site monitoring exercise focused on the construction and development of the zone.

Fifty-seat public buses line up for Foxconn in Pi County, Chengdu City, Sichuan. Drivers provide transportation service to Foxconn at government-discounted rates..

A government-printed banner on the side of the bus reads, "Use fighting spirit to overcome earthquakes and natural disasters to provide transportation for Foxconn."

Figure 5.2 shows how Foxconn draws up plans for student labor recruitment, then top-level provincial government officials lead work teams across different administrative levels (city, county, district, township, and village) to meet deadlines and quotas by securing cooperation of the vocational schools under their jurisdiction.

Between September 2011 and January 2012 (a school semester), more than 7,000 students were working on assembly lines in Foxconn Chengdu, contributing 10 percent of the factory labor force. One of the participating schools, Pujiang Vocational School, sent 162 students on September 22, 2011, to undertake three-month internships that were subsequently extended in accordance with iPad production needs. The larger Pengzhou Technical School recruited 309 students, who were accompanied by three male and three female teachers for the entire internship. This is typical of the 1:50 teacher-student ratio maintained throughout the Foxconn Chengdu internship program in 2011–2012.

Contrary to our findings, the Fair Labor Association (FLA) "found *no interns* had been engaged at [Foxconn] Chengdu since September 2011" (our emphasis).[25] The FLA assessors briefly visited the iPad factory in Chengdu on March 6–9, 2012, and their report failed to uncover the abuses of some 7,000 student interns there "since September 2011." Were they misled by Foxconn when conducting the pre-announced investigation and subsequent verification? Was Apple unaware of the massive use, and abuse, of some 7,000 teenage interns who assembled iPads day and night to meet its deadline? For whatever reason, the FLA team played down or ignored these and other labor abuses that were taking place at Foxconn Chengdu.

Figure 5.2. Foxconn student internship recruitment, Sichuan, 2011–2012.

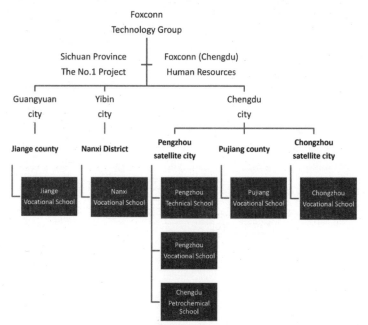

Note: For illustrative purposes, we simplify the multilevel power relationships in the recruitment of student interns through the triple alliance of Foxconn, local governments (from the provincial to the village level), and vocational schools under the jurisdiction of Sichuan province. The seven vocational schools that we specify were publicly reported in local news and/or on school websites as participating in the Foxconn internship programs. *Source:* Field data collected in Sichuan province.

Foxconn Mobilizing the Government

From Shenzhen to Chengdu to Zhengzhou, government officials staging "bidding wars" to attract and preserve investment have supported the huge labor recruitment assignments for Foxconn by targeting students and fresh graduates for internships and jobs. A township official-in-charge elaborated, "We were tasked by upper-level governments to eliminate negative social attitudes toward Foxconn after the 2010 suicide wave." The cross-departmental government team deploys messages across the internet, radio, television, posters, leaflets, telephone calls, door-to-door visits, and social media to publicize Foxconn's corporate culture, and "guide recruitment targets in correct thinking and understanding." The government is doing PR for Foxconn!

Villages, towns, and schools are saturated with propaganda to assure that Foxconn achieves the status of a household name and the company's labor recruitment quota is fulfilled. The division of labor among government departments in the service of Foxconn is summarized as follows:

1. The Human Resources and Social Security Department makes recruitment a top priority.

2. The Education Department arranges school-business cooperation, ensures that the number of graduates and interns meets the assigned goal, and arranges for their transportation on schedule and their proper supervision by teachers.

3. The Finance Department ensures that recruitment is adequately funded.

4. The Public Security Department completes job applicants' background investigations.

5. The Transportation Department assures appropriate transport capacity and safety.

6. The Health Department provides pre-employment physical examinations.

7. Other relevant departments ensure that recruitment progresses smoothly.

Governments have channeled financial and administrative resources to support Foxconn's search for labor at a time of rising costs and a tightening labor market.

As early as June 2010, the Zhengzhou Municipal Education Bureau in Henan province directed all vocational schools under its jurisdiction to dispatch students to intern in Foxconn's Shenzhen facilities 1,000 miles away.[26] This was to assure that students would be trained in time for the August opening of the new iPhone factory in Zhengzhou. Specifics of the sweeteners offered to support Foxconn Zhengzhou recruitment included the following:

1. Implement a policy of rewards for job introductions at the standard rate of 200 yuan per person from the designated government employment fund.

2. Give every successful worker (or intern) a 600-yuan subsidy from the designated government employment fund.

The Henan provincial government, using taxpayers' money, paid for incentives to schools or labor agencies ("the job introduction fee" of 200 yuan per person) to arrange for both employment and internships at Foxconn. In August and September 2010, local government officials divided the 20,000-recruit goal among twenty-three cities and counties and provided each new worker/intern with 600 yuan. For the targeted recruitment of 20,000 people, the government bill would be 16 million yuan (20,000 x [200 + 600] yuan). Each city or county government was assigned specific recruitment targets, with quotas within each district subdivided down to villages and towns. Table 5.2 shows the number of new Foxconn recruits that each of the twenty-three localities was ordered to produce.

Table 5.2. Government recruitment assignments for Foxconn, Henan, 2010.

	Name	Targets for August 2010 (persons)	Targets for September 2010 (persons)	Total (persons)
1.	Xinyang	1,000	1,000	2,000
2.	Zhoukou	940	940	1,880
3.	Luoyang	850	900	1,750
4.	Nanyang	850	850	1,700
5.	Shangqiu	850	850	1,700
6.	Zhumadian	850	850	1,700
7.	Puyang	750	700	1,450
8.	Xinxiang	680	680	1,360
9.	Anyang	650	650	1,300
10.	Pingdingshan	550	550	1,100
11.	Kaifeng	500	500	1,000
12.	Zhengzhou	200	200	400
13.	Hebi	200	200	400
14.	Jiaozuo	200	200	400
15.	Xuchang	200	200	400
16.	Luohe	200	200	400
17.	Sanmenxia	200	200	400
18.	Gushi	100	100	200
19.	Jiyuan	50	50	100
20.	Dengzhou	50	50	100
21.	Yongcheng	50	50	100
22.	Xiangcheng	50	50	100
23.	Gongyi	30	30	60
	Total	10,000	10,000	20,000

Note: The Henan provincial government established an interdepartmental committee to coordinate labor recruitment at Foxconn. The 20,000 new recruits included student *and* non-student job seekers. *Source:* Henan Provincial Poverty Alleviation Office (2010).[27]

It soon turned out that to recruit up to 10,000 student interns and fresh graduates for Foxconn in one summer month posed a great challenge to both teachers and officials. In early September 2010, an "urgent government recruitment directive" concerning student interns for Foxconn was cross-posted online at the All-China Federation of Trade Unions website. The core message of the original Education Department notice was that even if internships for final-year students had already been arranged, "the schools should redirect them to intern at Foxconn, to ensure that when Foxconn begins high-volume production, there will be an abundant high-quality workforce in Henan."[28] Such government effort on behalf of Foxconn bore all the hallmarks of a full-scale military mobilization, a people's war, waged by government on the economic front in the service of Foxconn.

In 2013, with the flexible labor of student interns and employees, Foxconn Zhengzhou "produced 96.45 million iPhones and exported 84.46 million of them," representing nearly 55 percent of the total value of exports of Henan province that year.[29] It also surpassed the Shenzhen facility to become the world's single largest iPhone production base, with local government offering one-stop export service at the prime location of the Zhengzhou Airport Economic Comprehensive Experimental Zone.[30]

The "well-choreographed customs routine," writes David Barboza of the *New York Times*, "is part of a hidden bounty of perks, tax breaks and subsidies" that has enabled Foxconn's rapid move to central China and its expansion. The local government of Zhengzhou municipality "promised discounted energy and transportation costs, lower social insurance payments, and more than $1.5 billion in grants for the construction of factories and dormitories that could house hundreds of thousands of workers."[31] This is but one of the many ways in which Chinese officialdom smoothed the path for Foxconn, as well as Apple, paving the way for growth in exports and local markets, but in this instance at the sacrifice of the interests of student interns.

Precarious Internships

"In electronics," Chad Raphael and Ted Smith comment, "lightning-fast product cycles and seasonal surges in consumer demand push suppliers to impose intense work hours and forced overtime, and to add droves of temporary workers to assemble the next new device to meet product launch deadlines determined by the brand owners."[32] Recruitment through vocational schools is an efficient way to add tens of thousands of students who can be mobilized for the company by the local labor and/or state agencies, and who can be terminated at will. In the context of China, with the tightening of labor law and employment requirements, such as restrictions over firings of long-serving employees, student interns have become low-cost substitutes for regular employees.[33]

A number of vocational schools we observed aspire to nurture young people to become the next Leonardo da Vinci, Albert Einstein, Thomas Edison, and the like, but under the crushing system imposed on the factory floor they are destined to fail, if the Foxconn internship program is any indication. In Shenzhen's Longhua Cultural Square, 16-year-old Zhang Lintong, whom we met at the opening of this chapter, talked about school life and music. An admirer of the nineteenth-century Russian realist artist Ilya Repin, he praised *The Song of the Volga Boatmen*, which reminds him of Repin's seminal painting *Barge Haulers on the Volga*.[34] *Barge Haulers* depicts a foreman and ten laboring men hauling an enormous barge upstream on the Volga. The men seem to be on the verge of collapse from exhaustion. The lead hauler's eyes are fixed on the horizon. The second man bows his head into his chest and the last one drifts off from the line, a dead man walking. The haulers, dressed in rags, are tightly bound with leather straps. The exception is the brightly clad youth in the center of the group, who raises his head while fighting against his leather bonds in an effort to free himself from toil. "I often dream, but repeatedly tear apart my dreams; like a miserable painter, tearing up my draft sketches ... I want to quit. But I can't," Lintong sighed.

Facing political and financial pressures from local governments, many schools—even the better ones—are unable to shield students from internships that violate the law and sacrifice students' interests as they play a government-supervised enforcer role in internship programs. Guy Standing, author of *The Precariat*, highlighted the fact that "internships are potentially a vehicle for channeling youths into the precariat," instead of providing a ladder to success.[35] None of the thirty-eight interviewed interns expressed interest in working for Foxconn after graduation. If they were interested in assembly-line jobs, they told us, they would have started working right after finishing middle school rather than seeking specialized training in multiple fields.

It is a cruel irony that internships are not performed for the benefit of the intern. As Ross Perlin comments in his book on American and European internship practices, *Intern Nation*, "The very significance of the word *intern* lies in its ambiguity."[36] We discovered that some employers went as far as renaming "internships" as "social practice programs" and "service learning" as a way to evade responsibility and monitoring, while maximizing their profits. In the case of such abuses, student interns are victimized in the service of the corporation and of corporate-state interests.

6

Fire and Brimstone

A Worker's Requiem

My body stretches long
lying within a bare building
obstructing the cityscape,
sealed tightly in cement
burying my story

With each mouthful of toxic dust inhaled
profit is exhaled
as prices rise and fall
each annual fireworks bash
burning my breath

Back bent I furtively twitter
computers nibble away life
backpack heavy on shoulder
muscles and bones strained to the limit
concealing my hardship

My body conveys a message:
reject this false prosperity
leave the corner of darkness—
strained body and soul embrace each other
still you and I will not yield

—Mininoise (Hong Kong grassroots folk band)[1]

iPad production and its upgrade to iPad 2 went smoothly at Foxconn Chengdu during the first half year of operations, drawing on the labor of student interns and rural migrant workers. But on March 11, 2011, Fukushima in northeast Japan was struck by the triple disaster of earthquake, tsunami, and nuclear meltdown. The disaster left close to 20,000 Japanese dead or missing, created 315,000 refugees, many of whom are still unable to return to their homes, devastated farms and fisheries, and left crippled nuclear plants with radioactive particles in the melted core of the containment vessels and in the soil of the surrounding areas. It was the world's worst nuclear catastrophe since Chernobyl in April 1986, with continuing repercussions extending across the Japanese economy and society and far beyond in a densely connected world.[2]

Foxconn was quickly alerted to the fact that imports of key components of the iPad, including Toshiba's flash memory (used for audio and video storage) and touch display screens, would be disrupted as Japanese ports and highways were incapacitated. The vulnerability of global supply chains that connected Foxconn, Apple, Toshiba, Japan, and China to electronics components and products essential to their success was dramatically revealed.

Chengdu: iPad City

By March 2011, Foxconn Chengdu's labor force had grown rapidly to fifty thousand employees. "Foxconn is hiring," a 17-year-old Sichuanese worker commented, "and the whole city has gone crazy. Local officials grab people and ask if they'd be willing to work at Foxconn. The government has made it an official task. Officials at each level have a recruitment quota. Isn't this crazy?"

At a government administrative building, employment officers helped walk-in job applicants fill out forms and arrange interviews at Foxconn. Such free administrative services lowered corporate recruitment costs. In addition, the production complexes and dormitories testified to Foxconn's westward advance, in which

abundant industrial land and subsidized utilities were provided
along with labor recruited in many instances by local governments.

*A government employment and social security office converted into a Foxconn recruitment
station at Hongguang Town, Pi County, in Chengdu City, Sichuan. The local state subsidizes Foxconn by providing free hiring services.*

"Work at Foxconn and swiftly move toward a prosperous life," a
recruitment slogan reads. Foxconn was quick to accelerate its move
to lower-wage inland locations in sync with the government's "Go
West" policy and lucrative offers from local governments eager to
secure the company's relocation. In Chengdu, workers soon learned
that the basic monthly pay was just 950 yuan (compared with
1,200 yuan in Shenzhen during the same period), far short of the
1,600 yuan that recruiters told them they would receive. Foxconn
justified this by explaining that the higher figure was their "comprehensive income," that is, the basic wage plus overtime premiums and bonuses.

Foxconn Chengdu's newly built eighteen-story factory dormitory, Block 2. Workers complained bitterly that living conditions were intolerable: noisy, dirty, smelly, and above all, lacking reliable water and electricity.

Foxconn ramped up iPad production at the renovated "northern plant" in the Export Processing Zone and was hurrying to move into the permanent "southern plant" in the Hi-Tech Zone of Chengdu. On the night of January 6, 2011, one of the two elevators in the dormitory was out of order. Thousands of workers, after an exhausting work shift, climbed the stairs to their rooms only to find that there was no hot water for showers. That month, the average temperature was between 34 and 41° Fahrenheit (1–5°C), and electricity and water supplies repeatedly failed.

One night, pent-up frustration exploded and several workers raced to the dormitory roof, smashed the water tank, switched off the power, and cut off the entire water supply system. Shouting workers rushed out of their rooms, trying to find out what was going on. In anger, some threw glass bottles, plastic basins, trash bins, stools, and fire extinguishers from the upper floors to the ground below. Foxconn management branded the workers' behavior "senseless." By 10:00 p.m., the police had arrested more than two dozen workers and a lockdown halted the protests. On the next morning, when workers returned to work there was no improvement in the dormitory environment.

iPad Workers

Production had begun on some factory floors even before auxiliary facilities such as toilets and canteens were fully accessible. Throughout the factory area, piles of sand, stones, and rubbish accumulated, and the roads were filled with potholes. The entrance to the factory had some crudely placed wooden boards, creating a small path between two uneven sand piles for workers to weave through as they entered and left through the makeshift pedestrian thoroughfare. Construction materials like steel bars and cement were stacked everywhere.

Construction material waste and rubbish litter the ground throughout the Foxconn Cheng-du factory complex.

"All of us log long hours of overtime with only two rest days in the entire month," an iPad-polishing worker explained in March 2011. Tracking demand worldwide, Apple's then chief operating officer Tim Cook put it this way, "Nobody wants to buy sour milk."[3] And elsewhere, "Inventory . . . is fundamentally evil. You want to man-age it like you're in the dairy business: If it gets past its freshness date, you have a problem."[4] The result is that supplier factories race against time at Apple's command to get the work done regardless of the toll on workers in terms of compulsory overtime and speedups.

Apple, by introducing myriad changes in the design of its devices, each with multiple variations to suit consumer tastes, sought to integrate hardware and a mobile operating system (iOS) "into an experience that's an 'aha' for the customer."[5] *Time* magazine recog-nized the original iPad as one of the "50 best inventions" of 2010.[6] Bill Gates, cofounder of Microsoft, mused that "we did tablets, lots of tablets, well before Apple did, but they put together the pieces in a way that succeeded," as Microsoft did not.[7] To meet Apple's aesthetic demands, Foxconn developed a one-piece precision mold so that the upgraded iPad 2 could be released on the market for as little as US$499—the same price that the original iPad debuted at the previous year.

An Apple press statement dated March 2, 2011, boasted, "While others have been scrambling to copy the first generation iPad, we're launching iPad 2, which moves the bar far ahead of the competition and will likely cause them to go back to the drawing boards yet again."[8] On the same day, more than two hundred Foxconn workers clashed with supervisors over job evaluations and wage adjustments that were supposed to take place after the probationary period. The aggrieved workers also demanded full payment of overtime premiums that had been withheld and overall improvement of working conditions. They had discovered a point of vulnerability for the manufacturing giant by launching their action at the moment when Foxconn was under pressure to produce a new iPad model.

Refusing to work after lunch, the protesting workers occupied the B22 factory canteen and demanded to negotiate with senior managers. When management stalled, at 3:30 p.m., they marched out of the canteen to the main entrance of the plant at Zone B in a bid to draw government attention to their case in order to increase pressure on the company. In less than ten minutes, traffic police and company security officers arrived on the scene. Only then did the manager agree to sit down and talk with workers, indicating the success of the strategy.

In massive strikes, either the employer or government officials require workers to elect representatives, generally limited to five, to engage in talks. Once worker representatives are elected, the company moves to take control. This intervention typically marks the beginning of the fragmentation, co-optation, and crushing of worker power. Frequently, the worker representatives are identified as troublemakers and dismissed.

Mingqi Chen, the Foxconn human resources manager who mediated the dispute, later recalled that the workers responded that they had no representatives. "We're all leaders," they told him. To prevent company retaliation, the workers had learned through bitter experience to protect each other in a collectivity that presented no visible leaders.

Foxconn was under intense pressure to make the second-generation iPads fast enough to meet global demand without delay, and management eventually compromised by agreeing to "increase workers' wages" on condition that eligible workers could pass the assessment at the end of the month. Meanwhile, Foxconn hired more student interns from vocational schools all over the country to fill the iPad assembly lines. On April 20, 2011, Apple's chief financial officer Peter Oppenheimer told investors in a conference call, "We sold every iPad 2 we could make."[9] If Foxconn could have produced more iPads, Apple would have reaped still greater profits.

Aluminum Dust

Wages were by no means the only issue that protesting workers contested. Foxconn's polishing workers are responsible for transforming raw aluminum into shiny, stainless iPad casings. Each polishing machine produces metallic dust as it grinds the casings with ever-greater refinement. Microscopic aluminum dust coats workers' faces and clothes. A worker described the situation this way: "I'm breathing aluminum dust at Foxconn like a vacuum cleaner." With the workshop windows tightly shut, workers felt that they were suffocating.

The monitoring of workplace hazards, including ductwork inspection and ventilation system review, was sacrificed to meet iPad production targets. "Some tearing and pain occurs as the tiny solid aluminum particles are rinsed from my eyes by tears," Ma Quan, a 20-year-old worker, explained to us in Sichuan dialect. He added: "Everyone in the workshop is wearing a thin gauze mask, with a center section of activated charcoal, but it doesn't have an airtight seal and provides no protection."

If the masks were useless for blocking the toxic effects of aluminum dust, they did help Foxconn pass factory inspections. Although workers were constantly coughing and complaining of sore throats, Foxconn managers, as well as the Apple engineers and product development teams dispatched to the Chengdu factory, apparently prioritized the hourly production figures over the health and lives of workers. Four of Quan's colleagues had already quit their jobs long before their probation ended.

In the polishing workshop, workers also wore cotton gloves, but the finest particles penetrated through the flimsy material to their hands. Workers simply washed their hands and bodies with soap and water, without knowing the exposure level of aluminum dust in their workshop. After work Quan took off his cotton gloves and looked helplessly at both his hands covered in aluminum dust.

This photo shows the skin-color contrast between the hand of the Foxconn polishing worker (after removing gloves) and the researcher. Workers were unaware that aluminum dust created by the polishing of an iPad could explode.

Polishing workers breathed in aluminum dust twelve hours a day during periods of peak production. Encouraged by fellow workmates, Quan relayed their shared health concerns to his line leader, only to hear words that left the workers feeling distraught: "The factory conditions are absolutely safe!" In other words, Foxconn refused to conduct a comprehensive risk assessment of its workplace health and safety conditions, or even to recognize the need for such an assessment.

Fire, Explosions, Death

On May 6, 2011, Foxconn released a media statement: "We have made tremendous progress over the past year as we work to lead our industry in meeting the needs of the new generation of workers in China and that has been confirmed by the many customer representatives, outside experts, and reporters who have visited our facilities and openly met with our employees and our management team."[10] Such public relations statements mocked the deep concerns expressed repeatedly by workers, which were first reported by the *Guardian* just before May 1, 2011, the International Labor Day.[11]

On one point, the company statement is all too accurate: "customer representatives," that is, Apple representatives, visited the facilities and raised no significant issues concerning health and safety. Two weeks passed. On May 20, an accumulation of aluminum dust in the air duct on the third floor at Foxconn Chengdu Building A5 fueled a deadly explosion. At about 7:00 p.m. the metallic dust was ignited by a spark in an electrical switch. Dense smoke rapidly filled the workshop. Firemen arrived at the scene around 7:30 p.m. Ambulances and company vans brought victims who were either seriously burned or had lost consciousness to the emergency units.

Four workers died and dozens were injured. "We barely escaped with our lives. It's terrifying," the surviving workers told us as they recalled the "black Friday evening." Remembering those who lost their lives in the midst of lightning and thunder that night, some workers could not hold back their tears.

Human Costs Are Built into an iPad

Immediately after the fatal accident, Foxconn confirmed that iPad production had been "suspended at the site of the explosion" in

Chengdu. "The safety of our employees is our highest priority and we will do whatever is required to determine and address the cause of this tragic accident," a Foxconn spokesperson said.[12] Apple's press statement echoed that message: "We are deeply saddened by the tragedy at Foxconn's plant in Chengdu, and our hearts go out to the victims and their families. We are working closely with Foxconn to understand what caused this terrible event."[13] The evidence on the ground, however, suggests that both Apple and Foxconn prioritized profit maximization, public relations, and damage control over protecting the health and lives of workers.

Internet censorship, along with company surveillance of the entire polishing workshop and the hospital, ensured a media blackout. Official notices read:

> The State Council Information Office: In regard to Foxconn's Chengdu plant explosion, all media and websites are to wait for an official report. No independent reports, re-posts, or recommendations will be allowed.

> The Sichuan Provincial Propaganda Department: With regard to Foxconn's Chengdu iPad 2 plant explosion, no independent reporting can be conducted. Unauthorized reports will be immediately deleted.[14]

Charles Duhigg and David Barboza, writing for the award-winning "The iEconomy" series of the *New York Times*, observed the harsh reality that "human costs are built into an iPad."[15]

Fire hazards and metallic dust explosions had put workers' lives at severe risk in other Apple suppliers. Seven months after the Foxconn tragedy, on December 17, 2011, combustible aluminum dust fueled another blast, this time at iPhone maker Pegatron in Shanghai, injuring sixty-one workers. In the blast, young men and women suffered severe burns and shattered bones, leaving many permanently disabled.[16]

7

Wandering the City

Shenzhen, Shenzhen

The years pass one after another
And I change one job for another
My earnings never amount to much
But I have accumulated fistfuls of grievances.

Shenzhen, Shenzhen,
Are you still the Shenzhen of my heart?
Or are you just a stop along the way?
When I leave you, where will I go?

—Power Bass D Worker Band[1]

Moving in and out of Foxconn, workers may suffer not only indus-trial accidents but also the "hidden injuries" that beset those of the lower social class. Richard Sennett and Jonathan Cobb, coauthors of *The Hidden Injuries of Class*, published in 1972, succinctly described an increasingly inegalitarian American society in which blue-collar workers were deemed to have less self-worth, life value, and social respect.[2] Similarly, manual laborers in today's China are struggling to earn a dignified living and livelihood security in Shenzhen and other big cities characterized by rising economic and social inequal-ities. For those who leave Shenzhen, where will they go?

The lyrics of the Chinese song "Shenzhen, Shenzhen" strike a chord with many among the working poor. They are desperate to make money to support their family and to marry. They are deeply troubled by the challenge of finding a home, not just a dormitory bunk bed, in the city. Those who are married are compelled to confront the reality of leaving behind their children and often a spouse in their birth village when they set out for factories far from home. Against this backdrop, Foxconn states that between 2014 and 2018 the company "helped 21,003 left-behind children in Sichuan and Henan,"[3] a welfare benefit offered to well-performing employees. Put another way, the stress of making a living for married workers with children is high.

The acute problems faced by male and female Foxconn employees, including those who have already married and have children, can be seen as a reflection of the larger Chinese society marked by rapid urbanization with widening regional disparity. Migrant parents with children face the dilemma of leaving them in the village with grandparents or other relatives, or bringing them to the city where most are ineligible for public education and must attend for-fee migrant schools.

Worker Dormitories in the City

Rural migrant workers face the difficult choice of either living in spartan conditions in factory dormitories, often sharing a room with seven or more fellow workers, or renting in the private housing market at higher cost. Looking back, in the Foxconn production base in Shenzhen during the late 1980s and early 1990s, the first floor of the factory compound was typically a canteen, the second to fifth floors the production lines, and the sixth floor the worker dormitory. The socio-spatial boundary between work and life was blurred, particularly for workers on compulsory overtime during busy seasons.

Fires and substandard structures at some enterprises were life-threatening. After the 1993 Zhili toy factory fire that took eighty-seven lives,[4] under mounting social pressure and international media scrutiny, the Shenzhen government passed a series of safety laws, requiring that all exits at workshops and dormitories be unlocked and clear, with exit signs and fire extinguishers in place. Worker dormitories were not to be located immediately adjacent to production workshops and warehouses, and they were to be subject to regular examination. At the national level, the government promulgated the Labor Law in July 1994, which came into force in January 1995, with provisions to protect workers including occupational health and safety.

In 1996, Foxconn upgraded building safety standards following the opening of the Longhua plant. Newly built dormitories have improved facilities and are equipped with metal lockers, shared TV rooms, and cafeterias. Nevertheless, the basic conditions remain: a shared dormitory room housing eight to twenty-four workers in double-decker bunk beds. Quarrels over toilet and shower use, noise, and security problems in the dormitories are frequent and demoralizing.

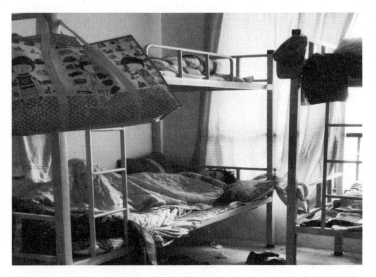

Sleep, eat, work, sleep—a Foxconn factory dormitory room with standard double-decker bunk beds. Eight men, on day and night shift, share one room.

Husbands and wives do *not* share a private dormitory room with their spouse, but are housed separately in male and female dormitories. Foxconn dormitory service managers talk about morality, cooperation, and obedience—all deemed essential to maintain the discipline of the workforce—but their regulations create barriers to communication between intimate partners. While working for the same boss, a husband and wife do not have access to an independent dormitory room unless they are high-level managers, who enjoy exclusive rights to company-provided housing benefits.

At Foxconn, and many other factories, the dormitory sections are segregated by gender, and visits to rooms of members of the opposite sex must be registered with the security management office. Workers entering the dormitory are required to swipe an electronic staff card and then wait for a green light before walking up the staircase or taking an elevator. Security officers monitor the dormitory gate around the clock and periodically inspect every floor.

A poster of Foxconn dormitory management rules and safety regulations. No. 5: "It is strictly prohibited to bring in or put up outsiders as guests, including workers who are not from this dormitory." No. 6: "It is strictly forbidden for male and female workers to drop in on one another."

The dormitory is not provided as a form of workers' welfare; it is rented, though at a price below that of apartments in the city. In the search for personal freedom and control over their private lives, some workers leave the dormitory and rent apartments as soon as they can afford to do so.

Searching for a Home

In June 2011, with the opening of the 20-kilometer Longhua Metro Line, the transportation network was extended from Longhua District, the location of Foxconn's massive factories, to Hong Kong's northern border. Large construction projects for shopping malls, homes, and hotels were approved one after another, transforming the new city center and urban landscape, pushing land and property prices as well as rents to new heights in the fast-growing metropolis of Shenzhen.

A worker explained the private housing market situation:

> Our landlord mistakenly believed that Foxconn had raised our starting wages to two thousand yuan per month. It's not true. Far from it! They don't realize that it's only after we work overtime that we have a bit more money to pay the rent. Our earnings have been eaten up by the landlords.

In old, densely packed migrant quarters, landlords used partitions to divide rental spaces into small rooms. In late 2011, the rent for a small room ranged from 380 to 580 yuan a month near the Foxconn Longhua factory, depending on the location and housing conditions. Utilities and property management fees varied widely. In comparison, Foxconn in 2010 deducted 40 yuan per month for a bunk-bed space in the dormitory to offset part of the increased wage, then raised the figure to 70 yuan, 110 yuan, and in 2011, 150 yuan.

The cheapest rental rooms frequently have no window. Some have a narrow window set high near the ceiling, which overlooks nothing but at least is a link to the outside world. Some complexes are infested with rats and cockroaches. Together with the burden of rent and the inflation that has driven food prices up for those who live outside the factory complex, workers continue to struggle to find decent accommodations and to make ends meet, despite sustained increases in basic wages.

In 2011, a hostel cost 25 yuan per night near the south gate of Foxconn Longhua, Shenzhen. The one-month special rate was 680 yuan. By contrast, a Foxconn bunk-bed space in a shared dormitory room cost 150 yuan per month.

Real estate developers transforming Shenzhen's industrial suburbs into middle-class homes have reaped lucrative returns. In February 2019, the minimum wage in Shenzhen was 2,200 yuan a month, second only to Shanghai (2,420 yuan a month). Foxconn workers, with overtime premiums, night-shift subsidies, and full-attendance allowances, could earn approximately 4,000 yuan a month. After deducting living expenses, the factory worker's personal savings did not go far in the local housing market where both rents and purchases had increased sharply. So what were the living options for migrant workers in the cities?

The all-in-one, multifunctional architecture of production workshops, warehouses, and worker residences was typical of early industrial districts, and is still common in poorly planned areas where low-income families concentrate. In terms of space, precisely when

Shenzhen had transitioned from village to metropolis to become a leading player in the international economy, migrant workers felt strong pressure to settle in an apartment of their own. However, they were frequently stymied by three factors: first, officials in Shenzhen, Beijing, Shanghai, and other medium-sized cities, large cities, and megacities denied rural migrants without stable income and employment the right to purchase apartments; second, prices on one- and two-bedroom apartments rose rapidly in step with urbanization and were well beyond the means of the vast majority of workers; finally, migrant workers were repeatedly evicted from even substandard rental housing, pushing them to the urban margins as cities sought to create "high-end," "smart," global cities, in part by eliminating rural migrants from the central city to the periphery. The hard labor of rural migrants was essential to the creation of the modern urban lifestyle, yet they were denied access to its benefits.[5]

In February 2019, the rent on a one-bedroom apartment with full-length windows like these rose to 1,500 yuan a month in the Qinghu community of Longhua District, Shenzhen. The minimum wage in the city was 2,200 yuan a month, placing such apartments well beyond the reach of factory assembly workers.

Living on the Margins

Several workers "escaped from the factory" to try something new, such as hawking food on the streets or starting other small businesses. Yu Xiatian, twenty-six, a tall, strong man in a black V-neck sweatshirt, was self-employed. "I disliked working for Foxconn. Day after day, my hope for a better life seemed to get further away. Last month I resigned."

In January 2012, Xiatian rented a van and began selling bananas. "I buy bananas directly from farmers at half-past five in the morning. Then I drive to the main footbridge opposite Foxconn Longhua Zone D, where workers pass through the factory gate to and from work. Several dozen hawkers sell oranges and other fruits and cooked food at these hot spots," Xiatian's voice rose as he talked about a good sale that morning.

Street hawkers at Zone D at the Foxconn Longhua factory (west gate), Shenzhen.

"If city officials don't show up to demand licenses and extort money, and gangsters don't demand protection, it's great. I sell cheap and in large quantities," Xiatian said. Time and again, however, four- to five-member gangs of thugs attacked him and other hawkers, demanding "protection fees." He told us, "It's pointless calling the police. We're not authorized to sell on the street. We don't have business licenses."

Many small businesses failed and their proprietors returned to factory work. "Since this January, I've kept telling myself I would never again enter a factory, but living at the margin it's not clear that I will be able to avoid returning to the factory," Xiatian said. Far from becoming middle-income earners in the city, most migrant workers continue to move in and out with a succession of industrial jobs.

Unlike Xiatian who is still single, Bu Hui is married with a child. He is a metal-polishing worker with eight years' experience at Foxconn.

The night was late. It was another sleepless night for Hui. In the online chat room, he shared his distress. "Lately I've been under a lot of pressure; I need to make some money. My son is only four years old. And my parents' health is not good. I've got to take care of my child and look after the elderly back home." He then asked, "Do you know how to find work in Hong Kong?"

Concerning his former wife, Hui lamented that a beautiful love had drifted away. "Mei had fallen in love with me at first sight at a skating rink," he recalled. They were nineteen years old. Soon they married. "We rented a room, just eight square meters." The living conditions were shabby.

Mei started working on the line at Foxconn, but she disliked the work and quit to sell shoes on the street. "I was busy working and did not have time to be with her. There was a lot of overtime, in peak periods as much as one hundred hours a month. Outside of sleep, there was just overtime," Hui recalled.

"Sometimes I worked the night shift. I would go to bed a little late or get up early to be with her." As Hui put it, "I always cared most about feelings; money is just a material possession."

After Mei gave birth to their child in his home village, she wanted to leave the house to find work. Following the Chinese New Year, Mei went to work in Guangzhou while Hui continued to work in Shenzhen. "I didn't want her to go, but I couldn't talk her out of it." The newborn was left in the village with his parents, joining the ranks of tens of millions of left-behind children, in this case from birth.

After parting, Hui and Mei's contact gradually faded away. "Married women like to compare themselves with others. We'd fight over money. With my low wages, I just couldn't satisfy her."

Mei's expectations created unbearable pressure on Hui. "I felt useless. I didn't have a house. I didn't have a car. I didn't know at first, then I found out that she despised me because I made so little money. I wanted to join her in Guangzhou, but she wouldn't let me." Their relationship had withered. He suspected that she had another man. Before long, they divorced.

For many rural residents, migration appears to open the only opportunities for advancement and higher incomes. The challenges facing young couples, however, are formidable. With husband and wife both frequently working very long hours, at times in different cities, they may feel overworked and stressed. The spheres of production and reproduction, as well as the workplace and the family, far from being integrated and mutually supportive, are divided and disruptive. Under these work and financial pressures, many workers find it extremely difficult to strengthen marital and familial relations.

On the Move

With the shift in location of Foxconn and its suppliers, Foxconn has transferred workers and staff to designated sites to meet its labor needs at reduced cost. This is an emergent pattern of corporate-led massive migration and labor flexibilization. For workers the move is not always voluntary or harmonious, putting it at odds with corporate publicity.

"Working close to home is really nice"—headline of Foxconn Weekly *of June 30, 2011. Faced with compulsory transfers to low-wage regions far from home, not all workers were smiling.*

Chen Chunhua, a 29-year-old Henan native with rural household registration, identifies Shenzhen as her home with an eye to permanently leaving the village behind. She lives with her partner in a rental room in Futian district, one of nine districts that make up the city. "Although our place is very small, we're content. Futian is convenient for public transportation. Not very far from here, we have many parks and green spaces." The Futian Port is connected with Lok Ma Chau Station, part of Hong Kong MTR's East Rail Line.

In Shenzhen, Chunhua would like to continue to work, and since beginning to work in 2006 she has enrolled in the government-administered social insurance program covering health care and pensions. "I was working at a French-owned company, Thomson Okmco, a Shenzhen-based subsidiary of Thomson Multimedia. One day, our director announced that Foxconn had signed a merger agreement with our company. He assured us that most of us would be given new contracts at the Foxconn Longhua plant."

Foxconn had hired Chunhua as a junior staffer in the Consumer and Computer Products Business Group (CCPBG). "My responsibility was to fill out product information sheets and prepare meeting minutes for the team leader. I worked the day shift in the office." Chunhua had become accustomed to the administrative work.

In September 2010, things changed unexpectedly for Chunhua, however. She was peremptorily ordered by senior management to move from Shenzhen to the Yantai Economic and Technological Development Zone. Located in Shandong province and bordered by the Yellow Sea and the Bohai Sea, the new job was 1,122 miles north, far from her partner and friends in Shenzhen. At that time, the local minimum wage in Yantai city was only 920 yuan per month, compared with Chunhua's pay of 1,360 yuan per month in Shenzhen.

Chunhua told her supervisor: "I am not prepared to go to Yantai. I'd rather take another office job under the same employment terms at Longhua."

From south to north, and from east to west, Foxconn explains its corporate expansion and relocation plans with characteristically altruistic claims: "We continue to prioritize placement of our manufacturing operations" in provinces where they are "the home regions of the majority of our employees." Then "workers can be closer to their families and friends, their traditional support network."[6] Some workers and managerial staff responded enthusiastically to the company's call to contribute to the local economy in their home provinces and to work closer to home. But many more, particularly those with jobs and families in southeast coastal regions, balked at accepting what they described as an "involuntary job transfer" involving a pay cut as well as disruption of family and other social networks, leaving them to start all over again far from Shenzhen homes.

According to Chunhua, "Workers received an ultimatum: transfer or quit." Foxconn refused to offer Chunhua either an office job or severance pay. She quickly learned that something was wrong. "That morning I found that my electronic work card was disabled. I was later assigned to an assembly line in another business group. My job classification was changed. I would also have to work at night. I was shocked."

When Foxconn redrew the territory of its manufacturing sites across China, "it moved workers around like any other commodity," Chunhua remarked. That afternoon Chunhua walked into the Employee Care Center to ask for help. "To my surprise, I was sent back to the very supervisor with whom I had strong disagreements." At night, "I was so angry that I could not eat or rest."

The next day Chunhua was admitted to the Shenzhen Futian No. 2 People's Hospital. "Foxconn had unilaterally and arbitrarily changed my main work responsibility, violating a labor contract that was based on mutual consent," she told us. "In retrospect, the day I said 'no' to going along with the transfer to Yantai, I was destined to leave without getting a penny."

In the course of the company-directed "harmonious labor migration" that was synonymous with the relentless territorial expansion of the Foxconn empire to new low-wage regions, many workers experienced a heightened sense of insecurity, accentuated by the uprooting of lives and the family separations.

Chunhua was hardly alone. Her colleagues in various divisions at Longhua, some of them married with school-age children in Shenzhen, had no alternative but to quit without compensation or severance pay. "Why? Our homes are here. We can't just leave and start everything all over."

Unsettled Lives

It is true that when Foxconn and other companies open factories in inland and western regions, there are increasing opportunities to find employment closer to home. Has this eased the strain for rural migrants? Liang Zhong, a 31-year-old migrant from a village in Yibin city in southeastern Sichuan, is a newly employed iPad assembly worker in Foxconn's plant in Chengdu. While Zhong and his parents, like other villagers, have cultivation rights to a small plot of agricultural land in their native village, he works away from home to support the family, providing the main source of cash for his wife, his daughter, and his parents.

Living in the factory dormitory, Zhong was able to send home 500 to 800 yuan a month on average. On special occasions, such as his parents' birthdays and relatives' weddings, he sent a thousand or so to the family by way of celebration. "Early this year, I squeezed into a bus to get home for the Spring Festival. Soon after, the nightmare started all over again as I traveled back to resume work," Zhong recalled of his week at home. Family relations were very important to him. However, Zhong could not afford to bring his parents to live under the same roof in the city. When he had enough savings, he took leave to go home. Although living only 160 miles from Chengdu, like most migrants to the coastal area, he was able to return home only once or twice a year.

China's "spring travel crush" at New Year's, the biggest holiday of the year, is also the world's biggest annual migration of people. For scores of millions of rural migrants, this is their only chance to visit home and reconnect with family. Zhong had been thinking about his wife while they were living apart. He passed us his smartphone and asked, "Is this kid cute?" Before we could reply, he said, "So cute, I really want to go home now. She's naughty!"

In February 2011, Zhong earned 1,870 yuan, including basic and overtime pay and a subsidy for night work. The cost of living and access to education for children remained his deep concerns. He alone was unable to provide funds sufficient for daily childcare. Due to the shortage of public kindergartens in both the countryside and the city, preschool education is not available for many children between the ages of three and six.[7] "Married workers like me have to scrimp on personal expenses while doing as much overtime as possible," he told us. His peers similarly struggled to keep their marital and personal lives together in the face of multiple crises, often separated from spouses, children, and parents except during a brief annual visit home. "There's a lot of pressure and the future is uncertain. I've wanted to quit to find better pay at another factory ever since starting my current job."

For the moment, however, Zhong would hold on to his position at Foxconn as he has neither the skills nor the capital to find a better job or to start his own business. "Life is insecure. I can't make enough if I go back home."

Eating on the street on the cheap: a street-side stall for workers.

How to Live a More Fulfilling Life?

When *Time* magazine nominated "workers in China" as runner-up in its 2009 Person of the Year issue, the editor commented that they have brightened the future of humanity by "leading the world to economic recovery."[8] But at what price?

According to one estimate by the Chinese Academy of Social Sciences and the World Bank, "co-residence of rural elderly with their adult children fell from 70 percent in 1991 to 40 percent by 2006," and the trend of rural to urban labor migration continues.[9] Stated differently, since the 1990s, large areas of the countryside have been depopulated as many youth migrate far from home, leaving primarily elders and children in the village. The nature of family ties and living arrangements is undergoing profound change.

Feeling homesick and, at times, a sense of loss is not a stranger to young adults who are on their own in the city. After finishing a long shift, Foxconn workers enjoy playing songs on their smartphones for relaxation. Here is one of the popular songs, "Embrace Life":

> We walk along the outskirts of the city
> Leaving footprints of world change
> Many wishes have become wisps of smoke
> Too much sweat has fallen
> Our lives are in a gray space
> Sleepless nights have nothing but stars to see
> Although life is always withering away
> Instead it has made the city's sky blue
> Walking alone on the city street
> Wanting to cry without the melancholy of tears
> But hope those vanished dreams can become memories . . . after we
>   succeed.[10]

The gigantic Foxconn factory city is a city that never sleeps. People there are assembling, uploading, and offloading throughout the long working night. Beneath the same starry sky, outside the factory wall, lovers find their limited free time for themselves. They take a walk along the river next to the Longhua complex, holding hands, and sharing soft words. With the relaxation of China's family policy, young people dream of marrying and having a happy family. How many of them would be able to buy an apartment and settle comfortably? Leaving Foxconn perhaps just means entering another, smaller Foxconn. Still, many are trying their luck by seeking a way out.

8

Chasing Dreams

"Birds, don't be silly, no one cares whether you're tired
from flying, people only care how high you fly!"

—Ou Yang, 19-year-old female Foxconn worker

Young workers, many now far from home villages of their birth,
are driven by the desire to broaden their horizons and experience
modern life and cosmopolitan consumption. Ou Yang dresses more
fashionably than most workers, favoring a dropped waist, knee-
length skirt. In her own words, we can hear the aspirations of this
new generation: "I want to secure a better life for my mother and
myself in the city." And she is hardly alone. Many are chasing their
dreams, big and small, of a good life, and of love, marriage, and
entrepreneurial triumphs.

Factory Girls

Ou Yang has begun supplementing her factory job with a part-
time job. "I like to wear makeup. I like to shop. Why should I
aspire to have less than others?" she asked. "I've joined a 'Perfect
Beauty' direct-sales training course. I hope to earn more money by
selling cosmetics."

"Someday I want to drive a brand new Honda and return home
in style!" Dreaming of helping her mother make a good life, Yang
plans to settle in Wuhan, the provincial capital of Hubei:

We can get up at six every morning hand in hand and walk in
the park, come back at seven and have breakfast, then sit on
rocking chairs holding a fan and chitchatting. At night we'll
eat some watermelon and watch television. Mother said that
if she is able to live like this, if only for a while, she will be
satisfied. She has had only two hopes in life, one is to live a life
of ease; the other is to visit Tiananmen Square in Beijing to see
the flag-raising ceremony. I don't think it's hard. I can help her
make it happen!

In the central China village where Yang was born, the most
important event for every household was the birth of a son. After
giving birth to a son, a family could hold its head high; those
who did not have a son were mocked. When Yang's mother was
pregnant for the second time, the entire family was brimming
with expectations. But alas . . . another girl! Her father was so dis-
appointed he sulked all day. Her grandmother, anxiously await-
ing a grandson to embrace, refused to give the new child a name.
Later, the family's hopes were shattered as Yang's mother gave
birth to two more baby girls while desperately hoping to produce
a male heir.

In the small traditional village, with the One Child Family policy in place for over a couple of decades through the 2010s, the son,
as the inheritor of the family, is preferred. He is supposed to care
for his parents in their old age in a system with little welfare for
rural folk. As time passes, the meanings of gender and family have
been changing. But the preference for sons remains deep-seated in
the minds of some, so much so that fines are paid to the authorities
after breaking the birth quota rules.

Yang's family turns out to have girls only. "When mother was
young, she was very beautiful, which is why my father married her.
Not long after they married, father always listened to her. But after
giving birth to four girls in a row, mother no longer had status in
the family. So father took control, and in our family his word is
final. Now he treats mother badly, even beating her."

To neighbors and family members, Yang's mother had become a woman to be bullied or pitied. From the time she was young, sensing her mother's pain, she felt a special love for her. When others, even her elders, criticized her mother for no reason, Yang would boldly stand up in her defense, raising her spirits, and attempting to protect her from tormenters. This earned her a reputation for being badly brought up.

Yang cultivated a strong, rebellious personality. She said: "I want the whole village to know, the girls in our family are extraordinary!" After graduating from middle school in her hometown, she hoped to enter a vocational school to study photography, but her parents refused to support her. Money was tight. At that time, her father sold building materials, but he did not earn much. Having four sisters in school at the same time was a great financial burden.

Whenever Yang thought about asking her parents for money, she felt ashamed. "I felt as if I was one of my parents' debts."

Yang left home to work when she was sixteen, determined to become independent. With her still-childlike face and a book bag on her back, she appeared at a garment factory in a nearby town where her cousin worked. It was the summer of 2008.

"I worked in the small garment factory for a year, each day consisting of one assembly line and three points—dormitory, factory, and canteen—life was pure and simple." But as if a restless spirit had crept into her body, one day, Yang decided to change her life. "Aside from the weather changing outside the window, nothing changes." She had grown weary.

Leaving the small town, Yang got a job at Foxconn near Shanghai. "My relationship with my line manager is good because I often treat him to meals. When other workers on the line have to do a lot of overtime, I can take off and run my own sales business." She hopes to become a sales professional—a path out of the factory to wealth and happiness.

Yang's story parallels that of the young migrants as portrayed by Leslie Chang, author of *Factory Girls*.[1] But unlike Chang, who wrote breathlessly about their prospects from the early to mid-2000s in her upbeat book, amidst China's deepening social and class inequality, Foxconn workers had rather different experiences. While dreaming of consumption and wealth, many quickly learned about the formidable obstacles that stood between them and success and encountered bitter disappointments.

Foxconn's Male and Female Employees

Foxconn is an enterprise defined by youth. In 2011, company statistics showed that 89 percent of the million-strong workforce at Foxconn was under thirty years of age.[2] Those who are approaching thirty feel stressed when discussing their personal income, private lives, and the future. By the end of 2017, as management faced increasing difficulties in recruiting and retaining young workers in a more competitive labor environment, Foxconn reported that the proportion of employees who were under thirty had fallen to 63 percent.[3] In 2018, while the number of resigned employees was not publicly reported, 73 percent of those who resigned from Foxconn were below thirty years old, most of them (68 percent) male employees.[4] The corporate profile reflects the mobility of labor and the shrinking population of working youth.

The gender composition of the Foxconn labor force has also changed over the last decade. In 2008, male employees made up a small majority (53 percent), reversing the longstanding industrial pattern of the feminized labor force. The increase in male employees continued in 2009 (59 percent), surpassed 63 percent in 2010, and has since stabilized. Between 2011 and 2018, nearly two-thirds of the Foxconn workforce was comprised of men (see figure 8.1). How can this new pattern be explained?

There are several reasons why male employees became the majority at Foxconn (and other electronics factories). Our interviews revealed that young men with moderate education enjoy better prospects at the company, ranging from assembly-line leaders to technical and managerial positions. In contrast, few women hold positions other than those of frontline workers and a small number of junior- to mid-level supervisors. As a result, some enterprising female workers quit to find jobs in salons, bars, and restaurants, where wages are not much better but working conditions may be less onerous and oppressive. In addition, pregnant women workers, unlike their managerial counterparts, typically resigned to give birth and care for newborns at home in the countryside, a situation partly exacerbated by the lack of maternity care and affordable nursery services at the workplace as well as the additional expense of city living. Finally, female interviewees revealed that at Foxconn (and not only at Foxconn) the "company culture" of sexual harassment and gender discrimination was a shared grave concern. Some line leaders kissed, touched, hugged, and commented on the women, rendering the working environment uncomfortable or even hostile to many.[5]

Figure 8.1. Foxconn employees by gender, 2008–2018.

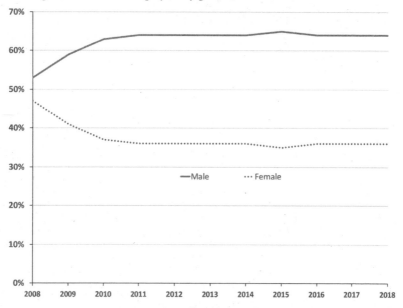

Note: Since 2008, company data indicating the gender ratio has been publicly available. *Sources:* Foxconn Technology Group (various years).[6]

To raise awareness of gender rights, Foxconn reinforces its code of conduct, stating that "any sexual harassment, sexual abuse, corporal punishment, mental or physical coercion or verbal abuse of workers" will not be tolerated but punished.[7] At the same time, a healthy relationship in the workplace is encouraged. For example, a column "Friends of Foxconn" was created in the *Foxconn Weekly*, the freely distributed company newspaper that sought to strengthen communication with employees in Foxconn's Shenzhen factories in October 2010. To make new friends, especially boyfriends and girlfriends, workers can submit their name, position, height and weight, hobbies and interests, as well as their photo, to the editors. A worker responded to our query about the popularity of the Foxconn "Friends" column: "Based on my rough estimate, there are showcases of only two females versus eight males in such an open forum mediated by the company. I think good girls are shy about asking men for dates."

Finding Love

Foxconn interviewees dream of finding their true love before thirty years of age. Zhou Lijuan, a counselor at Foxconn, observes, "Most Foxconn employees are pretty young, and at this age they are looking for love."[8] Among China's skewed youth population, with young men substantially outnumbering young women, the burden of finding a partner weighs heavily on men.[9] Men are desperate to save money for marriage given the gender imbalance that is acute in today's China. Some female workers, likewise, seek to earn more so that they may find an "ideal husband" and build a "sweet home" in the city together.

In recent years, Foxconn has sponsored large-scale social and entertainment activities to "make workers happy." These include hip-hop dancing nights called "I am on fire," singing contests, and tug-of-war team games. Chen Ximei, eighteen years old, is the youngest child in her family, which includes a brother. She loves movies and TV dramas, downloadable to smartphones at discounted fees. She joyfully shares with us, "I'm excited to learn that Foxconn is bidding for a big contract to produce Apple TVs."

Ximei dreams of saving enough to open a boutique or beauty shop in the city before marrying. On payday, "restaurants and shopping malls are flooded with Foxconn people," she cheerfully comments. Ximei is in the enviable position of being able to spend what she earns without having to save in order to provide financial support for her parents or her brother.

A rural migrant worker, born in 1992, poses for a photo with her newly bought bracelet at her lower-bunk bed in the Foxconn worker dormitory, Shenzhen.

Outside of the factory routines, workers hang out with friends at the Happy Together Ice Skating Rink, High Speed Internet Bar, OK Hair Salon, and discos and bars near the factory. Glitter balls in the dance halls reflect colorful light on youthful faces and bodies. The lights flicker to the rhythm of loud music. Provocatively dressed barmaids, some of them former Foxconn workers, shuttle between the seating and standing areas. After midnight on a Friday, a stream of customers begins to flood in. The entry fee at the disco is 5 yuan for men, but admission is free for women. "Young people are our main customers," said the disco bar owner. "People come, drink, and relax. They forget their troubles." At least for an hour or two.

Discos, boutiques, supermarkets, and brand-name stores target young consumers.

Many workers in their twenties and thirties are hoping to find romantic love when they go out to the discos and pubs. They do not necessarily go for one-night stands or casual sex. They wish to build their families and homes and live happily. However, these establishments may occasionally serve as sex clubs. A 21-year-old Foxconn worker talked freely about her offer of sexual services to colleagues:

> Where tens of thousands of single boys and girls live together, it's natural that such things happen. Since it is bound to happen, what's wrong with seizing the opportunity to make some money out of it? It's only necessary to provide contact details to join an online Foxconn Singles Club for fun and excitement.

The Singles Club regularly organizes parties for workers to meet other singles for potential dates. In the larger, consumerist society, Singles' Day—November 11 (the date 11/11 resembles four single people together)—has long been transformed by e-giant Alibaba from a day of celebration of Chinese youth singles into the world's largest online shopping festival. Flashing animated ads from Apple, Huawei, and other tech brands prompt shoppers to "click" and order their favorite items from Alibaba's platforms. Foxconn workers, single and married, seize the day to enjoy big discounts and celebrate "togetherness through consumption."[10] High-end devices such as smartphones are among the top-selling products.[11]

Apple's retail store on Beijing's Wangfujing Street promotes the sales of iPhone 8 Plus in April 2018. Foxconn is the world's largest manufacturer of iPhones.

Love and Consumption Desire

Apple has vastly expanded the number of retail locations and its geographical coverage. We can speak of a veritable cult of Apple, with tens of thousands of consumers tracking each corporate unveiling of a new design and lining up at Apple stores worldwide. As early as 2001, in the US, Apple opened its first retail store in Tysons Corner Center, Virginia, to increase sales and to bypass middleman competitors to capture profits. The company "turned the boring computer sales floor into a sleek playroom filled with gadgets," gushed the *New York Times*.[12]

The Apple Store combines the Genius Bar and product show rooms, consultation services, and interactive learning in a brightly lit space with superior visual articulation and access to technical advice. Patrons encounter myriad new products and are encouraged to problem-solve with the assistance of tech staff. In summer 2008, when China hosted the Olympics, Apple showed off its first store in Chaoyang District, the heart of the business center of Beijing. Over the next decade, Apple opened more than forty stores in major cities throughout China and partnered with all three state-owned carriers, namely, China Mobile, China Telecom, and China Unicom.[13] Through Amazon, Walmart, Carrefour, and e-commerce giants such as Alibaba and JD.com, in addition to its own online stores, Apple reaches out to consumers from all walks of life.

"Few brands are as loved in China as Apple," the *Economist* exclaimed in 2012.[14] In Apple's presentation of its products, laced with feel-good music and imagery, the corporate team sells more than a glitzy product. During the 2015 Chinese New Year, 16-year-old Eleanor Lee starred in the Apple TV ad "The Song."[15] In it she plays a guitar using GarageBand software on a Mac to reproduce an old Chinese song, "Eternal Smile," to the tune of a hit popularized by the pop singer and actress Zhou Xuan in cosmopolitan Shanghai in the 1940s. The digital song is a heartwarming gift prepared especially for her grandmother. When Lee's grandmother plays it on an iPad, her eyes fill with fond memories of love and happiness. By providing traditional cultural staples with a global face, Apple travels seamlessly through time and space, expanding its market share in China and afar.

On May 1, 2017, a public holiday, Apple released another ad, "The City."[16] It features a pair of young lovers enjoying adventure in the city, surrounded by hundreds of residents. Suddenly, it flips to portrait mode on the iPhone camera and the crowds vanish, leaving the two to share an intimate moment. It is a contemporary urban fantasy. They take photos on the streets, in the rain, at historic scenic sites, by the side of the Oriental Pearl TV Tower on the Bund, and in the Shanghai Ocean Aquarium. Bridging China and the world, Walter Martin (formerly of the Walkmen) and Karen O of the Brooklyn band the Yeah Yeah Yeahs intone "Sing to Me" in the background. Two partners have left everything else behind while roaming China's megacity alone. In the last shot, it reads, "Focus on what you love."

Dream It Possible?

China's leading phone producer and a challenger to Apple's supremacy, Huawei, presented its own #DreamItPossible brand theme song through a 2015 live performance in London at Abbey Road Studios. The following is an excerpt of the song's lyrics:

Dream It Possible
I will run, I will climb, I will soar
I'm undefeated
Jumping out of my skin, pull the cord
Yeah, I believe it
The past, is everything we were, don't make us who we are
So I'll dream, until I make it real, and all I see is stars
It's not until you fall that you fly
When your dreams come alive you're unstoppable
Take a shot, chase the sun, find the beautiful
We will glow in the dark turning dust to gold
And we'll dream it possible[17]

"Yeah, I believe it," pop star Jane Zhang croons as she performs the Chinese version of Huawei's song, literally translated as "My Dream."[18] It emphasizes individual efforts to make *my dream* come true.

How do workers navigate the new world of consumption, its fantasy, and reality? Manufacturers, from Apple to Samsung and Microsoft to Sony and Huawei, offer consumers compelling dreams of computerized consumption in some of the world's most successful advertising campaigns. They target consumers' emotions, encouraging them to believe that in buying their products they can achieve their dreams of love, entertainment, and success.

In a privately run "Real Woman Photoshop," young people lined up to pose for photos during their leisure time. Some of them came in pairs with their friends, lovers, or spouses. "The studio's inner walls are covered with colored scenes and dream landscapes," observed photographer Tommaso Bonaventura and documentary filmmakers Tommaso Facchin and Ivan Franceschini of *Dreamwork China*.[19] When asked about her dreams, a teenage worker responded, "Dreams cannot be realized, but everyone has a dream, isn't that so?"

Dreams of Marriage

At a noodle stand in the night market next to the Foxconn dormitory, we met Duan Dong, a 19-year-old school dropout. One night Dong brought his girlfriend to join us for a drink. They wore commitment rings, and the mood was very romantic. But when we asked about the rings, Dong said, "We wear them for play." When we further inquired about marriage, he looked very serious and said, "Marriage isn't just about feelings, it also takes a lot of money."

A year ago, Dong started smoking to relieve stress. At present, he and his girlfriend, like many couples who are short of cash, are living in the male and female factory dormitories, respectively.

Dong's anxiety over marriage is widely shared by young men. Zhu Weili was wearing blue jeans with Nike sneakers and a dark-blue Foxconn jacket when we met. While he affected a sporty, sunny look, he was anxious about his future, especially about having a family. At twenty-five years old, "I'm no longer able to muddle along at my job. If I marry, I will have to provide for a kid, and I really don't earn enough for that," he lamented.

Given the gender imbalance in China and that, according to estimates, young men outnumber women by between 20 and 30 million, the current pool of "excess males" will be unable to marry, or remarry—a source of deep tension among male youth facing a future of bachelorhood.[20] A "bare branch" refers to unmarried men who will never marry or procreate, a future that confronts many male workers.

Facing unresolved tensions at work, marriage, and family, as well as in life in general, some people have sought solace through Protestant churches. In Shenzhen, for example, the churches provide emotional shelters for a growing number of migrants, including Foxconn workers. After converting to Christianity, a worker reinterpreted labor discipline through religious discourse: "Now I realize that I am working for God. When you realize this, you feel peaceful and joyful, though the job is still tedious." Another worker commented, "The purpose of work is to glorify the Lord. If you have this attitude, you can keep peaceful no matter how they treat you."[21] The church also provided a community for young workers far from home and experiencing alienation to come together in a supportive environment. It remains difficult to know how many workers are followers of Jesus, but their numbers have been growing among rural people including migrant workers. If a more abundant life is deferred to the kingdom of heaven, in this corporeal world, pain and misery seems to be an integral part, particularly for the lower strata of the working-class majority.

9

Confronting
Environmental Crisis

Our generation drinks polluted water.
But the next generation will be drinking poisoned water.

—A coalition of environmentalists in China, 2011[1]

Worker well-being matters not only with regard to socio-psychological needs but also occupational health and safety. In *Challenging the Chip*, Ted Smith, David Sonnenfeld, and David Pellow propose a joint effort of workers and environmentalists to promote labor rights and protect the environment in the global electronics industry.[2] How have Foxconn workers and civil society organizations responded to occupational health hazards and environmental degradation in our times? The context is that ecological crisis is looming and capitalist destruction deepening.

Major tech brands, led by Apple, with their drive to encourage consumers to replace millions of phones and other equipment to gain access to each new model, should be held accountable for the "tech trash" that this rampant consumerism creates. They should be required to make the most eco-friendly production model feasible and be held financially responsible for the cleanup costs of trashing millions of perfectly usable electronics products. The same accountability should be required of governments with their prioritization of accelerated growth to fuel incessant consumption.

Labor and the Environment

Confronting the weak implementation of environmental and labor laws at both the national and international levels, workers and activists have pressured target corporations to clean up their transnational supply chains. The tagline of the 2007 Greenpeace campaign is "We love our Macs; we just wish they came in green." Utilizing social networking and digital media, conscientious consumers around the world urged Apple—*my* Apple—to go beyond the minimum to become a green leader in deeds, not just in words. The campaigners, many of whom are Mac users themselves, insisted that Apple take "producer responsibility," especially to reduce harm to workers' health and the environment throughout the manufacture and disposal of Apple products.[3]

In 2010, China's environmental groups initiated an important project to measure the discharge of heavy metals and wastewater by electronics manufacturers in rapidly industrializing regions. They collected and tested water samples in six major cities in coastal and interior China, including Beijing, Taiyuan (Shanxi), Kunshan (Jiangsu), Guangzhou (Guangdong), Wuhan (Hubei), and Chengdu (Sichuan). The surveyed firms were Foxconn, Kaedar Electronics (a subsidiary of the Taiwanese-owned Pegatron), Unimicron (a Taiwanese-owned printed circuit board firm), Meiko Electronics (a Japanese-owned manufacturer of printed circuit boards), and Ibiden Electronics (a Japanese electronics maker of integrated circuit substrates), which supplied parts or assembled products under contract with Apple, HP, Samsung, Toshiba, and others.[4] Environmentalists had raised concerns about a "polluting supply chain" that exposed workers and local residents to hazardous substances. The rivers ran black with sewage and were clogged with plastic waste. Threats to occupational and public health loomed.

Polluted Waste and Toxic Metals

In November 2011, Ding Yudong, deputy director of the Kunshan Municipal Environmental Protection Bureau of the Greater Shanghai region, eventually spoke about the "harmful chemicals" emitted from Kaedar Electronics in the face of media pressure. He sent off a team of inspectors to shut down ten spraying production lines of the Kaedar factory following the onsite audit. The effectiveness of the immediate government and corporate actions, as well as the long-term monitoring efforts, however, were difficult to assess because several village officials warned residents "not to talk to reporters about the pollution." Outside the Kaedar factory wall, journalist Rob Schmitz noted, "The air carries a strong chemical smell—like WD-40."[5]

Foxconn has been accused of discharging industrial waste into rivers and waterways.

Foxconn has also long been accused of causing pollution in the local community. In August 2013, a Foxconn Kunshan spokesperson countered that "wastewater emissions have been processed in accordance with all relevant government laws and environmental regulations."[6] But workers insisted that their "drinking water was foul-smelling at the factory and dormitory." Moreover, the Green Choice Alliance (a platform for consumers, civil society, and industries to promote responsible manufacturing processes) found that nickel levels in wastewater discharged by Foxconn and nearby factories were "almost 40 times over the limit."[7] Nickel is common in many alloys like steel.

Zhang Houfei, a team leader, had worked in the Foxconn electroplating workshop for nearly sixteen years before resigning for health reasons.[8] He explained:

> I oversee some one hundred workers on four assembly lines. To meet the company's demands for speed, all of us feel that we have no choice but to put aside our gloves because they eat into efficiency and slow down our work. Bonuses are tied to labor productivity. Although the total wages and benefits of our entire team are not among the lowest, turnover in our workshop remains fairly high. Why? Prolonged direct contact with nickel in metal alloys and electroplating materials affects human skin. If I already have a rash, it will itch even more.

Nickel is *not* a cumulative toxicant. That is, most of the nickel absorbed through drinking and direct contact with skin by humans, in theory, is removed by the kidneys and passes out of the body through urine. However, large doses or chronic exposure to nickel in 12-hour shifts can be damaging to one's health.

Workers were nearly unanimous in their evaluation that working conditions in the electroplating, polishing, metalworking, soldering, spraying, stamping, and molding workshops were poor. However, "the rapid churn of young employees through electronics factories and frequent changes in process chemicals," according to the analysis of Ted Smith and Chad Raphael, "make it difficult to trace long-term illnesses to workplace exposures."[9]

Industrial Poisoning

In February 2011, Apple finally responded to years-long charges concerning the "use of n-hexane" at its smartphone touchscreen supplier, Wintek. The internal auditors "discovered that the factory

[Wintek] had reconfigured operations without also changing their ventilation system. Apple considered this series of incidents to be a core violation for worker endangerment."[10] Apple has never, however, explained why it failed to prohibit the supplier's use of hazardous chemical substances in the first place.

Back in July 2009, in the Suzhou Industrial Park, about 100 kilometers northwest of Shanghai, 137 workers from a production department of Wintek were collectively poisoned by industrial chemicals. In the next two years, they underwent medical treatment while appealing to both Wintek and Apple for compensation through media activism.[11]

In May and June 2010, *GlobalPost* published a two-part investigative report entitled "Silicon Sweatshops," drawing public attention to n-hexane's damage to worker health. The news report noted that

> sometimes, deep and painful muscle cramps would wake the [Wintek] factory workers from their dorm beds. Weeks later, many of the workers simply couldn't walk right, staggering across the factory grounds, and struggling with once-nimble fingers to clean the delicate touch screens used in trendy gadgets. They had no idea that as they worked, the solvent they used to clean the screens was attacking their peripheral nerves. Unseen damage left them weak, shaky and often in pain. Sometimes their vision would blur. Headaches were common.[12]

In the factory dust-proof clean room, each worker was required to clean one thousand iPhone touchscreens per shift with n-hexane, a solvent that evaporates much more quickly than industrial alcohol. If n-hexane is used at all, workers should wear respirators and operate in a ventilated area. But this was not the case at Wintek.

The cat-and-mouse game was played this way: When an inspection team of the Suzhou Municipal Administration of Work Safety arrived at the factory, production managers immediately opened all the emergency doors to dilute the density of toxic chemicals in the closed environment. In the absence of inspectors, windows and doors were never opened during working hours.

When asked about workers' compensation in a media inquiry in February 2011, Kristin Huguet, a spokeswoman for Apple, "declined to discuss the Wintek case."[13] In our view, while suppliers are directly responsible for employees' occupational health and safety, Apple and other electronics corporations ultimately determine what chemicals and what processes go into manufacturing their products. They cannot simply claim that the sole responsibility is that of manufacturers such as Wintek or Foxconn.

Students and Scholars Against Corporate Misbehavior (SACOM) protested against unsafe and unhealthy working conditions in Apple's supply chains in May 2011, Hong Kong.

Greening the Apple

Facing bad press concerning suppliers' responsibility for adding to water pollution and heavy metal contamination, as well as worker victims' suffering from chemical poisoning, beginning in late 2011, Apple's CEO Tim Cook initiated "specialized environmental audits," along with labor, health, and safety inspections at "high-risk suppliers," in an effort to clean up the environment and quell protests. Apple pledged that its audits would cover "onsite inspections of wastewater treatment facilities, air emissions handling, solid waste disposal, and noise abatement systems both at the facility and in surrounding areas."[14] The company also proclaimed that "we don't allow suppliers to act unethically or in ways that threaten the rights of workers—even when local laws and customs permit such practices."[15]

Ma Jun, director of the Beijing-based nongovernmental think tank Institute of Public and Environmental Affairs, a recipient of the Skoll Award for Social Entrepreneurship, and formerly a senior figure in the state environmental protection agency, has led a series of environmental studies that provided the basis for negotiating with tech brands and their suppliers to stop pollution in China.[16] In August 2011, in an interview with chinadialogue, a nonprofit organization focusing on Chinese and global environmental issues, he highlighted the failure of Apple to disclose its supplier list, and by so doing, protecting itself from public scrutiny. He concluded that Apple has colluded with "polluting firms" to "poison China's environment and people—and make excessive profits."[17] It was not until January 2012 that Apple, for the first time, published a list of 156 companies on its website, which "represent 97 percent of Apple's procurement expenditures for materials, manufacturing, and assembly of Apple's products worldwide."[18]

In August 2014, five years after the Wintek n-hexane poisoning and hospitalization of more than one hundred workers in Suzhou, Lisa Jackson, Apple's vice president of environment, policy, and social initiatives and former administrator of the US Environmental Protection Agency from 2009 to 2013, finally announced the elimination of neurotoxins (such as n-hexane) from Apple products.[19] Apple's 2014 Environmental Responsibility Report reads: "We are committed to keeping our workers safe from harmful toxins."[20] The ban on these toxic chemicals in the manufacturing process, while long overdue, is an important victory for workers and their supporters who have fought to remove hazardous substances from electronics production.

New York–based China Labor Watch makes clear, however, that there is still a long way to go for Apple and other tech companies to achieve labor and environmental sustainability. In 2017 and 2018, the rights group found that Catcher Technology Company, a Taiwanese supplier of MacBook and iPhone parts and metal frames, had heavily polluted the waterways in the Suzhou-Suqian Industrial Park northwest of Shanghai. They pointed out that Catcher Technology directly dispensed "white, foamy wastewater into the public sewage system." The industrial hazard revealed not only the gross neglect of environmental authorities but also of the company. Moreover, Apple, one of the major buyers, should be held accountable. In an international media response to the *Guardian*, in January 2018, Apple acknowledged that "dozens of Apple employees are permanently on site, monitoring operations," but refuted the charges by claiming that, at the factory, "wastewater is treated appropriately and protective equipment is provided to employees who need it."[21] Apple's statement was nevertheless at odds with the wastewater sample testing results that were presented by the rights group. An analysis of wastewater from Catcher Technology found that it exceeded local government standards for "chemical oxygen demand, biochemical oxygen demand and levels of suspended solids—three common tests for water quality."[22]

Phone Story

Labor advocacy groups have continued to pressure Apple and other tech giants to stop the use of the most dangerous, toxic chemicals in supplier factories and replace them with safer alternatives. Environmentally conscious activists envisage a future in which "each new generation of technical improvements in electronic products should include parallel and proportional improvements in environment, health and safety, and social justice attributes."[23] Interestingly, as early as 2011, an Italian team from the video game developer Molleindustria contributed to the cause by introducing a satirical educational game, "Phone Story," just as the new iPhone was about to launch in the market. From raw materials extraction and child labor abuses in illegal mines, overtime pressures and speedups linked to worker suicides and injuries, consumerism and planned obsolescence, to e-waste dumping and environmental disasters throughout our planet, "Phone Story" walks players through the production, consumption, and disposal of the phone as a means of raising social awareness.[24] It exposes the truth behind Apple's self-promotion as a green corporation by highlighting the global environmental contamination and labor injustice that are built into the life cycle of an iPhone.

Ever vigilant to threats to its corporate image, Apple removed "Phone Story" from its App Store within hours of its launch. The American multinational justified killing the game in this way: "Apps that depict violence or abuse of children will be rejected" and "Apps that present excessively objectionable or crude content will be rejected."[25] But what is "objectionable"? The depiction of corporate abuse by Foxconn and Apple, or the abuse itself that threatens the lives of miners and workers?

The educational game app nevertheless remains available online to users of the Android (although banned at the Apple Store). It provokes smartphone users and the wider society to rethink the relations among technology, people, and the environment.

Just before Christmas, in 2014, the BBC program *Panorama* aired a one-hour feature entitled "Apple's Broken Promises."[26] The film crew found an exhausted workforce making iPhones in Pegatron's Shanghai plant in eastern China, and children toiling in tin mines in Indonesia to supply materials for the phones, facing threats of landslides. The TV report documented the fact that tin, tantalum, tungsten, cobalt, and rare earths (a group of seventeen chemically similar elements) are massively extracted to manufacture high-tech electronics products, including the iPhone. The sourcing of these minerals could be particularly deadly to the most vulnerable child workers.

Sean McGrath, senior reporter for *MicroScope* and a defender of Apple, characterized BBC's efforts as "irresponsible journalism," claiming that the public broadcaster "took a cheap shot" to single out Apple as an easy media target.[27] In our understanding, however, the program provided compelling evidence of ongoing systemic problems that urgently require resolution at Apple, among many key players in the industry. Jeff Williams, Apple's senior vice president of operations, responded quickly that "more than 1,400 talented engineers and managers were stationed in China" to manage engineering and manufacturing operations at large production sites, who worked and lived "in the factories constantly."[28] But the presence of Apple staff did not prevent the occurence of labor and environmental problems at its huge China supply base. Dangerous industrial practices directly impinging on worker and community health have caused and continue to cause irreversible destruction to our planet and its people.

Green Growth

A green economy that emphasizes environmental sustainability will bring long-term social benefits and economic growth. In 2016, Apple issued a US$1.5 billion green bond to finance environmental projects, including renewable energy initiatives.[29] The company prioritized displacing fossil fuel–based energy sources and eliminating greenhouse gases in its operations at home and abroad. By April 2017, Apple reported that it had "installed 485 megawatts of wind and solar projects across six provinces of China," thereby creating new clean energy at its large production sites.[30] It boasts of promoting low-carbon operations in its supplier factories, data centers, offices, and retail stores. If the programs succeed, "over 20 million metric tons of greenhouse gas pollution" will be avoided, "equivalent to taking nearly 4 million passenger vehicles off the road for one year."[31]

In addition to Apple's much-vaunted improvements, Dai Fengyuan, Foxconn's chief technology officer, hailed his firm's innovative and safe production methods:

> Rather than spray paint onto its smartphones, the usual method where 70 percent of paint is wasted and chemical fumes are released into the air, we're now using a special mold process where less than 1 percent of the paint is lost. . . . Similarly, the traditional film used in smartphone touchscreens has been replaced by a new carbon nanotube film, which requires 80 percent less energy to produce and cuts water use to near zero.[32]

Foxconn has constructed new solar photovoltaic panels to produce electricity in manufacturing, thus reaping the environmental and economic benefits of clean energy. Its vision is to build an industrial system that utilizes wind energy and other renewable power to fuel big data centers, research and development labs, and manufacturing complexes. Foxconn's Guizhou plant, for example, is made with recycled steel and heat-reflective laminated glass for all windows to cut energy use while operating.

"Can we power a global business with the sun, wind, and water?" This is only one of the many "bold questions" raised by Apple's environmental policy team.[33] Apple highlights its achievements in reducing its carbon footprint in the realm of renewable energy generation and in disassembling iPhones for recycling at factories in China and elsewhere. At the same time, vice president Lisa Jackson advised Apple to "focus on building durable products" because "by focusing on durability," the company "can minimize both repairs and replacements."[34] Wise advice. Yet, with the corporate drive to produce every new iPhone and cannibalize all previous models, the green revolution proclaimed by Apple and its suppliers is being overwhelmed by a combination of corporate greed and consumer demand for new products.

Greenpeace's senior corporate campaigner Elizabeth Jardim believes that the "brightest designers can create toxic-free gadgets to last, be repairable, and ultimately be transformed into something new."[35] At present, however, environmental degradation and health endangerment are epidemic in transnational production, notably in the electronics industry. In Shenzhen and Guangzhou, for example, Heather White and Lynn Zhang filmed the lives of dozens of factory workers who have contracted occupational leukemia while working for contractors and subcontractors for global electronics corporations.[36]

Smartphones—Not So Smart for the Planet

Outside of China, Hsin-Hsing Chen has pointed out that long before the emergence of Foxconn, "Taiwan's history of economic growth" was also "a history of technological catastrophes," a reference to the suffering and deaths of electronics workers from heavy industrial pollution associated with the country's rapid development.[37] Specifically, RCA (Radio Corporation of America) workers, mostly young women, were exposed to toxic chlorinated organic solvents during the two decades of the company's operations between 1970 and 1992. In late 2009, the Taipei District Court finally heard a collective lawsuit filed by former RCA workers and their families, the first of its kind in Taiwan. The ultimate victory of winning compensation for 445 workers came in April 2015, with support from a coalition of civil society groups, including professionals, students, and teachers, as well as activists from all over the country.[38] But such victories have been few and far between.

Workers' campaigning efforts pale in the face of corporate expansion, which has led to massive deleterious environmental consequences throughout the world. Samsung races to outpace competitors by introducing Galaxy Z Flip smartphones, pushing new demands for precious raw materials in electronics manufacturing while pledging to protect and preserve the environment. In North

America, Washington, DC–based Green America, building on the momentum from the Apple campaign, has called on Samsung to monitor and remove hazardous chemicals from its factories and suppliers in South Korea, China, Vietnam, and other countries in order to prevent cancer, birth defects, miscarriages, and nerve damage.[39] In South Korea, Samsung workers' struggle for compensation has dragged on for years. In the tragedy, at least 370 semiconductor and screen display assembly workers were diagnosed with cancer caused by benzene (a sweet-smelling, carcinogenic cleaning solvent) and other hazardous substances in the course of their work. By July 2017, more than 130 workers had passed away from leukemia, while the survivors had serious disabilities.[40]

The time is long past to put an end to widespread occupational disasters in the electronics supply chain. Who is going to compensate sick, injured, and deceased workers and their families for both industrial disabilities and the environmental consequences of corporate campaigns that generate massive production of waste? Considering the lack of government monitoring in China and elsewhere, the combination of weak deterrent effects of existing laws and regulations, and official and corporate corruption, it is clear that workers have scant protection.

10

Dead Man Walking

We were a very happy family.
But Tingzhen does not look like my son anymore.
Since his accident, every day is like living death.

> —Zhang Guangde, 50-year-old father
> of a brain-damaged son[1]

On Wednesday, October 26, 2011, a work accident shattered the lives of a four-person family. Zhang Tingzhen suffered an electric shock while repairing a spotlight outside the E12(A) Building at the Foxconn Longhua complex. He fell from a ladder after being shocked by a high-voltage electric current. Falling from four meters, he landed hard on his head. He had been provided with neither electricity-proof gloves, nor a helmet, nor an industrial safety belt. Admitted to the nearest hospital, he underwent emergency brain surgery. Half of his left brain had to be excised because of severe bleeding and trauma. Doctors replaced a large portion of his skull with synthetic bone and implanted a tube in his body to drain fluid from his brain cavity to his bladder. Three weeks passed, and it was not until November 16, after anguished demands by his parents, that Foxconn transferred Tingzhen to the Shenzhen No. 2 People's Hospital for specialized diagnosis. He underwent four additional surgeries in the following five months to save him each time his condition became critical. He was twenty-five years old when the accident occurred.

"What is Tingzhen's future? I'd been looking forward to seeing him married. I dare not think about this anymore. . . . If there had been adequate protective equipment, the accident could have been avoided," his father sighed. In February 2014, Guangde mustered the courage to petition the central government in Beijing to demand a speedy resolution to compensate and care for his severely injured son. It turned out to be a futile attempt. By then, more than two years had passed.

Tingzhen, a graduate of a technical college in Henan, was employed as an equipment and facility technician. Foxconn's lawyer defended the position that while Tingzhen had worked at the Shenzhen Longhua plant for eighty-four days, during this time his wages and social insurance benefits were paid by Foxconn Huizhou. Huizhou city, lying some 70 kilometers from Hong Kong, borders Dongguan to the southwest and the provincial capital of Guangzhou to the west. Both enterprises—Jizhun Precision Industry Company (known as Foxconn Huizhou) and Hongfujin Precision Industry Company (known as Foxconn Longhua)—are directly owned by Foxconn, as attested by business registration certificates. Foxconn insisted that Tingzhen's social insurance contributions had been made directly to the human resources and social security bureau in Huizhou, not to the government unit in Shenzhen.

The critical point is that work-related injury insurance benefits are higher in the first-tier city of Shenzhen than in Huizhou. "Tingzhen's basic wage was 2,500 yuan per month, starting from August 4, 2011. With the addition of overtime premiums and benefits, his average income during the nearly three months of employment before the accident was over 4,000 yuan per month," said Guangde. The Zhang family and Foxconn were unable to agree on the medical care expenses and economic compensation. Guangde then filed a claim on behalf of his son against Foxconn with the local labor dispute arbitration committee in Shenzhen.

Labor Dispute Acceptance

Arbitration committees are government organizations mandated to bring together labor and management to resolve work-related conflicts. The Chinese state, in response to the rising tide of labor unrest, sought to expand the legal rights of workers and to redirect conflict from strikes and other forms of collective action to the courtroom to the extent that some now hold that "the law has become the pivotal terrain of labor politics."[2] The number of labor disputes submitted for arbitration has soared since the mid-1990s, when officials started encouraging protesters to resolve disputes through mediation and arbitration rather than taking grievances to the streets.

Government records indicate that in 1996, 48,121 labor disputes (including individual and collective cases) were accepted for arbitration, involving 189,120 persons nationwide (see figure 10.1). In 2008, at the start of the global economic crisis when tens of millions of workers were laid off, the number of cases involving nonpayment of wages and benefits and illegal termination of employment contracts skyrocketed to 693,465, involving more than 1.2 million laborers across the country. "The wave of filings initiated by workers against their employers," Mary Gallagher and Baohua Dong report, "can be seen as a type of bottom-up enforcement of the new law;" however, the disputants often face long, drawn-out, and bitter disputes even when the legal process is streamlined.[3]

Following economic recovery, newly accepted arbitration cases fell to 600,865 in 2010 and 589,244 in 2011. In 2012, however, the total number of labor dispute cases rebounded to 641,202, reflecting widespread rights violations in a slowing economy and popular use of the law in the service of rights defense. New legal provisions tested by workers in conflict resolution cases, and particularly worker victories (with full or partial payments in accordance with legal standards), have boosted confidence in and consciousness of rights among workers. In 2016, the official number of disputed cases reached new heights to 828,410, involving over 1.1 million workers, alerting governments at all levels to growing willingness on the part of workers to file grievances. This was a seventeen-fold increase in arbitrated disputes in the two decades between 1996 and 2016. In 2017, while standing at a high level, the number slightly dropped to 785,323 cases, involving 979,016 workers.

Table 10.1. Arbitrated labor disputes in China, 1996–2017.

Year	Laborers involved in arbitration (persons)	Arbitrated labor disputes (cases)
1996	189,120	48,121
1997	221,115	71,524
1998	358,531	93,649
1999	473,957	120,191
2000	422,617	135,206
2001	467,150	154,621
2002	608,396	184,116
2003	801,042	226,391
2004	764,981	260,471
2005	744,195	313,773
2006	679,312	317,162
2007	653,472	350,182
2008	1,214,328	693,465
2009	1,016,922	684,379
2010	815,121	600,865
2011	779,490	589,244
2012	882,487	641,202
2013	888,430	665,760
2014	997,807	715,163
2015	1,159,687	813,859
2016	1,112,408	828,410
2017	979,016	785,323

Note: Cases of individual *and* collective labor disputes are included. From 2009 collective labor disputes have been officially defined as disputes involving at least ten workers (previously a collective dispute was defined as one joined by three or more employees). *Source: China Labour Statistical Yearbook 2018* (2019).[4]

Figure 10.1. Arbitrated labor disputes in China, 1996–2017.

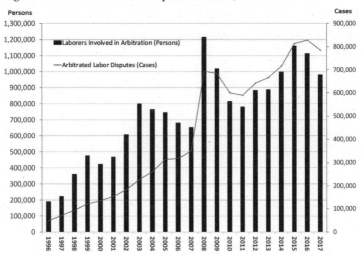

Note: Cases of individual *and* collective labor disputes are included. From 2009 collective labor disputes have been officially defined as disputes involving at least ten workers (previously a collective dispute was defined as one joined by three or more employees). *Source: China Labour Statistical Yearbook 2018* (2019).[5]

Arbitrated labor disputes distinguish individual and collective cases. In the event of insufficient evidence, such as the lack of an employment contract to prove the existence of a labor relationship, officials will not accept the case. Even when some workers succeed in filing for arbitration, they face many challenges. For working people, particularly low-income rural migrants, access to affordable and effective legal representation is hard to come by. According to lawyer Aaron Halegua, "since 2007, workers have become less likely to 'totally win' and more likely to only 'partially win' in labor arbitration."[6] The fact that the institutional barriers such as the time and costs needed to complete the legal processes are so high doubtless have discouraged many from pursuing this route. At the same time, stability-obsessed officials have also relied on informal means to dissuade victims from making their case in court, thereby reducing the caseloads.

Nevertheless, every year hundreds of thousands of aggrieved Chinese workers, at times in excess of one million, have sought to use the law to defend their rights. In *Against the Law*, Ching Kwan Lee observed that plaintiffs "do not necessarily see the law or the courts as a neutral or empowering institution in their fight against official corruption and abuse of power." Still, without better alternatives, "many continue working through and around the law and its related trappings in the state apparatus."[7] In the arbitration process, the authorities regularly seek to divide collective cases into individual ones, thereby raising the cost of filing suit for workers and undermining the possibilities for labor solidarity. Patricia Chen and Mary Gallagher argue that "the atomizing effects of court procedures and legislation" has partially restrained "the development of a labor movement" in China.[8] The legal path of winning grievance suits is extremely difficult for workers, even at a time when the Chinese state has promoted the "rule of law" to boost its legitimacy and governance.

Labor Arbitration

Against all odds, the Zhang family managed to submit an application for labor arbitration on behalf of Tingzhen within the one-year statutory limit after the accident. The case rested on claims to medical insurance and compensation for the complete loss of work capability. According to the "Regulations on Work-Related Injury Insurance," in effect from January 1, 2011, workers who are disabled in workplace accidents and covered by government social insurance are eligible for compensation payments in accordance with local standards. The insurance claims are evaluated following the completion of disability assessment at authorized hospitals within two years of the accident. The age of the victim, type of injury, degree of disability, extent of employer negligence, and related workplace factors determine the amount of compensation that an injured worker will receive. Payments for medical treatment and disability support differ from city to city, taking into consideration the local cost of living.

On December 3, 2012, Guangde finally received a five-page arbitration statement from the Shenzhen authorities. The arbitrators ruled that "no contractual relationship" existed between Tingzhen and Foxconn Longhua. They endorsed Foxconn's claim, as stated in the employment contract that the company presented as evidence, that Tingzhen had been hired by its Huizhou facility. Although the tragic accident had occurred at the Shenzhen workplace, Foxconn Longhua could not be held legally responsible for compensation.

Appeals to the Courts

Under Chinese law, workers can reject arbitration decisions and appeal to basic-level courts when they perceive arbitrators' judgments to be unjust. Within fifteen days of an arbitration ruling, workers have a right to apply for a retrial of the original dispute. Such appeals have become increasingly common as aggrieved workers anticipate that "judges will grant them higher compensation than the amount of the arbitral awards."[9] If either side is dissatisfied with the verdict, it can appeal to a higher court, whose judgment is final.

Such cases are typically filed by individual workers with no support from the labor union. Tingzhen's father appealed to the court: "Was the Foxconn employment contract forged? From the day of employment [on August 4, 2011] to the moment of the accident [on October 26, 2011], Tingzhen worked at the Shenzhen Longhua plant." Having raised the question, Guangde concluded that his son "should be entitled to full medical treatment and occupational injury compensation right here in accordance with local standards." What Foxconn has done to Tingzhen, in his understanding, "lacks morality and humanity!"

Tingzhen's recovery was painfully slow. He continues to require careful monitoring and medical care twenty-four hours a day. In

the prolonged legal battle, Tingzhen's family was at a severe dis-
advantage in taking on the Foxconn legal department. On April
4, 2014, the Shenzhen Intermediate People's Court proceeded to
the second and final trial in Tingzhen's case. The Zhangs lost the
lawsuit, thereby exhausting their legal remedies.

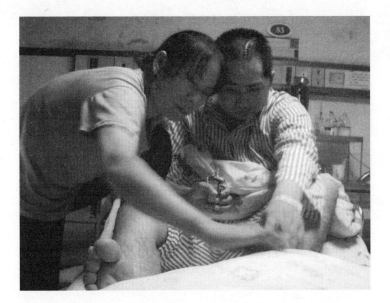

*In the Shenzhen No. 2 People's Hospital, Tingzhen's mother declared: "We want the
government to hold Foxconn accountable and to prevent similar tragedies from happening!"*

Grief

In a subsequent private settlement Guangde had no choice but to
accept a one-off medical fee from Foxconn. The condition was that
the Zhang family agree to terminate the employment relationship
between Tingzhen and Foxconn.

Before departing for his old home in rural Henan, Guande,
revealing pent-up anger and helplessness, showed us a large glass
bottle with a bone that had been removed from Tingzhen's crushed
skull.

11

Strikes and Protests

Workers come second to, and are worn out by, the machines.
... But I am *not* a machine.

—Cao Yi, a 20-year-old Foxconn worker activist

In 1973 Huw Beynon published a book, *Working for Ford*. Over the previous six years, when he conducted fieldwork at Ford's Halewood plant on Merseyside in England, a worker told him, "It's got no interest. You couldn't take the job home. There's nothing to take. It's different for them in the office. They are part of Fords. We are not, we are numbers."[1] A half century later, Cao Yi, a young migrant, described comparable conditions facing workers at Foxconn in China: "In the production process, workers occupy the lowest position, even below the lifeless machinery. Workers come second to, and are worn out by, the machines." A *Modern Times* in modern times: repetitious work tasks, atomized lives, and desperate efforts to support families.[2] "But I am *not* a machine," he said firmly.

Mass Incidents in China

Foxconn workers have repeatedly fought for individual and collective rights and interests through legal and extra-legal means. Labor incidents at numerous Foxconn sites are part of a pattern of growing worker unrest across coastal and inland China.

From the early 1990s, a period of accelerated market-oriented reforms and rapid social change, conflicts multiplied between employees and management. Public security officials began to release statistics on "mass incidents." This all-encompassing category included strikes, protests, riots, sit-ins, rallies, demonstrations, traffic blockades, and other unspecified forms of unrest. The mass incidents ranged widely from protests against unpaid wages and illegal layoffs, to labor and environmental disputes, to religious, ethnic, and political clashes involving workers and other victims who resisted rights encroachment by targeting authority in diverse ways.[3]

The number of mass incidents each year increased from 8,700 in 1993, the first year for which official data is available, to 32,000 in 1999.[4] And the number "continued to increase at more than 20 percent a year" between 2000 and 2003.[5] In 2005, the official record noted 87,000 cases, rising to 127,000 in 2008 during the world recession—the last time the Chinese Ministry of Public Security released figures.[6] Did the rising numbers raise official concern? Major protests, defined as those involving more than one thousand participants, frequently prompted police intervention and the arrest or detention of protest leaders. The main goal of the police in most cases was to disperse the protest to prevent it from disrupting social order or blocking traffic.

Although official statistics appear to be a study in obfuscation that conceals not only the nature of strikes and protests but even their numbers, they still seem to reflect increased worker agitation overall. For the present, we must rely on other sources of macro data and fine-tuned studies of specific protest actions.

In China, the official count of strikes is *not* publicly available. As early as 1975, a provision for the "right to strike" was incorporated into the amended Constitution of the People's Republic of China. The constitution enacted in 1978 also stipulated that citizens had the "freedom of strike" and other civil rights. The "freedom of strike" stipulation, however, was removed from the 1982 constitution, showing the Communist Party–dominated state's tightening of its rule in response to democratic protests taking place in Beijing and Eastern Europe at that time.[7] The revocation of the legal right *did not* end labor strikes, however.

To better understand the causes and patterns of strikes and labor protests, from January 2011, the Hong Kong–based China Labour Bulletin (CLB) began to collect internet sources covering Chinese news and social media reports to create an open access "Strike Map."[8] During the first five years of President Xi Jinping's rule from 2013 to 2017, for example, CLB recorded "8,696 collective worker protests." Geoffrey Crothall, communications director of CLB, estimates that the Strike Map at best "accounts for about five to ten percent of all incidents of workers' collective action in China" during the period of a five-year study.[9] In light of the state's ubiquitous censorship, coupled with technological limitations that only provide access to the public domain, the available data captured only a small subset of "the population."

Labor Actions at Foxconn

At Foxconn, China's largest manufacturing firm, sudden spikes in orders, at the time of introduction of new models and during the holiday season, have frequently resulted in speedups, compulsory overtime, increased safety and health hazards, heightened tensions in supervisor-worker relations, and even outbreaks of violence on the factory floor. In response, Foxconn managers repeatedly joined hands with local governments, the trade unions, and police officers to suppress workers' strikes and protests. Yet workers have again and again organized to defend their dignity, health, rights, and interests.

At the key node of transnational production, Foxconn workers leveraged their power to launch coordinated actions during critical moments in the densely connected, just-in-time manufacturing process. Beverly Silver, author of *Forces of Labor*, explains: "Workplace bargaining power accrues to workers who are enmeshed in tightly integrated production processes, where a localised work stoppage in a key node can cause disruptions on a much wider scale than the stoppage itself."[10] The primary goal for labor was to force management and/or government representatives to respond to its demands. Those demands have been *both* economic and political, that is, reforming the trade unions, while the party-state has repeatedly extended its reach to the workplace level to ensure control and "social harmony."

Over the recent ten-year period of rapid business growth since 2010, when the company's revenues doubled, Foxconn workers and managers were "flexibly" transferred between jobs to reach ever-higher productivity and profit goals, culminating in multiple labor and social crises. Striking workers are *not* legally protected. Workers staging protests and strikes can be charged with disrupting public order. But workers again and again mobilized to resist oppression, as discussed below, even when the state assured that labor actions were short-lived and limited to a single workshop or factory.

Work Slowdown

During the first five months of 2010, when Foxconn accelerated the pace of work to satisfy demand for the updated iPhone against the backdrop of employee suicides, a woman worker recalled: "Production output of iPhone casings was previously set at 5,120 pieces per day; but in July, it was raised by 25 percent to 6,400 pieces per day. I'm completely exhausted." During months of peak production, workers voiced their "exhaustion to the point of tears." And the iPhone assembly line was not alone in placing increasing pressures on workers. The Kindle e-reader workshop was likewise riddled with tensions over speed.

Amazon, creator of the Kindle, was founded by Jeff Bezos in 1994 and grew quickly to become a leading e-commerce corporation. The American giant, like Apple, has long contracted Foxconn to build its products in China, including the Kindle, Echo Dot smart speaker, and tablet. At Foxconn, the Technology Merging

Services Business Group assembles e-book readers for Amazon. Facing speedups and heavy overtime that routinely accompany the unveiling of new models, on October 20, 2011, Foxconn's Amazon product line in the Longhua factory reported a work slowdown.

Sixty workers of the A1 Line, forty-one male and nineteen female workers, handled the night shift. Cao Yi complained vociferously, "We've been pushed like mad dogs to meet impossible production targets!" Working at Foxconn for the last two months, Yi went on: "Our hands and our minds never rest. There was no way we could work fast enough to meet the new production quota, so we decided to ease off!" His workmates supported the decision to stage a slowdown. "This week, the output quota was adjusted upward for the second time, from 1,800 units to 2,100 units; it's really too much," Yi's friend echoed.

The A1 Line workers took action after the midnight meal break. Yi was responsible for product quality assurance in the middle of the line. There were two other quality checkers, one each at the first quarter and third quarter positions on the line. "I instructed the first process-checker and the workers at the front of the line to slow the pace, so that workers on the whole line could comfortably handle the work," Yi explained. In the factory canteen some twenty workers listened to Yi attentively and nodded. In the following four hours after work resumed, the Kindles flowed slowly along the conveyor belt. Every worker on the line was either actively or passively participating in the slowdown.

At the early breakfast hour, Yi and three leading workers celebrated their small victory. However, the coordinated action by several dozen workers immediately drew supervisory attention and tighter surveillance. Workers were ordered to meet the production quota. In response, Yi came up with a new strategy: to creatively make defective products.

In the male factory dormitory, Yi and his coworkers spread word of the proposed action, involving as many workers as possible so that no individual could be identified as the leader or singled out for punishment. Mutual protection and trust among "underground activists" and fellow workers were critical. They held small-group discussions in rooms, turning the dormitory into a space for worker resistance.

Using smartphones, they texted the "call for action" message to fellow workers, a key medium of wider communications. Indeed, Foxconn workers have built QQ groups to link fellow workers in their business groups, in addition to their own friends and families. That Thursday night, many workers on the A1 Line intentionally left out a screw on the Amazon Kindle casing. Others did not affix the bar code in the right place.

"Guarantee product quality, take it all to heart," is a Foxconn slogan. As product quality was crucial, the line leader had to check each and every work procedure. The speed of the line slowed to a crawl. Workers had joined together to score a victory in the struggle to halt the company's relentless speedups. In this way, Yi and his coworkers challenged their subordinate position and inhumane treatment, so glaringly at odds with the managerial discourse of love, care, and support. And they did so in ways that the company could neither ignore nor tolerate.

Coordinated actions like the slowdown and sabotage of the product sent a clear message of protest to the company, despite being limited to one assembly line. It was a self-protective act to avert burnout. However, management had weapons to restore order and discipline. Within two weeks, the A1 Line was thoroughly reorganized, and Yi and his workmates were dispersed throughout the F4 and F5 factory complexes. Industrial engineers reset the "standard work pace" at high speed.

Suicide Threats

In contrast to covert actions, the threat of mass suicide emerged as a staged performance to force managers to accept immediate negotiations. In Hubei's East Lake High-Tech Development Zone,

known as Optics Valley, on January 3, 2012, 150 Foxconn workers
threatened to jump from the roof of the factory if managers refused
to solve the conflict, which linked job transfer and a wage dispute.
The key issue was their forced transfer from Shenzhen to Wuhan
(provincial capital of Hubei) in the latest round of interprovincial
business reorganization that was sending workers from Shenzhen
to inland regions. The specter of suicide, which had taken so heavy
a toll earlier at Foxconn facilities in Shenzhen, now haunted central
China.

Foxconn Wuhan assembled desktop computers and video game
consoles for Microsoft. It paid workers, including newly transferred
employees, a basic wage of 1,350 yuan per month, 200 yuan lower
than the entry-level wage in Shenzhen. Standing on the roof, workers posted their news in real time on the internet via smartphones.
In the wake of the "Foxconn jumpers," government mediators
quickly arrived at the scene, and took pains not to add fuel to the
fire. At this point, officials were drawn into the mass suicide protest.

Arriving at Foxconn, local party committee members, trade
union officials, lawyers, and plainclothes police gathered intelligence. The cross-departmental government team also called a
closed-door meeting with senior managers. Finally, the chief government mediator offered the protesters a stark choice: "Continue
working at the Wuhan plant or leave now with severance pay." To
prevent widening worker unrest, the use of discretionary power—
instead of adhering to the preexisting, formal legal procedures—
was to reach resolution as quickly as possible.[11] Those who chose
severance would receive compensation calculated at the higher
Shenzhen wage level that they had been receiving, that is, 1,550
yuan per month. But such a quick fix failed to address the core concerns of agitated workers, who had been fighting for "fair wages,"
specifically their former wage, following their move. At best the
government had opened a door for those workers who were most
upset to "exit" with a modest severance payment. In total, forty-five

workers took the severance payment and left the company. The collective protest then quickly crumbled.

In confronting this high-profile mass suicide threat, the official representative pressured Foxconn Wuhan management to grant minor economic concessions to the most adversely affected workers, specifically those who were prepared to leave the company, in order to encourage a settlement. However, concessions were limited to those who opted for severance. The company and the local government left the great majority of workers, those who chose to continue working at the plant, with a wage of 1,350 yuan per month, well below their former wage in Shenzhen and for a job far from their original workplace and home. A sense of anger and frustration was rampant.

In Wuhan, the East Lake High-Tech Development Zone trade union federation, which had initially failed to support workers' wage demands, in the end did nothing to help the remaining one hundred-plus protesters to bargain for higher wages in their new workplace. Management insisted on "paying 1,350 yuan to everyone equally," regardless of their previous salaries, so those who had been dispatched from Shenzhen to Wuhan and stayed on the job were forced to accept the company's "standard pay" in Wuhan.

Three months after the January conflict, some two hundred workers launched another protest, this time to demand payment of welfare benefits that had disappeared as a result of the relocation. Nineteen-year-old Su Hualing explained: "My health insurance plan cannot be transferred from Shenzhen to Wuhan. Are my employer's contributions to the Shenzhen social security scheme over the past two years all gone? I am told that I can only claim my own premiums, not those paid by the employer." This was despite the fact that she remained a Foxconn employee. The truth is, the employer's contribution was indeed lost.

The Shenzhen government pocketed the 10 percent monthly contributions that Foxconn had made based on Hualing's and all other transferred workers' pay toward their pensions during 2010 and 2011. Hualing and her coworkers could only withdraw their individual payments from the insurance account administered by the Shenzhen Human Resources and Social Security Bureau because, they were informed, "there was no way for the Shenzhen office to set things up when they moved to Wuhan." Despite the fact that it was the company that transferred them to Wuhan, they were unable to recoup the payments that Foxconn had made in their names through Shenzhen's social security unit. Foxconn explained that the officials would not permit the company to carry forward the insurance premiums for its transferred employees. The workers could only swallow their rage. Characteristically, the company trade union did not support the aggrieved workers' claims to their entitlement to social insurance.

Lower basic pay and loss of benefits were not the Foxconn workers' only grievances. The company found myriad ways to nickel-and-dime workers. In the Personal Computing Electronics Business Group, managers canceled workers' weekend overtime pay, replacing it with compensatory time off. This "flexible time" policy was designed to eliminate overtime payments with the result that many workers lost income, despite putting in "tens of hours of overtime work on weekends during February and March." That was because workers were no longer paid double wages for overtime work on Saturdays and Sundays; instead, the company offered workers "free time" during slack periods in lieu of the overtime wages that should rightfully have been paid.

On the morning of April 25, two hundred mold-stamping workers (including those who were transferred from Shenzhen and others who had been working in Wuhan) walked off the factory floor over the loss of overtime payments. It is noteworthy that they did not face obstruction from their line leaders during the walkout. Wang Shuping, a 23-year-old line leader, explained, "We were concerned about the problem since our own rights and interests had been similarly hurt. The loss of overtime premiums reduced everyone's wages by about one-third." In this case, the economic interests of frontline workers and line leaders were aligned.

On the roof of the three-story factory building, angry workers chanted, *"Wo yao jiaxin!"* (I want a raise!) and *"Li Wenzhong, gundan!"* (Down with Li Wenzhong [the business group leader]!). After a standoff of more than ten hours, city officials stepped in to promise increased wages, thereby averting the possibility of a prolonged walkout or worker suicides. The protesting workers did not succeed in their demand to remove the business group chief from his position, but they did win weekend overtime wages stipulated in the law that the company had sought to deny them.

In this and many other encounters, officials had developed a wide repertoire of "protest absorption" techniques to resolve labor disputes, just as workers had learned to bargain collectively. "Bargained authoritarianism," in the analysis of Ching Kwan Lee and Yonghong Zhang, could sometimes serve the short-term interests of workers through a compromise between government negotiators and protesters, yet efforts to achieve a more thorough labor reform to enshrine workers' bargaining power through responsive unions stalled.[12]

Speaking to Reuters, Foxconn spokesman Simon Tsing said nothing about the wage and benefit cuts workers had experienced as a result of transfers from Shenzhen, or the terms of the agreement, merely stating that the dispute had been peacefully settled after "negotiations involving the human resources and legal departments as well as the local government."[13] But management was particularly sensitive to the challenges of an alliance between workers and line leaders. It moved aggressively to assure that line managers adhere to company discipline, demanding of line leaders acceptance of the following terms:

> As a manager of the company, regardless of the reason, I will not insinuate, instigate or incite employees to use improper means to express their demands. Under no circumstance will I participate in an illegal assembly, march, demonstration, organization or

activity. Should I discover employees participating in an illegal assembly, march, demonstration, organization or activity, I will persuade them to stop and report it immediately.[14]

Senior managers subsequently adopted stricter measures, such as firing and blacklisting, to deter workers and staff from uniting to press for change, according to interviewed workers.

Riot

Repression has sometimes prompted powerful reactions among the repressed. Yu Zhonghong, a 21-year-old high school graduate who had worked at the Taiyuan Foxconn site for two years, wrote about the suppression of a factory riot in September 2012. His firsthand report took the form of an open letter to Foxconn's chief executive Terry Gou. It circulated through a number of social media platforms before being quickly removed by internet censors.

A Letter to Foxconn CEO, Terry Gou

If you don't want to be loudly awakened at night from deep sleep,
If you don't want to constantly rush about again by airplane,
If you don't want to be investigated again by the Fair Labor
　　Association,[15]
If you don't want your company to be called a sweatshop,
Please treat us with a little humanity.

Please allow us a little human self-esteem.
Don't let your hired ruffians rifle through our bodies and
　　belongings.
Don't let your hired ruffians harass female workers.
Don't let your lackeys treat every worker like the enemy.
Don't arbitrarily berate or, worse, beat workers for the slightest
　　mistake.

You should understand that working in your factories:
Workers live at the lowest level,

Tolerating the most intense work,
Earning the lowest pay,
Accepting the strictest regulation,
And enduring discrimination everywhere.
Even though you are my boss, and I am a worker:
I have the right to speak to you on an equal footing.

—Yu Zhonghong, a Foxconn Taiyuan worker[16]

As Zhonghong's letter made clear, the balance of power between managers and workers was highly skewed in favor of management. In the face of despotic management, he spoke of "right" and human dignity, not something narrowly confined to the realm of legal rights. On behalf of the workers living "at the lowest level" in the company, he called for a public discussion with CEO Terry Gou "on an equal footing." Demanding that Gou, senior management, and the company union act responsibly toward workers, his letter ended with three reminders:

1. Please remember, from now on, to treat your subordinates as humans, and require that they treat their subordinates, and their subordinates, and their subordinates, as humans.

2. Please remember, from now on, those of you who are riding a rocket of fast promotions and earning wages as high as heaven compared to those on earth, to change your attitude that Taiwanese are superior.

3. Please remember, from now on, to reassess the responsibilities of the company union so that genuine trade unions can play an appropriate role.[17]

How would Foxconn senior leadership respond to protesting workers' demands? And how did the workers' riot start, and how did it end? On September 23, a siren pierced the night at the 80,000-worker Taiyuan plant as rioting erupted. Zhonghong recalled, "During the previous month workers had clocked as many as 130 hours overtime." Overtime was compulsory. This was more than three times the maximum 36-hour limit of overtime per month allowed under Chinese law. Put another way, workers were subjected to 13-to-1, and under extreme conditions, 30-to-1 work-to-rest schedules, that is, just one day off every two weeks or one day off a month in the pressure-cooker months preceding the release of the new iPhones. Fatigue and bodily pain aside, workers experienced being severely ill treated.

"Over the past two months," Zhonghong continued, "we couldn't even get paid leave when we were sick." The ever-tightening production cycle pressured workers to speed up. Days off were canceled and the sick were pressed to continue to work. The upgraded iPhone was hailed as a thinner, faster, and brighter model. In stark contrast, workers experienced some of their darkest days on the production floor.

Worker fury was fueled by security staff brutality at the male workers' dormitory. Zhonghong explained: "At about 11:00 p.m., security officers severely beat two workers for failing to show their staff IDs. They kicked them until they fell to the ground." This beating of workers by security officers touched off the riot.

By midnight, thousands of workers had had enough. They smashed company security offices, production facilities, shuttle buses, motorbikes, cars, shops, and canteens in the factory complex. Some grabbed iPhone back-plates from a warehouse. Others broke windows, demolished company fences, pillaged factory supermarkets, and overturned police cars and set them ablaze. The company security chief used a patrol car public address system in an attempt to get the workers to end their "illegal activities." But as more and more workers joined the roaring crowd, managers called in the riot police.

By 3:00 a.m., five thousand riot police in helmets with shields and clubs, government officials, and medical staff had converged on the factory. Over the next two hours, the police took control of the dormitories and workshops of the entire complex, detaining the most defiant workers and locking down others in their dormitory rooms. More than forty workers were beaten, handcuffed, and sent off in half a dozen police cars. The factory was sealed off by police lines on all sides, so that workers were contained and onlookers were prevented from joining in. While police repression could demobilize, defuse, and crush worker actions, such methods could also highlight the depths of conflict and might even intensify it.

In emergency mode, Foxconn announced "a special day off" for all workers and staff at the Taiyuan facility. Local officials were sensitive to the fact that riots could undermine economic goals, thereby provoking the wrath of higher authorities if grievances were not quickly resolved and worker insurgency suppressed. The iPhone parts factory reopened after a one-day lockdown.

The timely shipment and continuous flow of products appeared to have remained Apple's overriding concerns. On the same day that the riot occurred, Apple CEO Tim Cook assured the world that retail stores would "continue to receive iPhone 5 shipments regularly and customers can continue to order online and receive an estimated delivery date."[18] But as international news headlines blared "China Apple Factory Riot"[19] and "Riot Reported at Apple Partner Manufacturer Foxconn's iPhone 5 Plant,"[20] Apple was compelled to reassure consumers around the world, including Chinese consumers, that it was not running sweatshops.

Apple quickly looked beyond the riot that had engulfed Foxconn and proclaimed: "We are in one of the most prolific periods of innovation and new products in Apple's history. The amazing products that we've introduced in September and October [2012], iPhone 5, iOS 6, iPad mini, iPad, iMac, MacBook Pro, iPod touch, iPod nano and many of our applications, could only have been created at Apple."[21] Perhaps so. But perhaps it is no less true that the intense pressure on the factory workers was "created at Apple" working hand in glove with its chief supplier, Foxconn.

Strike

Foxconn workers face intense pressure to make each delicate part flawlessly, often under punishing overtime conditions and demands for ever-greater speed. Speaking of the design process, as Apple's senior vice president of hardware engineering Dan Riccio put it, "Every tenth of a millimeter in our products is sacred."[22] The products are indeed sacred to the company. But there is no compelling evidence that the welfare of the human beings who produce them is sacred.

With Apple pressing Foxconn to fulfill production targets as consumer excitement about the new iPhone surged, workers shrewdly recognized that the time was ripe to display their power. Less than two weeks after the Taiyuan workers' riot, in early October 2012, more than three thousand Foxconn workers from one production department in the Zhengzhou factory protested against management's "unreasonable demands for quality control." The Taiyuan plant manufactured iPhone casings, which were sent to a larger Zhengzhou complex in adjacent Henan province for final assembly.

Following the long-awaited iPhone 5 debut, American consumers complained about scratches on the casing of a particular batch of new iPhones, leading to product quality control investigations of final assembly at the Zhengzhou plant. Li Meixia, a 19-year-old female worker, recalled:

> We had no time off during the National Day celebrations, and we were forced to fix the defective products. The precision requirement for the screens of the iPhone, measured in two-hundredths of a millimeter, cannot be detected by the human eye. We use microscopes to check product appearance. It's impossibly strict.

The new quality standards caused workers painful eyestrain and headaches. When several workers were penalized for not meeting the 0.02 mm standards, quarrels erupted between workers and quality control team leaders.

On October 5, production managers screamed at workers and threatened to fire them if they did not "cooperate and concentrate." Workers would tolerate no more. They walked out. The strike paralyzed dozens of parts-processing lines in Zones K and L from late afternoon to night. Following the stoppage during the day shift, senior managers imposed stringent quality standards on night-shift workers. The brief strike put the company on notice but failed to win the rest periods that workers sought.

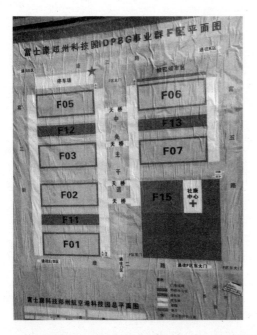

iDPBG (integrated Digital Product Business Group) assembles iPhones exclusively for Apple. It is the largest business group at the Foxconn "iPhone City" at the Zhengzhou Airport Economic Zone, Zhengzhou city, Henan province. The twelve Foxconn Zhengzhou factory zones (A, B, C, D, E, F, G, H, J, K, L, and M) are further subdivided into multistory, multifunction blocks (numbering from F01 to F15 of Zone F).

To sum up, Foxconn workers at the Taiyuan and Zhengzhou factories waged significant actions at the critical moment when Apple launched its signature product that would soon elevate it to a position as the world's most profitable company. Nevertheless, they were unable to build a sustained wider movement, despite the fact that the two plants played complementary roles in the final stages of the iPhone manufacturing chain. As a result, no breakthrough occurred on a plant-wide or company-wide basis, and the company union retained its position despite its passivity in the face of worker actions. The question remains: How long will Foxconn and the Chinese state be able to quell discontent and block the emergence of effective workers' representation and the securing of fundamental worker rights?

Foxconn Trade Union, or Company Union?

The Foxconn Trade Union, like many other enterprise-level unions, from its inception has been an integral part of company management, the very paradigm of the *company union*. Chen Peng, special assistant to CEO Terry Gou, chaired the union for more than a decade beginning in January 2007. Under her leadership, between 2007 and 2012, the Foxconn Trade Union's executive committee expanded from four representatives to twenty-three thousand representatives, as union membership reached 93 percent of its million-strong workforce in China.[23] The year 2012 was the peak of Foxconn's effort to build union membership, a key provision of the Fair Labor Association's remedial action plan. Foxconn is currently not only China's largest private employer, it also has the country's biggest union.

The Chinese Trade Union Law stipulates that all types of enterprises with twenty-five employees or more are supposed to have "basic-level trade union committees" on the shop floor. An enterprise union shall be approved by the next-higher-level trade union, and the topmost decision-making power is to be centralized and exercised by the All-China Federation of Trade Unions. The trade union federation is a constitutive institution of the party-state. In retrospect, despite official efforts since the early 1990s when labor strikes and protests were growing, only 33 percent of the some 480,000 foreign-funded enterprises, and less than 30 percent of private enterprises, had set up unions by mid-2005.[24] Later, Guangdong, the heart of labor activism, took the lead to step up its unionizing drive, aiming to "see trade unions in 60 percent of the foreign-invested enterprises" in the province by the end of 2006.[25] Finally, on January 1, 2007, Foxconn announced the establishment of its union in Shenzhen, having previously ignored the law since 1988. By December 2009, "unions had been set up in 92 percent of the Fortune 500 companies operating in China."[26]

Kong Xianghong, vice-chair of the Guangdong Federation of Trade Unions, emphasizes that unions "must represent the interests of their members or they will be rejected."[27] When union representatives are appointed by and responsive to management, rather than elected by their members, workers frequently are unaware of their union membership, and many who are aware have little confidence in them. This situation prevails to this date at Foxconn.

Union Elections

Worker protesters have repeatedly demanded that Foxconn hold union elections to improve corporate transparency and accountability and secure worker rights. In 2013, Foxconn proclaimed that "a pilot program for union leadership elections had been implemented to improve union representation, and candidates can participate in the election on a voluntary basis."[28] But the selection of candidates and the election process have remained opaque and election methods have never been specified.

In March 2015, a Foxconn Longhua worker interviewee recalled the so-called union election that had taken place earlier that year. He said:

> Not many workers knew about the company union elections. The promotional posters were placed in dark corners of the factory. Management did not do it for our information. They did

it only to complete the standard process. It was a show for the
Shenzhen authorities and the company's biggest customers.

Apple, Foxconn's biggest customer claimed, "Our efforts range
from protecting to empowering to improving the lives of everyone
involved in assembling an Apple product. No one in our industry
is doing as much as we are, in as many places, touching as many
people as we do."[29] But the worker's testimony was tantamount to
a slap in the face for Apple. The truth is that union rights remain
severely restricted for workers at Foxconn and many other workplaces throughout China.

Even worse, on several occasions, supervisors manipulated the
elections by instructing workers to cast their votes for designated
candidates. Out of fear of retaliation, workers followed these
instructions. As one Foxconn worker from the Communication and
Network Solution Business Group (a Cisco Systems server assembly
group) candidly told us:

> We're asked by our supervisors to check the right box. What's
> laughable is that all the candidates are complete strangers to me.
> Afterwards, I checked the information about the winner, and
> found out that he's a senior manager from the same department
> as me! But I've never heard of him. I believe that all the winners
> were handpicked by senior management.

Another worker commented sarcastically: "After all, we have no
idea who's running in the elections. Perhaps only our boss knows
about them!"

Clearly, the new rounds of elections of union leadership at Foxconn were conducted as a formality that would leave intact the
structure of power of the company union. Some workers learned
about the very existence of their unions only when they received
souvenirs, such as water bottles bearing the red union logo, from
union staff members.

The Foxconn Trade Union, in the face of numerous labor protests, increasingly felt the need to address the gaps in union-worker

communications to preempt unrest. The company placed feedback boxes inside the main production complexes and dormitories. "Satisfaction surveys" about canteen food quality, dormitory services (such as free laundry services), and employee assistance programs, among others, were regularly conducted, and the results were published in the *Foxconn Weekly*. "When there's trouble, look to the union," was reiterated by the 24-hour company union hotline. The company offered psychological consultation and advice to workers facing family distress, financial problems, and other personal problems. But in the absence of effective grievance resolution procedures at the workplace, many problems festered.

Building a Workers' Union

Beyond Foxconn, some workers pooled efforts to form better functioning unions, with varying success. Following a 2007 strike, for example, the Yantian International Container Terminal trade union conceded to worker demands to implement a system of annual collective bargaining. The elected union representatives serve dockworkers' interests to negotiate with management on a regular, rather than a one-off, basis. One critical factor in the longshore workers' success is the militancy of crane operators—middle-aged male rural migrants with low turnover—who wield a high degree of bargaining power at one of the world's busiest ports in the capital-intensive sector in South China. In and through strikes, they caused "costly disruptions via direct action at the point of production."[30] Disruptions negatively affected the upstream and downstream linkages of the entire logistics and maritime and ground transportation chain. In this case, dockworkers exercised their "associational power" at the workplace through participation in union-led collective bargaining, while accepting the institutional supervision of the union across different levels.[31]

By the end of 2016, there were 2.8 million enterprise-level trade unions in China, with more than 302 million registered members throughout the country.[32] In comparison, the International Trade Union Confederation (ITUC) represents 200 million workers in 163 countries and territories.[33] Clearly, the number of Chinese union members is super large, and it has been increasing. However, true worker representation remains very rare at the workplace level.

"When There's Trouble, Look to the Union"—But How?

The gains of tech brands in transnational production chains rest squarely on the value created by workers at Foxconn and other suppliers. In the context of expansive global capital, the discrepancy between fair labor policies (as proclaimed by Amazon, Microsoft, and Apple in their supplier codes of conduct) and the reality on the Foxconn factory floor remains huge. For one thing, union rights are unprotected.

Foxconn, not unlike many other enterprises, represses workers' demands for union representation responsive to worker interests. In contrast to the decline of union representation in the US and many other Western countries, Foxconn and many other large-scale Chinese enterprises are fully "unionized" through the All-China Federation of Trade Unions. Formalities aside, workers lack voices and democratic participation in the unions, which are subordinate to the Chinese Communist Party.

In the wider context, as labor shortages have become widespread, human resources agencies have offered cash bonuses to attract temporary workers through "signing bonuses" to be paid to new recruits after the completion of the first or second month of employment. Some workers seek to improve their conditions by pursuing these short-term signing bonuses with other enterprises, but for the most part, the result is simply to perpetuate the growing temp economy, with increasing numbers of temporary and subcontract workers, which undermines worker networks and organizing capacity and creates a situation in which workers frequently fall prey to the illicit tactics of recruiters.[34]

In December 2018, for example, dispatch workers of Foxconn Zhengzhou, the iPhone maker in central China, complained that they were not paid the "large bonus" of 6,000 yuan per person after having worked fifty-five days, as agreed, to meet the demand for iPhones for the Christmas holiday season. The joint legal responsibility of the agencies and Foxconn remains ambiguous. What is not ambiguous is the fact that many workers, who confided to us via WeChat, failed to receive promised bonuses. Perhaps not surprisingly, the pro-management Foxconn Trade Union did not support workers in the disputes.

Apple, Foxconn, and the Lives of China's Workers

For My Departed Brothers and Sisters
I'm like you

I was just like you:
A teenager leaving home
Eager to make my own way in the world

I was just like you:
My mind struggling in the rush of the assembly line
My body tied to the machine
Each day yearning to sleep
And yet desperately fighting for overtime

In the dormitory, I was just like you:
Everyone a stranger
Lining up, drawing water, brushing teeth
Rushing off to our different factories
Sometimes I think I'll go home
But if I go home, what then?

I was just like you:
Constantly yelled at
My self-respect trampled mercilessly
Does life mean turning my youth and sweat into raw material?
Leaving my dreams empty, to collapse with a bang?

I was just like you:
Work hard, follow instructions and keep quiet

I was just like you:
My eyes, lonely and exhausted
My heart, agitated and desperate

I was just like you:
Entrapped in rules
In pain that makes me wish to end this life

Here's the only difference:
In the end I escaped from the factory
And you died young in an alien land
In your determined bright red blood
Once more I see the image of myself
Pressed and squeezed so tightly I cannot move.

—Yan Jun, a female migrant worker[1]

Many of Yan Jun's generation, working far from home, miss parents and loved ones. They have fled stagnant villages whose youth have departed for urban jobs thousands of miles away, leaving behind only children and the elderly. The world outside is harsh. Some think of going home, yet the hopes and dreams of most migrant workers remain fixed on the cities.

Chinese Rural Migrant Labor

China has witnessed the world's largest labor migration—internal migration—over the past four decades. Since the 1980s, successive waves of predominantly peasant villagers have seized newfound opportunities to find work in booming industries and services in cities across the country. As of 2018, 51.5 percent of rural migrant workers were born *after* 1980. Of the post-1980 generation, three cohorts can be differentiated: those who were born in the 1980s (50.4 percent), in the 1990s (43.2 percent), and after 2000 (6.4 percent).[2] Young workers at Foxconn, like their peers elsewhere, aspire to earn a living wage,

develop technical skills, enjoy comprehensive welfare benefits, marry, and secure the full range of citizenship rights in the cities they
inhabit. Indeed, as early as 2011, a government survey covering one
thousand enterprises in twenty-five cities and districts found that as
many as 42.3 percent of the 2,711 respondents were concerned about
"searching for self-development opportunities"—not just about making money—when going out to work.[3]

China's eastern coastal provinces and their major cities, including
Shanghai, Shenzhen, and Beijing, have been, and remain, the most
popular destinations for rural migrants. In 2018, eastern China was
the major location with over 100 million of the internal migrant
working population (36.1 percent) (see table 12.1). At the same time,
macro-economic transformations and new development projects
have yielded significant results. Both the central (33 percent) and
western (27.5 percent) regions reported an increase in the number of
rural migrant workers, with the largest increase in labor in the western provinces (up 5.4 million people). With rapid urbanization and
industrialization in interior provinces, short-distance labor migration became possible for many.

Table 12.1. Chinese labor migration by region, 2015–2018.

	2015	2018	Change	Change
	(in millions)			
Eastern China	103.0	104.1	1.1	1.1%
Central China	91.7	95.4	3.7	4.0%
Western China	73.8	79.2	5.4	7.3%
Northeastern China	9.0	9.7	0.7	7.8%
	277.5	288.4		

Notes: Eastern China includes three provincial-level municipalities (Beijing, Tianjin,
and Shanghai) and seven provinces (Hebei, Jiangsu, Zhejiang, Fujian, Shandong,
Guangdong, and Hainan); central China includes six provinces (Shanxi, Anhui,
Jiangxi, Henan, Hubei, and Hunan); western China includes Chongqing, six
provinces (Sichuan, Guizhou, Yunnan, Shaanxi, Gansu, and Qinghai), and five
autonomous regions (Guangxi, Inner Mongolia, Tibet, Xinjiang, and Ningxia); and,
northeastern China includes three provinces (Liaoning, Jilin, and Heilongjiang).
Sources: National Bureau of Statistics of the People's Republic of China (2017, 2019).[4]

Urban-rural and inter-regional income and wealth dispari-
ties remain wide, despite government rebalancing efforts, such as
improving infrastructure and financial support for underdeveloped
interior regions. Researchers Yujeong Yang and Mary Gallagher
suggest that, under China's massive industrial relocation and new
investment,

> the movement inland may create a different (and better) kind
> of industrialization because inland localities will be much more
> dependent on local and nearby workers to fuel their own in-
> dustrial transformation. Inland local governments may be de-
> veloping a governance style that is qualitatively different from
> that pursued by coastal local governments. Built on the notion
> of "coordinated rural-urban development", cities like Chengdu
> are becoming more inclusive and responsive to their population,
> which is expanding as nearby rural areas are absorbed into sub-
> urban and peri-urban areas.[5]

Referencing our own decade-long study, we are not fully
convinced by Yang and Gallagher's "moving in and moving up"
thesis. Foxconn's employment profile does fit the pattern of reduced
jobs in eastern regions and increased jobs centered in central and
western regions. Although this has led to increased incomes in provinces with lower levels of industrialization, many Foxconn workers,
specifically those transferred from relatively high-minimum-wage
areas such as Shenzhen and Shanghai, have experienced a "race to
the bottom," that is, the forced transfer from coastal jobs and homes
to lower-wage inland locations. Much else remains unchanged. For
example, at Foxconn Chengdu, the dormitory labor regime is repro-
duced to enable iPad production on a 24-hour basis at the lowest
possible cost. The minimum and actual wages of inland workers
remain substantially below those in coastal areas and many find
themselves in temporary, subcontract, and informal employment.
Rural migrant workers, who have neither personal assets nor access
to government-subsidized urban housing, lead lives of insecurity,

drifting between factory dormitories and small rental rooms on the periphery of rapidly changing cities.

Young and Old Migrant Workers

As of December 2018, by official reckoning some 288 million rural migrants had been drawn into manufacturing, service, and construction sectors in towns and cities all across the country, accounting for one-fifth of the total Chinese population. The annual rate of growth of rural migrant labor, however, declined from 5.4 percent in 2010 to 0.6 percent in 2018 in sync with China's demographic transition.[6] With the tightened supply of youthful workers and rising life expectancy, at present, a high proportion of the elderly continue to work until late in life, as clearly tracked by government data.

Figure 12.1 shows the changing age distribution of Chinese rural migrant workers between 2008 and 2018. Over that period, the largest change was in the 16- to 20-year-old bracket, which declined from nearly 11 percent in 2008 to 2.4 percent in 2018 (16 is the statutory minimum age for work in China). The 21-to-30 age cohort also dropped from 35 percent in 2008 to 25 percent in 2018. At the same time, older cohorts expanded steadily. Those in the 41-to-50 group rose sharply from 19 to 26 percent (the solid line) while those over 50 increased even more rapidly from 11 to 22 percent (the dotted line).

To summarize, rural migrant workers—a significant part of the Chinese working population and the overwhelming majority of Foxconn workers—are getting older. Social policy intervention, notably government welfare provisions to needy workers and families, is more urgent than ever before.

Figure 12.1. Chinese rural migrant workers by age, 2008–2018.

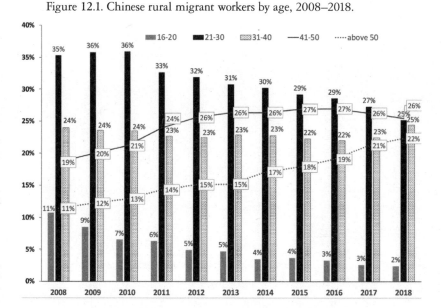

Note: The earliest government survey data of Chinese rural migrant workers available online is for 2008. Age groups are divided into five categories: 16–20, 21–30, 31–40, 41–50, and above 50 (with no further breakdown for those age 60 and older). *Sources:* National Bureau of Statistics of the People's Republic of China (2013, 2019).[7]

Student Labor in China

China's pool of young workers is diminishing. In this context, interning students could play a significant role in national development if they were to receive appropriate training that raises their skill levels and enables them to find better jobs requiring mastery of higher technology and specialized knowledge. Scott Rozelle, co-director of the Rural Education Action Program in the Freeman Spogli Institute for International Studies at Stanford University and a long-time researcher in rural China, commented:

> In our experience, Apple is a leader in ensuring that student workers thrive, working closely with suppliers to institute practical standards and innovative strategies for protecting student

workers. We're working with Apple to assess the quality of vocational schools—the main source of student workers in China.[8]

Since 2013, with the support of the global electronics association
the Electronic Industry Citizenship Coalition (rebranded the Responsible Business Alliance in 2017),[9] Rozelle has created a monitoring and evaluation program of China's vocational schooling system. Its objective is to achieve "responsible vocational education,"
beginning with a project of 118 vocational schools in Henan province.[10] In June 2016, the project team created a list of twenty-two
credentialed vocational schools to benchmark teaching standards,
school resources, and student learning experiences against a set of
criteria.[11]

Using the list as a reference, the Henan provincial government
encouraged companies to select students and graduates from quality schools for internships and employment, thereby providing economic incentives for both teachers and students to improve their
performance. Cooperating schools were promised increased government funding for long-term educational development. This was
framed by the Stanford University research team as a "win-win-
win action research" effort to strengthen collaboration between the
government, schools, and companies.[12]

While holding the vocational schools directly accountable for
poor learning experiences and internship arrangements, the Stanford University researchers seemingly neglected the heavy responsibility of both Apple and Foxconn, in collaboration with provincial
and municipal Chinese governments, for sustaining what we have
called "precarious internships." These are internships in name only
as these programs recruit technical school students as cheap and
disposable labor at Foxconn factories and provide no student training. In our assessment, the blame cannot be attributed primarily to
the failure of the schools. It is above all the product of strong collaboration between corporate giants and the Chinese government
in bending internship rules and regulations to their own advantage
at the expense of students.

Exposés by the media demonstrated that Foxconn student interns—some as young as fourteen years of age—were essentially engaged in thinly disguised child labor that made a mockery of the intern program.[13] These "sheep-like internships" left their victims confused and helpless, like sheep without a shepherd. With students becoming a significant proportion of the workforce at Foxconn and other large firms, questions of educational and labor rights protection during internships deserve urgent attention.[14]

Regulating China's Intern Economy

Legal practitioners Earl Brown and Kyle deCant argue that when internship programs are "devoid of any relevant educational component and maintained solely for the benefit of the employer's bottom line ... interns should be afforded the full protection of China's labor laws."[15] We have shown that Foxconn's internship program is precisely such a program, devoid of an educational and skills training component. In a long-awaited response to intern abuse, the Chinese central government in 2016 belatedly took some of the first steps to protect the basic rights of student interns.

Specifically, vocational schools are instructed to manage student internships in accordance with the "Regulations on the Management of Vocational School Student Internships." Under the new regulations, effective April 11, 2016, the duration of workplace-based internships should normally be six months. Vocational schools and enterprises are required to jointly provide interns with commercial general liability insurance. The regulations also require that student internships have substantial educational content and work-skills training provisions, along with comprehensive labor protections for student interns such as eight-hour working days, no overtime, and no night shifts. Above all, no more than 10 percent of the labor force at "any given facility," and no more than 20 percent of the workers in "any given work position," should consist of student interns at any point in time.[16]

However, the government left intact incentives for corporations to continue to prioritize student interns as cheap and expendable labor. The 2016 regulations stipulate the statutory minimum level for paying interns: "Wages shall be *at least* 80 percent of that of employees during the probationary period" (emphasis added).[17] In other words, interns are to be paid for their labor, but employers are permitted to pay them just 80 percent of the minimum income offered to employees. Employers save further since interns, defined as students rather than workers, receive no corporate payments toward retirement.

Fundamentally, the interests shared by companies and local governments are intertwined to the detriment of student interns. In 2019, Foxconn Hengyang in Hunan province, whose primary contracts were with Amazon, reportedly violated limits on the number of intern and dispatch workers (also known as agency workers), who made up, respectively, 21 percent and 34 percent of the 7,435 workers. Under the law, dispatch workers should not exceed 10 percent of the company's workforce. The proliferation of "flexible" employment has adversely impacted not only dispatch workers. Regular workers would also encounter greater difficulty in making collective demands on employers as they now must compete with contingent laborers in the workplace. Worse, student interns were illegally required to work 10-hour shifts, day and night, including two hours of forced overtime.[18] The super-exploitation of Chinese student labor has in fact gone far beyond Foxconn to e-commerce giants such as JD.com, and from manufacturing to the services industry.[19]

Labor Rights Struggle

The clashing interests and intentions *within* and *across* the many elements of the Chinese state are complex. The Communist party-state—nominally "a socialist state" under the people's democratic dictatorship led by the working class—has introduced new labor laws and regulations and extended them to the vast population of rural migrants, including, more recently, interning students or, more accurately, "student workers." But workers themselves often have to fight to secure their hard-earned wages and compensation.

Moreover, Chinese trade unions, which should protect worker interests, are subject to managerial domination and state control. Tim Pringle, in charting the priorities for Chinese union reforms in light of growing worker demand for better conditions, stresses the need for "more accountable enterprise-level union chairpersons and committees," as well as "more supportive, interactive, and, at times, directive relationships between the higher trade unions and their enterprise-level subordinates."[20] Conspicuously silent about policies to strengthen worker rights has been Wang Dongming, the Beijing-based trade union federation chairperson who assumed office in March 2018. The result, with respect to Foxconn's labor struggle and other cases, is his tacit endorsement of company and state control over workers. A notable example illustrative of the failure of union organizing is the experience at Jasic Technology, a welding machinery factory based in Shenzhen.

At Jasic, an alliance between workers and their supporters developed between summer 2018 and early 2019 was crushed. The immediate background was that Jasic management had repeatedly ignored strong worker demands over wages and benefits, as well as occupational health and safety. Fines and draconian punishments were rampant. In July 2018, Jasic workers gathered eighty-nine signatures out of a workforce of one thousand to file a union membership application (far more than the minimum legal requirement of twenty-five applicants). Although exercising their legal rights by setting up a union in accordance with the Chinese Trade Union Law, they faced heavy-handed repression.

The subsequent firing of Jasic labor activists drew not only the attention of fellow workers but also a few dozen left-wing university students, Maoists, and Marxists throughout the country. In response, in the fall and winter of 2018, the government cracked down on the emergent worker-student coalition and mobilization in support of Jasic workers on university campuses in Beijing, Nanjing, Guangzhou, and other cities.[21] In Au Loong Yu's critical analysis, "Though Xi Jinping continues to demand the people learn from Marxism-Leninism and Mao's thought, the state continues to crack down on any independent and collective effort at seriously studying left classics—and to crack down even harder when these efforts carry an aspiration to sympathize with working people."[22] By January 2019, three Jasic workers, along with a former worker, had been detained for six months before finally being released. Ten leaders of the Jasic Workers Support Group were similarly detained and denied access to lawyers and families; worse, they were forced to testify that they broke the law in video "confessions."[23] Clearly, both management and the government remain vigilant to prevent the emergence of autonomous unions that might empower workers.

Government Responses to Workers' Actions

Rights-claiming workers, as vividly discussed by Mary Gallagher in her book, *Authoritarian Legality in China*, are expected to act as "firefighters" who self-enforce their rights by sounding the "fire alarm" at labor departments and courts to alert higher officials to abuses and encourage them to uphold labor standards.[24] If workers sound the alarm by filing cases and the government consistently enforces worker protections, employers may anticipate the risk of a dispute and avoid the problem. But if enforcement is lax, employers may ignore the letter and spirit of the law, and the conflict is likely to be perpetuated. Local governments often prioritize attracting investment rather than enforcing laws and regulations. A persistent pattern is established: despite efforts by workers to sound the alarm, serious problems such as abuse by management continue and remain unresolved.

Suicide involves an intensely personal, and social, struggle on the part of the individual. In November 1970 in South Korea,

23-year-old textile worker Chun Tae-il poured gasoline on himself and set himself ablaze in the hope of rallying fellow workers to demand that the Park Chung-hee dictatorship protect worker rights. His suicide inspired the labor and democratic movements that followed and helped transform South Korean civil society. As Kim Hyojoung puts it, Chun galvanized "collective action by mobilizing the 'hearts and minds' of the target audience."[25] In China, Foxconn employees who committed suicide in 2010 and after also issued a cri de coeur in response to the harsh conditions that confronted workers. The tragic loss of young lives reverberated throughout society and internationally, inspiring a call to guarantee worker rights and strive to prevent more deaths. But will their deaths and the responses to them set in motion fundamental changes in labor conditions and the nature of state power in China?

Under President Xi Jinping's leadership, from 2013, the political environment for those working on labor rights issues in China, including grassroots social organizations, students, scholars, and lawyers, has been severely constrained. The shutdown of "illegal," nongovernmental labor rights organizations in Guangdong province in December 2015 and the heightened surveillance and massive arrest of worker activists (including feminists and social media editors) in recent years have undermined worker-led and worker-student networks.

Effective from January 1, 2017, with the passage of the Law on the Management of Overseas Nongovernmental Organizations' Activities within Mainland China (also known as "the Foreign NGO Law"), the oversight of Hong Kong and international NGOs by the Chinese authorities has strengthened. In fact, the Ministry of Public Security now reserves the right to "manage" foreign NGOs' daily operations on the mainland. Police can request specific information like membership and activities, as well as the source of funding. The growth of civil society, within which labor organizing exists, has been severely restricted.[26]

In October 2017, President Xi delivered a three-and-a-half-hour speech stressing the priority of developing "socialism with Chinese characteristics in the new era" and achieving a "moderately prosperous" society by 2020, wherein all citizens would enjoy comfortable and affluent lives. On October 24, the National People's Congress closed its weeklong meetings with the following prospectus for its future:

> In the first stage from 2020 to 2035, we will build on the foundation created by the moderately prosperous society with a further 15 years of hard work to see that socialist modernization is basically realized. In the second stage from 2035 to the middle of the 21st century, we will, building on having basically achieved modernization, work hard for a further 15 years and develop China into a great modern socialist country that is prosperous, strong, democratic, culturally advanced, harmonious, and beautiful.[27]

The paths to prosperity, democracy, socialism, cultural advancement, social harmony, and ecological civilization, however, remain elusive even as Xi touts the broad objective of rejuvenating the nation "in the new era."

"Realize the great Chinese Dream," exhorts a government banner. The definition of that dream and the determination of who may claim it remain fiercely contested. In March 2018, the Communist Party's central committee removed the two-term, ten-year limit for president and vice president from the Constitution (a two-term limit for the posts was ratified in the 1982 Constitution). The move would allow Xi to stay in power beyond his due retirement in 2022, perhaps serving as president for life.

Whose Chinese Dream?

As worker protests crescendoed, some took up their cause in poems and other writings, and in discussion with fellow workers. Worker-poet

Xiaoxiao memorialized the twelve workers who committed suicide at the two Foxconn Shenzhen factory complexes in the first five months of 2010. His poem uses the Chinese character for *tiao* (jump or leap) twelve times to represent each of the desperate workers whom he identifies as "our martyred workmates."

Grieving for Our Martyred Foxconn Workmates
Leap
I use my life to end your glee
Leap
I use my life to stop the production line
Leap
I use my life to proclaim to the people
Leap
I use my life to protest against the times
Leap
I use my life to peel away your cloak
Leap
I use my life to let people see you reek of blood
Leap
I use my life to reveal people's needs
Leap
I use my life to awaken them from their anesthesia
Leap, Leap, Leap
We use our lives to excavate a deeper passage
Leap
I use my life to seek human dignity.

—Xiaoxiao, a migrant factory worker[28]

Writing in the first person, Xiaoxiao powerfully identified with his fellow workers, "Leap, Leap, Leap." The intensity of suicides reached its peak in May 2010, when the thirteenth suicidal worker slit his wrists after failing to jump from the heavily guarded factory dormitory. Then the poet shifted from the singular to the plural, speaking not only for the author, but for the workers who sacrificed their lives. "We use our lives to excavate a

deeper passage." Here Xiaoxiao looked beyond the acts of atomized workers to suggest the possibility of a collective understanding of their acts as part of a process that could bring together
individuals in ways that make possible "a deeper passage." The
pathway to "seek human dignity."

Behind the façade of prosperity exemplified by the Shenzhen
skyline, a worker named Xu Lizhi ended his life at Foxconn Longhua on September 30, 2014. He was twenty-four years old. A native
of rural Guangdong, his multiple attempts to find employment
that would allow him to escape from the assembly line, such as a
position as a librarian in the on-campus Foxconn University, had
failed. He left this, his last poem, next to his deathbed:

On My Deathbed
I want to take another look at the ocean,
Behold the vastness of tears from half a lifetime
I want to climb another mountain,
Try to call back the soul that I've lost
I want to touch the sky,
Feel that blueness so light
But unable to do any of these, I'm leaving this world.
Everyone who's heard of me
Shouldn't be surprised at my leaving
Even less should you sigh or grieve
I was fine when I came, and fine when I left.

—Xu Lizhi, a Foxconn migrant
worker, September 30, 2014[29]

Some of Lizhi's most poignant poetry conveys a sense of life and
death on the assembly line, here capturing the exhaustion of the
poet and fellow workers on the line falling asleep while standing:

Falling Asleep While Standing
The paper before my eyes fades to yellow
With a steel pen I chisel on it uneven black
Full of working words

Workshop, assembly line, machine, work card, overtime, wages . . .
They've trained me to become docile
Don't know how to shout or rebel
Don't know who to complain to or denounce
Only how to silently endure exhaustion

When I first set foot in this place
I hoped only for that grey pay slip on the tenth of each month
To grant me some belated solace
For this I had to grind away my rough edges, grind away my words
Refuse to skip work
Refuse to take sick leave
Refuse leave for private reasons
Refuse to be late
Refuse to leave early
By the assembly line I stood straight as iron, with versatile hands
On many days, many nights
I fell asleep while standing

—Xu Lizhi, August 20, 2011

Later Lizhi wrote of a screw that fell to the ground in perhaps
his most desolate reflection on life and death at Foxconn.

A Screw Fell to the Ground
A screw fell to the ground
In this dark night of overtime
Plunging vertically, lightly clinking
It won't attract anyone's attention
Just like last time
On a night like this
When someone plunged to the ground

—Xu Lizhi, January 9, 2014

As Lizhi recorded, the rat race of life on the line clashed with the
best instincts and highest aspirations of humanity.

Toward a Stronger Social Movement

In contemporary Chinese development, although both government initiatives and workers' demands have resulted in expanded employment and renewed calls for expanded workplace rights, many of those rights remain aspirational, that is, as yet unrealized. President Xi reiterated in an October 2018 meeting with the new union leadership in Beijing:

> Trade unions should adhere to the employee-centered working approach; focus on the most pressing, most immediate issues that concern the employees the most; and fulfill the obligation of safeguarding workers' rights and interests and sincerely serving workers and the people.[30]

Rhetoric aside, the anti-suicide nets and locked and barred windows surrounding the manufacturing buildings and worker dormitories installed in May 2010 and remaining today are a grim reminder of worker hardship and the shared corporate failure of Foxconn, Apple, and other tech companies, as well as the failure of the Chinese state to guarantee worker rights.

In our analysis, a significant cause of the tragedies of 2010, and continued tensions thereafter, was the fact that workers, employed under pressure-cooker conditions, were deprived of the right to leverage their trade unions to collectively challenge enterprise decisions shaping conditions that heightened the risk of employee suicide. Life-threatening risks of industrial injuries and occupational illnesses that plague those working in electronics manufacturing, in part as a result of union subservience to corporate power, remain sources of deep labor discontent. Legal rights have frequently been treated like a commodity, with contenders, employers, and government officials bargaining for the price, rather than it being arbitrated and litigated.

Workers strive to take direct action as a means to voice shared grievances. They support each other to demand better conditions and greater participation in trade unions. Indeed, some worker protesters have moved ahead to establish their own organizations to carry on their fight after being fired or released from prison, a practice that Feng Chen and Xuehui Yang call "exit with voice." Outside the factory gate, these workers-turned-activists continue to serve workers' diverse needs by adapting to the arduous economic and political contexts.[31] They aspire to build networks to educate and organize more workers for the common good, generating new ideas and strengthening ties with the community. This growth of autonomous, local, and underground self-organizations is increasingly important at a time when workers' centers—*including* those formally affiliated with the government trade union or women's federation through state-administered service subcontracting contracts—are being shuttered.[32]

To conclude, workers' struggles and social activism toward strengthening labor rights face formidable state and corporate challenges in China, as they do in many parts of the world. At the same time, workers—in and through their successive struggles—have accumulated organizing experience, leadership skills, and the capacity to present collective claims. If labor protest is to transcend localized actions in dispersed sites of resistance to span whole industries, it will be necessary to build a broad-based social movement that wins support at home and abroad.

Epilogue

There's a right way to make products.
It starts with the rights of the people who make them.

—Apple Supplier Responsibility (2016)[1]

In 2016 Apple released its tenth Supplier Responsibility Progress Report. "There's a right way to make products," the company proclaimed. "It starts with the rights of the people who make them." That's *supposed* to be the Apple way to make products. Through interviews, poems, songs, letters, blogs, photos, and videos, Chinese workers revealed a different world: we learned that our beloved high-tech gadgets are not produced in a Silicon Valley paradise. Indeed, while designed in Silicon Valley, they are not produced there at all.

While Foxconn should seriously examine the link between suicide and employment conditions, and develop effective policies not only to prevent employee suicides but to guarantee the welfare of its nearly one million employees, we have shown that the lives of Foxconn workers are not only constrained by management policies but in the first instance are shaped by the brand whose products are being produced. That is, above all, Apple, but also Samsung, Microsoft, Amazon, and other leading global buyers of electronics products.

Can Apple Serve Humanity?

Transnational corporations have benefited tremendously from the speed, flexibility, and efficiency of China's supply chain and its workers. In return, Apple proclaims its dedication to "educating and empowering supplier employees," stating that "every workday should include opportunity and enrichment."[2] At the 2016 World-wide Developers Conference, CEO Tim Cook prioritized the use of new technology to advance social good and closed his presentation with this message: "At Apple, we believe that technology should lift humanity and should enrich people's lives in all the ways that they want to experience it."[3] On June 9, 2017, Cook delivered MIT's commencement address, proclaiming once more the Apple mission: "To serve humanity. It was just that simple. Serve humanity."[4] In 2019, he opened the Apple Supplier Responsibility Progress Report with the following: "We believe that business, at its best, serves the public good, empowers people around the world, and binds us together as never before."[5] Presumably, Cook was referring not only to the consumers of Apple products but the workers who produce them, the vast majority of them working at Foxconn. Can we say that Foxconn workers' lives have been changing for the better? Are the workers and student interns who produce Apple's products part of that humanity?

Apple has engaged with business leaders, technology experts, and social scientists to address critical concerns. "The same leverage [of large firms] that can be used to demand lower prices and better quality from suppliers," pinpointed by Frederick Mayer and Gary Gereffi, "can also be used to press for better labor practices."[6] The key is closer collaboration between buyers and suppliers to advance mutual benefits by overcoming labor governance problems, that is, placing the welfare of workers to the fore. In 2013, in the wake of the tragedies of suicides, explosions, and poisonings in large supplier factories in China (notably, Foxconn, Pegatron, and Wintek), Apple established an academic advisory board for its Supplier Responsibility program. The eight advisors initially appointed were global supply chain, labor, and China specialists from leading US universities: Richard Locke (Brown University), Mary Gallagher (University of Michigan), Mark Cullen (Stanford University),

Margaret Levi (Stanford University and University of Washington), Dara O'Rourke (University of California, Berkeley), AnnaLee Saxenian (University of California, Berkeley), Charles Sabel (Columbia University), and Eli Friedman (Cornell University).[7] With access to "Apple's audit data, program results, and supply chain information," the advisory board was offered the opportunity to develop projects that could be incorporated into Apple's Supplier Responsibility program.[8]

Locke, an authority on international labor rights and corporate responsibility, served as chair (2013–2016) of the Apple Academic Advisory Board and has been provost of Brown University since July 2015. He expressed hope that the advisory board will "shape the practices of Apple and its suppliers so that all employees involved in Apple's supply chain . . . are paid living wages, work within the legal work hour regimes, work in environments that are safe and where they can express their rights as citizens." Under his coordination, the academic advisors planned to first, "study and make recommendations to Apple about current policies and practices"; second, "conduct or commission new research on labor standards within Apple's supply chain"; and third and finally, "share existing research which may help improve those policies and practices."[9]

Writing for the May 2013 *Boston Review* special issue, Locke commended not only Apple but also Nike and HP for their commitment to voluntary regulation of their labor policies: "These businesses have committed to using private, voluntary regulation to address labor issues traditionally regulated by government or unions. And for the most part, the companies have acted on these commitments."[10] At the same time, Locke acknowledged that what he described as the huge efforts of companies to improve workers' well-being had produced only limited results on the ground. His collaborative research on global supply chain governance led him to conclude that the effectiveness of corporate attempts to regulate labor practices may depend less on the programs implemented and more on the national political economy context.[11]

Market reforms, conducted under the auspices of the Chinese state, have indeed reclassified the rights, status, and benefits of different segments of workers. The older generation of state sector workers have lost their job security in successive waves of enterprise restructuring, mergers and acquisitions, and privatization since the late 1990s. At the same time, younger cohorts, the great majority being rural migrants, at best receive inferior health insurance, pensions, maternity packages, and other benefits, and are paid less than local workers. With business reorganization and massive layoffs, urban state sector and collective enterprise workers find it necessary to compete for jobs with rural migrants. The divisive hiring system, which includes both direct and indirect labor, gives rise to new forms of social conflict and inequality as workers doing identical tasks working side by side may have different conditions, including wages and security. This both keeps labor cost down for the company and increases its flexibility to hire and fire workers.

But it is important to reiterate that Apple and other international companies are responsible for rights violations at Foxconn and other supplier factories. Leading American and European firms, having actively shed domestic employment through outsourcing and other forms of subcontracting, have failed to honor labor rights in the companies that now produce and assemble their products, whatever their company codes state. Fundamentally, the buyer-driven business model functions to assure "a rise in profitability for [companies that] operate at the top of industries and increasingly precarious working conditions for workers at lower levels."[12] This situation has driven workers and their supporters to join hands to launch anti-sweatshop campaigns to forge solidarity with workers in China and worldwide.

Global Anti-Sweatshop Campaigns

Foxconn's expansion from Taiwan to coastal China was a springboard for operations that eventually spread throughout China, and then Asia, Europe, and the Americas. The company's international links and its global exports are the heart of its economic prowess, but they also render it vulnerable to a transnational movement that seeks to secure labor and environmental justice.

In the wake of the plague of suicides at Foxconn, across the straits beginning in June 2010, Taiwanese scholars Lin Thung-hong and Yang You-ren issued an open statement with more than three hundred signatories and held a press conference in Taipei to condemn Foxconn management for its brutal treatment of mainland workers. They confronted Terry Gou, the head of the Foxconn Group, as he promised to increase wages. Noting that "recent pay raises" at Foxconn did not address the deep-seated problems confronting workers, they concluded, "We believe that the Foxconn suicide cluster is a bitter accusation made with 11 young lives against the inhumane, exploitative labor regime."[13]

Thousands of miles away in Mexico, workers at Foxconn Guadalajara launched solidarity actions to protest labor oppression in China. Their support included creating a makeshift cemetery to allow the workers to rest in peace and draw media attention to their plight worldwide.[14] They also read out a press statement in Spanish calling on not only Foxconn but also Apple, Dell, HP, Sony, Nokia, and other global brands to take responsibility for the unfolding labor crisis in China.

In the US, university students and faculty members, union organizers, and labor rights groups protested outside Apple's flagship New York store to demand justice for Foxconn workers. They decorated the surrounding sidewalk with photos of the young Foxconn victims and a funeral bouquet.[15] On the West Coast, San Francisco's Chinese Progressive Association held a candlelight vigil for the Foxconn victims and their families. The memorial featured solemn teenagers holding signs with the names of Foxconn workers who had taken their own lives.[16]

Thirteen young activists picketed an Apple store in San Francisco on June 17, 2010. They carried placards showing the names and ages of twelve of the thirteen Foxconn suicide victims whose names are known, and an unnamed placard for the thirteenth. They had a moment of silence for each of them. The iPad placard "DEATH PAD" reads, "Gongren yao zhengyi" (Workers Want Justice).

On June 14, 2010, United Students Against Sweatshops, working with a nationwide network of over 250 American college and high school chapters, sent an open letter urging Apple CEO Steve Jobs to "address the problems in Shenzhen by ensuring payment of living wages, legal working hours, and democratic union elections in Foxconn supplier factories." The letter was copied to our campaign allies, including Hong Kong–based Students and Scholars Against Corporate Misbehavior (SACOM), San Francisco Chinese Progressive Alliance, and Washington, DC–based Worker Rights Consortium (an independent labor rights monitoring organization that investigates working conditions in factories around the globe).[17] They received no response from Apple. Clearly, it is necessary for the campaign to continue to expand and deepen, reaching out to corporate management and concerned citizens through coordinated actions.

"iSlave" at Ten: 2017—The Campaign Continues

The year 2017 saw the launch of the campaign "#iSlaveat10—No More iSlave." Ten years earlier, Apple had entered the mobile phone market with the launch of the iPhone. As time passed, consumer awareness of the links between electronics manufacturing and the plight of workers grew, and as Apple became a global behemoth, more consumers demanded that the company act responsibly and transparently.[18]

On November 3, 2017, Apple released iPhone X, priced at US$999. SACOM (Students and Scholars Against Corporate Misbehavior) held a banner "iSlave at X" to protest the company's labor policies at the Apple store in Festival Walk, Hong Kong.

In the wake of consumer movements focused on Nike, Adidas, and other makers of sneakers, has Apple become more sensitive to the ability of school- and university-based consumer actions to stage boycotts? A substantial part of Apple's market is education generated, and its claims to ethical practices directly impinge on students and faculty, among other consumers. This could open the way for strong pressure on the company in the many countries that constitute its global market.

Besides updating its smartphone with the launch of iPhone 11 in September 2019, Apple has been promoting its app development curriculum for high school and community college students at home and abroad. "The app economy and software development are among the fastest-growing job sectors in America and we're thrilled to be providing educators and students with the tools to learn coding," enthused CEO Tim Cook.[19] The company proposes that every child be taught how to code at school and notes that Swift, Apple's primary programming language, is an ideal vehicle for learning. In a seamless digitized ecosystem, Apple's apps are linked with virtual classrooms such as iTunes U by utilizing iPhones, iPads, Macs, TVs, Watches, and other Apple products.

"Education is at the core of Apple's DNA and iTunes U is an incredibly valuable resource for teachers and students," trumpeted an Apple company statement.[20] What goes unmentioned is an open secret: the exploited student interns in Foxconn's factories are excluded from Apple's worldwide educational initiatives. Working day and night to make the iPhones and iPads, they have no time to rest properly, let alone to study coding.

In shining a bright light on Apple, anti-sweatshop activists simultaneously seek to stimulate further inquiry into the labor conditions of Samsung and of the entire electronics industry, thereby hoping to promote an industry-wide solution to the chronic problems in China and other countries.[21]

Is Foxconn a Global Predator?

No one is free when others are oppressed. This book, sparked by the rash of suicides and grounded in research on Foxconn, Apple, and the Chinese state, has attempted to inform and heighten social consciousness concerning labor issues to inspire transnational activism in opposition to the oppression of labor wherever it is found. A collectivity between workers and environmentalists has been emerging. Despite pressures from both the Chinese authoritarian state and global corporations, labor organizing for sustainable change continues. Given the economic prowess of Foxconn and its durable relationship with major clients, including notably Apple, our engagement with Foxconn workers is strategically important to leverage for long-term change in an entire industry that has global ramifications.

Foxconn has striven to move up the value chain by striking sweetheart deals with governments all over the world, as revealed by international studies and mainstream media reports. The Taiwanese multinational has frequently captured new markets by circumventing labor, social, and environmental regulatory controls and taking advantage of China's massive global investment under the Belt and Road Initiative. Even when Foxconn's attempts to replicate its early successes in China through large-scale investments globally have encountered challenges and resistance from workers, residents, environmentalists, progressive politicians, and concerned citizens, its expansion has continued.

While China remains the heart of the Foxconn empire, the company operates six factories in Eastern Europe, including two Czech, one Slovak, one Hungarian, and one Russian (in St. Petersburg). It also has a complex in Turkey (100 kilometers west of Istanbul in a European Free Trade Zone). These Foxconn manufacturing complexes, all of them small compared with the company's China plants, serve fast-growing European, Middle Eastern, and African markets.[22] Foxconn relies heavily on agencies to recruit temporary workers for its two Czech factories, thereby increasing organizational flexibility and lowering operating costs in response to rapidly changing production needs.

Foxconn has five manufacturing sites in Mexico—a series of *maquilas*—in Ciudad Juárez (the largest city of Chihuahua), San Jerónimo (a port of entry in Chihuahua), Reynosa (a border city in northern Tamaulipas), Tijuana (the largest city of Baja California), and Guadalajara (the capital of Jalisco). The Mexican sites allow Foxconn, Apple, Sony, Amazon, and other brands to enjoy zero tariffs on goods imported to the US. As of 2015, Foxconn had twenty-two thousand employees in Ciudad Juárez, making it one of the largest foreign investors in Mexico.[23]

In 2011 Foxconn proposed major investments at six facilities in Brazil (in the states of São Paulo, Amazonas, and Minas Gerais). The plan called for a US$10 billion investment that would create 100,000 jobs in what was projected to be the largest iPhone production site outside of China.[24] By 2017, however, Foxconn employed just 2,800 workers and most of the proposed sites were abandoned. The company discovered that in Brazil, as elsewhere, it could not duplicate the synergies of East Asia centered on China, nor reap the advantages of Chinese state support and control of the labor force for jobs averaging US$2.50 per hour in plants in Eastern Europe or Latin America. In any event, the Brazilian government that had cut the deal with Foxconn was soon immersed in corruption charges and the Dilma Rousseff administration was impeached, ending, at least for the time being, Foxconn's plans for the construction of plants in Brazil.[25]

In March 2017, Foxconn entered into partnership with Chinese manufacturer Xiaomi to make smartphones at Sri City in Andhra Pradesh, India.[26] Local authorities granted duty exemptions and tax concessions to big investors that are said to be even more favorable than those offered in China. Foxconn has negotiated with officials in Maharashtra, Uttar Pradesh, Tamil Nadu, Haryana, and Telangana to expand its manufacturing capacity.[27] However, while continuing to hold out the prospect of creating fifty thousand jobs in Maharashtra, as of 2019, plans remained at the level of talk.[28]

Foxconn had similarly announced plans to establish a smartphone assembly plant in the university town of Yogyakarta in Java, Indonesia. As early as 2014, the company claimed that it would invest US$1 billion within three to five years, turning Indonesia into the "most important growth area aside from Taiwan and China." Foxconn boasted that it is "not just building a factory" but bringing in "a whole high-tech supply chain," including machinery development, optics, and semiconductor businesses.[29] However, after one year, plans to build the Indonesian factory were canceled. In 2017, with news of Apple's investment in a research and development center in Tangerang of Banten, west of Jakarta, there was again talk of Foxconn ramping up production of smartphones in Indonesia.[30]

Perhaps the most powerful incentive for diversifying Foxconn's production portfolio is the attack on Chinese imports that has emerged as a centerpiece of the Trump administration's "America First" drive, resulting in the imposition of crippling tariffs on Chinese products and continued threats to raise those tariffs yet further. In the US, Foxconn quickly joined the parade of companies responding to President Trump's attacks on China's and others' "unfair trade practices" with its own initiatives designed to protect its access to the US market. Other corporate giants followed suit, including the Chinese internet giant Alibaba, whose chairman Jack Ma told Trump that he would create one million jobs in the US, and Japan's Softbank founder Masayoshi Son, who dangled a US$50 billion investment in the US before the president.

With high-profile support from then Wisconsin Governor Scott Walker and House of Representatives Speaker Paul Ryan, President Trump and the media were quick to hail Foxconn's Mount Pleasant project in Wisconsin. As early as 2017, Foxconn announced plans to manufacture large displays for TVs, with a prospective budget of "more than US$10 billion."[31] In return, Mount Pleasant's Village Board of Trustees secured 2,800 acres of farmland, roughly four square miles, to build the Foxconn manufacturing hub.[32] In 2018, Foxconn began to build a manufacturing campus at a site dubbed "Wisconn Valley" in Wisconsin, attempting to smooth the waters at the time of an emerging US-China clash over trade imbalances.[33]

From land acquisition to road improvements to support services, Wisconsin committed more than US$4.5 billion in subsidies to close the Foxconn deal. It was the largest public subsidy package for a foreign corporation in American history. One estimate suggests that the Foxconn incentives are "more than 10 times greater than typical government aid packages of its stripe."[34] The plant would impose other costs on the state. It is estimated that the Foxconn LCD screen factory "would require an average-day demand of 5.8 million gallons [of water] per day" and another 1.2 million gallons would be needed "for adjacent operations related to the factory."[35]

Boosters envisioned Wisconsin's transformation into a midwestern high-tech hub. By December 2018, however, Foxconn had hired a grand total of 178 full-time employees in Wisconsin, along with 854 employees involved in the construction, falling far short of the hiring target for the year.[36] The original production plans were significantly reduced, even as Foxconn held job fairs in Mount Pleasant, Racine, Green Bay, Eau Claire, Milwaukee, and elsewhere. In light of angry popular denunciations of Wisconsin's lavish subsidies, Foxconn's promise of creating thirteen thousand jobs in Wisconsin seems dead in the water, if indeed the plant is ever completed. Critics also note that the projected composition of the Foxconn Wisconsin workforce has shifted from blue-collar workers to knowledge workers such as engineers and R&D scientists, thus undermining President Trump's goal of reinvigorating the American industrial labor force. As of February 2019, Foxconn had taken steps to build a Generation 6 facility, rather than a more advanced Generation 10.5 plant that would be capable of producing large screens. And in October, the plan for a Generation 6 facility was also scrapped in favor of a smaller factory under its Foxconn Industrial Internet (FII) subsidiary to make small LCD screens as well as automotive controls, servers, and various other devices."[37] In short, the original grandiose plans for the Wisconsin high-tech hub have been scaled back to what will be at best a modest facility.

In summary, Foxconn's worldwide expansion extends its impact on labor and the environment but on a scale that is a small fraction of both its Chinese operations and its much-touted global plans. When workers, with support at home and abroad, unite to reclaim their dignity and right to fair labor, the case of Foxconn—both its present international profile of plants in twenty-nine countries and territories, and its proposed extensions to the US, Europe, Asia, and the rest of the world—could inspire a new round of global labor struggles.

Acknowledgments

Foxconn workers have made iPhones, Kindles, Xboxes, and many more products for a global clientele that significantly includes the US, China, Europe, and Asia. They have also made this book by sharing their dreams and hopes for a brighter future. With the emergence of the coronavirus disease outbreak from late 2019, and World Health Organization recognition that it is a world pandemic in March 2020, many multinational corporations are reconsidering the opportunities and risks of global supply chains, particularly those based entirely or primarily in China. Less studied is how hundreds of millions of Chinese workers are facing health and livelihood threats, ranging from chronic labor and environmental hazards to loss of income from factory closures and inability to travel.

If not for the loss of more than a dozen young migrant workers' lives, in 2010, we might not have had the opportunity to learn about Foxconn and the lives of its workers. We are deeply saddened. At the same time, we are grateful for the trust and confidence of Foxconn employees, who share the conviction that this research and writing could contribute to bettering working lives in China and beyond. For this reason, we dedicate this book to workers of Foxconn and everywhere.

Through face-to-face meetings, video calls, and emails, we exchanged numerous ideas about the book. As we were finishing it, we joked that we, too, were working as "iSlaves." True, but more to the point, we had joyful experiences of learning, excitement, discovery, and a sense of accomplishment, as well as many productive struggles, in the course of the teamwork that culminated in this book.

Jeffery Hermanson, Amanda Bell, Greg Fay, Matthew A. Hale, and friends translated workers' poems and songs from Chinese to

English with linguistic grace and cultural sensibility. Ralf Ruckus, Daniel Fuchs, Andrés Ruggeri, Florencia Olivera, Ferruccio Gambino, Giorgio Grappi, Devi Sacchetto, Celia Izoard, Thierry Discepolo, and Liu Xinting translated our text into German, Italian, French, Spanish, and Chinese.

International campaign organizers and labor researchers facilitated publication and the organization of press conferences, including Debby Chan, Yiyi Cheng, Michael Ma, Sophie Chen, Parry Leung, Ken Yau, Vivien Yau, Sophia So, Yun-chung Chen, Mirana Szeto, Kenneth Ng, Lin Lin, Suki Chung, Kap Su Seol, Elaine Hui, Ellen David Friedman, Li Qiang, Ted Smith, Garrett Brown, Pauline Overeem, Esther de Haan, Alejandro González, Scott Nova, Isaac Shapiro, Diana Beaumont, Björn Claeson, Peter Pawlicki, Anne Lindsay, Eric Lee, Kimi Lee, Alex Tom, Shaw San Liu, Liana Foxvog, Brigitte Demeure, Olga Martin-Ortega, Chantal Peyer, Jane Slaughter, Paul Garver, Jason Judd, Katie Quan, Lynda Yanz, Tim Beaty, Liana Dalton, Kevin Lin, Ivan Franceschini, Nicholas Loubere, Christian Sorace, Anja Höfner, and Vivian Frick. We are thankful for the inspiration and comradeship of Earl V. Brown Jr. (1947–2017) and William (Willy) Brown (1945–2019).

Journalists Aditya Chakrabortty, Jonathan Adams, Kathleen McLaughlin, John Sexton, Yuan Yang, Tom Hancock, Christian Shepherd, Gerry Shih, Pak Yiu, Daniel Denvir, Louisa Lim, Graeme Smith, Charles Duhigg, Keith Bradsher, Michelle Chen, David Barboza, Javier C. Hernández, Richard Swift, Dinyar Godrej, Cissy Zhou, Grace Tsoi, Daniel Suen, Peter Bengtsen, Shai Oster, Joshua Bateman, Dominic Morgan, Michael Ortner, Leen Vervaeke, Lena Hallwirth, Robert Foyle Hunwick, Saif Malhem, and many others disseminated our key findings by interviewing us.

In academia, Elizabeth Perry, Ching Kwan Lee, Mary Gallagher, Dimitri Kessler, Michael Burawoy, Margaret Abraham, Dorothy Solinger, Marc Blecher, Joel Andreas, Richard Appelbaum, Nelson Lichtenstein, Ralph Litzinger, Deborah Davis, Yan Hairong, Stephen Philion, Jack Qiu, Eric Florence, Thung-hong Lin, Daniel

You-ren Yang, Fred Chiu, Chu-joe Hsia, Hsin-Hsing Chen, Jieh-min Wu, Pei-Chia Lan, Shen Yuan, Lu Huilin, and Guo Yuhua provided detailed comments and probing criticisms of selected chapters or earlier drafts. We appreciate their generosity and insights that have helped make this a much better book. We thank Marilyn Young (1937–2017) for her useful suggestions.

In presentations and writings, we received informed commentary from our mentors and colleagues, including Anita Chan, Jonathan Unger, Peter Evans, Ruth Milkman, Mark Anner, Chris Tilly, David Goodman, Yingjie Guo, Sally Sargeson, Philip Huang, Yin-wah Chu, Alvin So, Tai-lok Lui, Stephen Chiu, Daya Thussu, Anita Koo, Ben Ku, Chris Chan, Kaxton Siu, Susanne Choi, Minhua Ling, David Faure, Rutvica Andrijasevic, Jan Drahokoupil, Kees van der Pijl, Richard Maxwell, Karl Heinz Roth, Marcel van der Linden, Chris Smith, Jos Gamble, Tim Pringle, Jude Howell, Andreas Bieler, Chun-Yi Lee, Jane Hardy, Jane Holgate, Gabriella Alberti, David Harvey, Joonkoo Lee, Minqi Li, Jennifer Jihye Chun, Joshua Cohen, Jeffrey Henderson, David Fasenfest, Dae-oup Chang, Ngai-Ling Sum, Bob Jessop, Ian Cook, Debra Howcroft, Philip Taylor, Tony Dundon, Adrian Wilkinson, Paul Ryan, Jamie Doucette, Jamie Peck, Jackie Sheehan, Niall Duggan, Jenny Butler, Tom Fenton, Aaron Halegua, Nicki Lisa Cole, Genevieve LeBaron, Neil Howard, Eli Friedman, Sarosh Kuruvilla, Stephen Cowden, Christian Fuchs, Anne Alexander, Miriyam Aouragh, Mark Graham, Andrew Lamas, Dev Nathan, Daniel Spencer, John Gittings, Sarah Waters, Rina Agarwala, Alexander Gallas, Ben Scully, Karin Pampallis, Jörg Nowak, Zoë Svendsen, Simon Daw, Beth Walker, Paul Jobin, Rudolf Traub-Merz, Rachel Murphy, Paul Irwin Crookes, Anna Lora-Wainwright, Patricia Thornton, Henrietta Harrison, Margaret Hillenbrand, Barend ter Haar, Rana Mitter, Matthew Erie, David Johnson, Greg Distelhorst, Nandini Gooptu, Teresa Wright, Manfred Elfström, Lu Zhang, Christian Göbel, Richard Smith, Nancy Holmstrom, David Armstrong, Maurizio Atzeni, Immanuel Ness, Robert Ovetz, Elsa Lafaye de Micheaux, Chloé Froissart, Karin Fischer, Florian Butollo, Boy

Lüthje, Sarah Swider, Chris Rhomberg, Manjusha Nair, Julie Greene, Heidi Gottfried, Eileen Boris, Jill Jensen, Matthew Hora, Matthew Wolfgram, Charles Kim, Gay Seidman, Mark Frazier, Wanning Sun, Joshua Freeman, Ho-fung Hung, Beverly Silver, Susan McEachern, Ellen Schrecker, and others who must remain anonymous.

Over this decade-long research and writing endeavor, we have been fortunate to receive support from the Research Grants Council of Hong Kong, the Hong Kong Polytechnic University, the University of Hong Kong, Peking University, Tsinghua University, the University of Oxford, and the University of Oxford's Kellogg College, among other sources.

Anthony Arnove, Julie Fain, Nisha Bolsey, Rachel Cohen, and Rory Fanning collaborated to publish this book with Haymarket Books, to which we are very thankful. Ashley Smith provided insightful editorial suggestions in reading the manuscript for the press. Dana Henricks offered valuable support throughout the copyediting process. David Shulman, Florence Stencel-Wade, Emily Orford, Chris Browne, James Kelly, Kieran O'Connor, David Castle, Robert Webb, Brekhna Aftab, and Melanie Patrick of Pluto Press, together with colleagues, prepared the United Kingdom edition with enthusiasm and professionalism.

Last but not least, we wish to express our heartfelt gratitude to our families, whose love has enriched and continues to enrich our lives. Kyoko Iriye Selden is especially remembered for generously sharing her knowledge and passion for life. Chan Wai Tak, Jenny's elder brother, passed away in his thirties after battling with a decade-long illness in 2014; he will be dearly missed forever by his family and friends. Auntie Jean Wager lives in Jenny's fond and loving memory. We extend our love, faith, and hope to the workers and their families we have profiled in this book.

Jenny Chan, Mark Selden, and Pun Ngai
Hong Kong, China, and New York, USA
March 2020

Appendix 1

Our Book Website

This book is accompanied by a website to make available firsthand documents, color photographs, and audiovisual records that are the products of our research. Workers' blog posts, poems, songs, photos, videos, and open letters, along with company documents and government publications, were collected during multiple research trips to Foxconn's major production cities in China from 2010 to 2019.

Dying for an iPhone is accessible online:

Haymarket Books:
www.haymarketbooks.org/books/1468-dying-for-an-iphone

Pluto Press:
www.plutobooks.com/9780745341286/dying-for-an-iphone/

Authors' book website:
www.dyingforaniphone.com

We have rights to the two following coproduced documentaries that will be made available at the site:

The Truth of the Apple iPad (2011, 6 min.)
Wong Tinshing and Lilian Lui
In collaboration with Students & Scholars Against Corporate Misbehavior (SACOM)

iProtest (2011, 24 min.)

Al Jazeera

James Leong and Lynn Lee

In collaboration with Students and Scholars Against Corporate
Misbehavior (SACOM)

Additional video clips and footage on Foxconn worker interviews
and labor campaign actions are available on SACOM's YouTube
channel: https://www.youtube.com/user/sacom2005/.

*SACOM (Students and Scholars Against Corporate Misbehavior) unfurls a 6-meter high
banner from the third floor of the Hong Kong Apple Store in the International Finance
Center on its opening day, September 24, 2011.*

Appendix 2

Suicides and Attempted Suicides at Foxconn in China, 2010

Name	Gender	Age	Native place	Foxconn facility	Date of suicide	Remarks
1. Rong Bo	M	19	Hebei	Langfang	Jan. 8, 2010	Jumped from the 8/F
2. Ma Xianqian	M	19	Henan	Guanlan	Jan. 23, 2010	Fell from building
3. Li Hongliang	M	20	Henan	Longhua	Mar. 11, 2010	Jumped from the 5/F
4. Tian Yu (#)	F	17	Hubei	Longhua	Mar. 17, 2010	Jumped from the 4/F
5. Li Wei (#)	M	23	Hebei	Langfang	Mar. 23, 2010	Jumped from the 5/F
6. Liu Zhijun	M	23	Hunan	Longhua	Mar. 29, 2010	Jumped from the 14/F
7. Rao Shuqin (#)	F	18	Jiangxi	Guanlan	Apr. 6, 2010	Jumped from the 7/F
8. Ning Ling	F	18	Yunnan	Guanlan	Apr. 7, 2010	Jumped from building
9. Lu Xin	M	24	Hunan	Longhua	May 6, 2010	Jumped from the 6/F
10. Zhu Chenming	F	24	Henan	Longhua	May 11, 2010	Jumped from the 9/F
11. Liang Chao	M	21	Anhui	Longhua	May 14, 2010	Jumped from the 7/F
12. Nan Gang	M	21	Hubei	Longhua	May 21, 2010	Jumped from the 4/F
13. Li Hai	M	19	Hunan	Guanlan	May 25, 2010	Jumped from the 4/F
14. He (surname; given name unknown)	M	23	Gansu	Longhua	May 26, 2010	Jumped from the 7/F
15. Chen Lin (#)	M	25	Hunan	Longhua	May 27, 2010	Slit his wrists after failing to jump
16. Liu (surname; given name unknown)	M	18	Hebei	Nanhai	Jul. 20, 2010	Jumped from building
17. Liu Ming	F	23	Jiangsu	Kunshan	Aug. 4, 2010	Jumped from the 3/F
18. He (surname; given name unknown)	M	22	Hunan	Guanlan	Nov. 5, 2010	Jumped from building

(#) Survived with injuries.

Appendix 3

Fieldwork in China

From the summer of 2010 to December 2019, during multisited field research, we conducted interviews with former and current Foxconn managers, workers, student interns, teachers supervising internship programs, local government officials, and nongovernmental labor rights groups in China. We traveled to twelve cities across China where major Foxconn complexes are concentrated.

City	Foxconn Field Sites in China
Shenzhen	Longhua and Guanlan technology parks, Shenzhen City, Guangdong
Langfang	Technology Industrial Park, Langfang City, Hebei
Tianjin	Tianjin Economic and Technological Development Zone
Shanghai	Songjiang Export Processing Zone, Shanghai
Kunshan	Beimen Road, Kunshan City, Jiangsu
Nanjing	Pukou High-Tech Zone, Nanjing City, Jiangsu
Hangzhou	Qiantong Science and Technology Park, Hangzhou City, Zhejiang
Taiyuan	Economic Development Zone, Taiyuan City, Shanxi
Wuhan	East Lake High-Tech Development Zone, Wuhan City, Hubei
Zhengzhou	Export Processing Zone and Airport Economic Comprehensive Experimental Zone, Zhengzhou City, Henan
Chongqing	Shapingba District, Chongqing
Chengdu	Import and Export Processing Zone and High-Tech Industrial Development Zone, Chengdu City, Sichuan

We particularly wished to know whether the working conditions of Foxconn have improved since the 2010 spate of suicides. What factors are in play that might sustain or lead to the reform of dominant business practices? During fieldwork, we supplemented interviews with workers' wage statements, employment contracts, internship agreements, work-injury medical reports, labor dispute legal documents, company publications (including employee handbooks, newspapers, magazines, recruitment posters, notices, annual reports, and press releases), and government data (including educational directives and local labor laws and regulations). Everywhere we went—Foxconn production complexes, dormitories, food stalls, tea houses, internet cafés, basketball courts, discos, shopping malls, parks, community service centers, and hospitals—we met with workers (who could be clearly identified by their staff cards and uniforms) and student interns introduced by friends and colleagues. Through professional contacts, we also talked with government officials at the township, county, and municipal levels.

Following Foxconn's inland expansion and relocation, in early 2011 we went to "iPad city" in Chengdu, southwest China. We learned of workers' afflictions as a result of iPad aluminum dust in poorly ventilated workshops. In fact, we collected a bag of aluminum dust onsite during the first hour of our visit. In the ramp-up for the upgraded iPad, a deadly aluminum dust explosion occurred on May 20, 2011. To understand and convey to others the underlying causes of the "industrial accident," we collaborated with SACOM (Students and Scholars Against Corporate Misbehavior) to film the workers and the witnesses as part of our investigation.[1]

In the school year 2011–2012, we met student interns and their teachers from eight vocational schools at Foxconn complexes in Chengdu (Sichuan), Zhengzhou (Henan), and Shenzhen (Guangdong). In subsequent years, in major cities where Foxconn ramped up its production of iPhones, iPads, and game consoles, we learned that provincial governments provided special funds for schools that met the company's labor quotas, thus firming up close ties linking local governments, schools, and corporations. The involuntary character of student intern labor was unveiled in our in-depth research.

In relatively safe spaces, we reconstructed mobilization processes during protests and strikes by listening to worker testimonies and assessing their accounts in light of manager interviews, company media statements, and journalistic reports. The acute conflicts were centered on wage and social insurance disputes, injury compensations, refusal of time off during the peak production months, abuses of teenage interns, and the ineffective organization of a trade union. And these tensions were intensified when Foxconn was pitted against other suppliers to fight for the orders of Apple and other tech giants.

In the course of Foxconn's territorial expansion, the workers and managers facing "forced transfer" had to accept jobs at substantially lower wages from their present positions or leave the company without severance pay. Some protested wage and benefit cuts following the move. Significantly, we learned that worker leaders took advantage of the opportunities for collective action available to them during new product launches and holiday sales. They engaged with local and international media to pressure image-conscious brands to respond to their demands.

Whenever possible, we used encrypted communications apps (such as Signal and Wire), especially in 2017 when the WhatsApp messaging app was blocked by the Chinese authorities.[2] We found numerous examples of grassroots labor strategies, including instances of partial worker victories in specific assembly workshops and factories. But we also learned about the Chinese state's ability to restrict labor actions in both space and time, prioritizing "social stability" even in cases where some worker demands were accepted. These are important experiences to share with workers and their supporters, as well as consumers, around the world.

Over the past decade, we carried out fieldwork with the cooperation of a team of colleagues and students based in Hong Kong, mainland China, Taiwan, the US, and Europe. For security, we preserve the anonymity of the researchers involved in undercover fieldwork, interviews, and media production.

Appendix 4

Foxconn Facilities around the World

Country	City
Taiwan	Tucheng, New Taipei City, the company headquarters, and other manufacturing sites
China	Beijing, Tianjin, Shanghai, Chongqing; Anqing (Anhui), Xiamen (Fujian), Lanzhou (Gansu), Shenzhen, Huizhou, Dongguan, Foshan, Zhongshan, Zhuhai, Guangzhou (Guangdong), Nanning (Guangxi), Guiyang (Guizhou), Haikou (Hainan), Langfang, Qinhuangdao (Hebei), Zhengzhou, Jiyuan, Hebi, Puyang, Lankao (Henan), Wuhan (Hubei), Hengyang, Changsha (Hunan), Nanjing, Kunshan, Huai'an, Changshou, Funing (Jiangsu), Fengcheng (Jiangxi), Changchun (Jilin), Shenyang, Yingkou (Liaoning), Yantai (Shandong), Taiyuan, Jincheng, Datong (Shanxi), Chengdu (Sichuan), Hangzhou, Ningbo, Jiashan (Zhejiang), and other smaller production bases and research centers
Japan	Toyko, Sakai, Kyoto, Nagano, Chiba, Yokohama
South Korea	Seoul
Australia	Rydalmere (New South Wales)
New Zealand	Wellington
Canada	Toronto
United States	Mount Pleasant (Wisconsin), Chicago (Illinois), Boston (Massachusetts), Raleigh (North Carolina), Sunrise, St. Lucie (Florida), Indiana (Indianapolis), Memphis (Tennessee), Dallas, Fort Worth, Austin, Houston (Texas), San Diego, Los Angeles, San Francisco, San Jose, Santa Clara, Fremont (California), Hillsboro (Oregon), Sandston (Virginia)

Mexico	Ciudad Juárez, San Jerónimo (Chihuahua), Reynosa (Tamaulipas), Guadalajara (Jalisco), Tijuana (Baja California)
Brazil	Jundiai, Itu, Sorocaba, Indaiatuba (São Paulo), Manaus (Amazonas), Santa Rita do Sapucaí (Minas Gerais)
Turkey	Corlu
Czech Republic	Pardubice, Kutna Hora
Hungary	*Pecs, *Szekesfehervar, Komarom
Slovakia	Nitra
Germany	Düsseldorf
Austria	Vienna
The Netherlands	Amsterdam, Eindhoven, Heerlen
Denmark	Copenhagen
Sweden	Lund
Finland	Helsinki
Russia	St. Petersburg, Moscow
Scotland	Glasgow
Ireland	Limerick
United Arab Emirates (UAE)	Dubai
India	*Chennai, Sriperumbudur (Tamil Nadu); Sri City (Andhra Pradesh), Jaipur (Rajasthan)
Vietnam	Bac Ninh, Bac Giang
Malaysia	Kuala Lumpur, Penang, Kulai (Johor)
Singapore	Ruby Land Complex, 54 Genting Lane
Indonesia	Yogyakarta

Note: *Foxconn factories that have been closed. *Sources:* Foxconn Technology Group websites (1974–2020).[1]

Notes

Preface

1. This post, along with other firsthand research data, is available at our book website (see Appendix 1). All translations are ours unless otherwise stated.
2. We have translated the excerpt into English. The full statement dated May 18, 2010, in Chinese, is on file with the authors.
3. See Appendix 2 for the names of the eighteen workers at Foxconn in 2010 who attempted suicide (including the fourteen successful suicide attempts).
4. Hon Hai (Foxconn), "Competitive Advantages—Foxconnian Belief" (2019), http://www.foxconn.com/GroupProfile_En/CompetitiveAdvantages.html.
5. Kaityn Stimage, "The World's Largest Employers," WorldAtlas, February 15, 2018, https://www.worldatlas.com/articles/the-world-s-largest-employers .html.
6. Foxconn's official web-based reporting on its contributions to Chinese imports and exports in 2018 (in Chinese), http://www.foxconn.com.cn/ GroupProfile.html; also, see Foxconn Technology Group's "2017 Social and Environmental Responsibility Report" for the 2016 data (3.6 percent) for comparison (2018), 11, http://ser.foxconn.com/javascript/pdfjs/web/viewer .html?file=/upload/CserReports/2e4ecfaa-df6f-429a-88cd-cf257828b0a7 _.pdf&page=1.
7. Foxconn Technology Group, "2018 Social and Environmental Responsibility Report" (2019), 11, http://ser.foxconn.com/javascript/pdfjs /web/viewer.html?file=/upload/CserReports/5b75b277-d290-45f4-a9e1 -efe87475543b_.pdf&page=1.
8. Foxconn Technology Group, "2018 Report," 11.
9. Timothy Sturgeon, John Humphrey, and Gary Gereffi, "Making the Global Supply Base," in *The Market Makers: How Retailers Are Reshaping the Global Economy*, ed. Gary G. Hamilton, Misha Petrovic, and Benjamin Senauer (Oxford: Oxford University Press, 2011), 236.
10. Leander Kahney, *Tim Cook: The Genius Who Took Apple to the Next Level* (New York: Portfolio/Penguin, 2019).
11. Foxconn's seven-page statement dated December 31, 2013 (signed off by Martin Hsing, executive director of Foxconn Global Social and Environmental Responsibility Committee), and Apple's email reply on February 18, 2014 (sent out by Jacky Haynes, senior director of supplier responsibility at Apple), are on file with the authors. They are available at our book website, along with our December 16, 2013, letters.

12. See Appendix 3 for our fieldwork sites and research design at Foxconn factories and major cities across China between 2010 and 2019.

13. See Appendix 4 for Foxconn's production sites based in Taiwan, China, and other countries around the globe (1974–2020).

Chapter 1: A Suicide Survivor

1. Tian Yu is her real name, used with permission given the extensive press coverage of her attempted suicide. The authors and their research team conducted the interviews for this book. The names of all interviewees are aliases unless otherwise stated.

2. *Shenzhen Daily*, "Non-Hukou Population Sees 1st Drop," April 13, 2012, http://english.sz.gov.cn/news/latest/201204/t20120413_14893232.htm.

3. According to the 2010 Population Census of China, 61 million rural children (under eighteen years of age) were left behind as either one or both parents migrated. In 2015, the number of left-behind children increased to 69 million. See UNICEF report entitled "What Census Data Can Tell Us about Children in China: Facts and Figures 2013," 9 (figure 9), and UNICEF Annual Report (2017), 3,https://www.unicef.cn/media/10621/file /Census%20Data%20About%20Children%20in%20China%20Facts %20and%20Figures%202013.pdf; https://www.unicef.org /about/annualreport/files/China_2017_COAR.pdf.

4. The "one-child policy," which was rigorously enforced in urban China from its inauguration in 1980 to its abolition in 2015, was more relaxed in some rural areas, with families finding ways to have two to three children. Others who succeeded in having a second or third child were fined heavily.

5. QQ (founded in 1999) is a social media platform owned by the Chinese corporate giant Tencent, the same company that owns WeChat. QQ facilitates its users to sort their online contacts into groups, for example, "friend," "special friend," "family," "colleague," "stranger," or any custom-designed group they may wish to create. QQ and WeChat are digital spaces for creating new relationships and strengthening old ones.

Chapter 2: Foxconn: The World's Largest Electronics Manufacturer

1. Chang Dianwen, *Decoding Terry Gou's Quotations* (Taipei: CommonWealth Magazine Company, 2008), 23 (in Chinese).

2. Hon Hai Precision Industry Company (Foxconn), "Company Milestones," 1974–present, http://www.foxconn.com/GroupProfile_En /CompanyMilestones.html.

3. *Harvard Business Review*, "The Best-Performing CEOs in the World 2018," November–December 2018, https://hbr.org/2018/11/the-best-performing -ceos-in-the-world-2018.

4. Steve Jobs, "Stanford University Commencement Speech," June 12, 2005, https://www.english-video.net/v/ja/720.

5. *Bloomberg Businessweek*, "The Tao of Gou," September 13–19, 2010, https://www.yumpu.com/en/document/read/17853759/bloomberg -businessweek-ftp-directory-listing.

6. Frederik Balfour and Tim Culpan, "A Look Inside Foxconn—Where iPhones Are Made: A Postmodern Chinese Industrial Empire That Was Blighted by Suicides," *Bloomberg Businessweek*, December 9, 2010, http://www.nbcnews.com/id/39099077/ns/business-us_business/t/look -inside-foxconn-where-iphones-are-made/#.Xc5atFczaUk.

7. Henry Wai-chung Yeung, *Strategic Coupling: East Asian Industrial Transformation in the New Global Economy* (Ithaca, NY: Cornell University Press, 2016).

8. On September 22, 1985, the finance ministers and central bank governors from the US, the United Kingdom, West Germany, France, and Japan signed an accord to control currency markets at the Plaza Hotel in New York City. The US, then running enormous deficits, devalued its currency to make its exports competitive, while the Japanese yen and various East Asian industrializing economies' currencies were strengthened.

9. Gary G. Hamilton and Cheng-shu Kao, "The Asia Miracle and the Rise of Demand-Responsive Economies," in *The Market Makers: How Retailers Are Reshaping the Global Economy*, ed. Gary G. Hamilton, Misha Petrovic, and Benjamin Senauer (Oxford: Oxford University Press, 2011), 181–210.

10. You-tien Hsing, *Making Capitalism in China: The Taiwan Connection* (New York: Oxford University Press, 1998), 8.

11. Dieter Ernst, "From Partial to Systemic Globalization: International Production Networks in the Electronics Industry," Berkeley Roundtable on the International Economy Working Paper 98 (1997), p. 40, https://brie .berkeley.edu/sites/default/files/wp_98.pdf.

12. Yu-ling Ku, "Human Lives Valued Less Than Dirt: Former RCA Workers Contaminated by Pollution Fighting Worldwide for Justice (Taiwan)," in *Challenging the Chip: Labor Rights and Environmental Justice in the Global Electronics Industry*, ed. Ted Smith, David A. Sonnenfeld, and David Naguib Pellow (Philadelphia: Temple University Press, 2006), 181–90.

13. Hongbin Li, Lei Li, Binzhen Wu, and Yanyan Xiong, "The End of Cheap Chinese Labor," *Journal of Economic Perspectives* 26, no. 4 (2012): 57.

14. Ho-fung Hung and Mark Selden, "China's Post-Socialist Transformation and Global Resurgence: Political Economy and Geopolitics," in *The Cambridge History of Communism*, ed. Juliane Fürst, Silvio Pons, and Mark Selden, vol. 3 (Cambridge: Cambridge University Press, 2017), 502–28.

15. Suzanne Pepper, "China's Special Economic Zones: The Current Rescue Bid for a Faltering Experiment," *Bulletin of Concerned Asian Scholars* 20, no. 3 (1988): 7.

16. Phyllis Andors, "Women and Work in Shenzhen," *Bulletin of Concerned Asian Scholars* 20, no. 3 (1988): 22–41.

17. William Hurst, *The Chinese Worker after Socialism* (Cambridge: Cambridge University Press, 2009), 16.

18. Albert Park and Fang Cai, "The Informalization of the Chinese Labor Market," in *From Iron Rice Bowl to Informalization: Markets, Workers, and the State in a Changing China*, ed. Sarosh Kuruvilla, Ching Kwan Lee, and Mary E. Gallagher (Ithaca, NY: Cornell University Press, 2011), 17.

19. Foxconn has released eleven social and environmental responsibility reports since 2009 (covering the fiscal year from January 1 to December 31, 2008). Ten of those reports, published in 2010 and thereafter, were made available online in Chinese and English. See Foxconn Technology Group (2009, p. 11; 2010, p. 5; 2011, pp. 4, 14; 2012, pp. 3, 12; 2013, pp. 4, 12; 2014, pp. 3, 12; 2015, pp. 15–16, 25; 2016, pp. 14–15; 2017, p. 2; 2018, p. 2; 2019, p. 11), http://ser.foxconn.com/viewCserReport_listYearReport.action.

20. Foxconn Technology Group's company milestones (1974–present): http:// www.foxconn.com/GroupProfile_En/CompanyMilestones.html.

21. Elaine Huang, "Hon Hai Precision: You Are Your Own Greatest Enemy," *CommonWealth Magazine*, October 16, 2014, https://english.cw.com.tw /article/article.action?id=340.

22. Tse-Kang Leng, "State and Business in the Era of Globalization: The Case of Cross-Strait Linkages in the Computer Industry," *China Journal* 53 (2005), 70.

23. Foxconn Technology Group (2009, p. 11; 2010, p. 5; 2011, pp. 4, 14; 2012, pp. 3, 12; 2013, pp. 4, 12; 2014, pp. 3, 12; 2015, pp. 15–16, 25; 2016, pp. 14–15; 2017, p. 2; 2018, p. 2; 2019, p. 11), http://ser.foxconn.com /viewCserReport_listYearReport.action.

24. Thomas Dinges, "Is There Trouble on the Horizon for Contract Manufacturers?," EBN (The Premier Online Community for Global Supply Chain Professionals), October 31, 2012, http://www.ebnonline.com/author .asp?section_id=1096&doc_id=253427.

25. Charlie Z. W. Chiang and Ho-Don Yan, "Terry Gou and Foxconn," in *Handbook of East Asian Entrepreneurship*, ed. Fu-Lai Tony Yu and Ho-Don Yan (Abingdon, Oxon, UK: Routledge, 2015), 300–312.

26. Panasonic (Fortune Global 2019), https://fortune.com/global500/2019 /panasonic.

27. Xiaomi (Fortune Global 2019), https://fortune.com/global500/2019/xiaomi.

28. Foxconn Technology Group, "2018 Social and Environmental Responsibility Report" (2019), 11, http://ser.foxconn.com/javascript/pdfjs /web/viewer.html?file=/upload/CserReports/5b75b277-d290-45f4-a9e1 -efe87475543b_.pdf&page=1.

29. Apple, "Annual Report for the Fiscal Year Ended September 29, 2018" (2018), 21, https://d18rn0p25nwr6d.cloudfront.net/CIK-0000320193/68027c6d-356d -46a4-a524-65d8ec05a1da.pdf.

30. Filtered by tech sector and ranked by profits, search Global 500 (2019) at: https://fortune.com/global500/2019/search/?profits=desc&sector=Technology.

31. Quoted in Zhang Shidong, "Why Stock Traders Are Dumping Apple Supplier Foxconn Industrial," *South China Morning Post*, July 8, 2018, https://www.scmp.com/business/companies/article/2154130/why -stock-traders-are-dumping-apple-supplier-foxconn-industrial.

32. Filtered by tech sector and ranked by profits, search Global 500 (2019) at: https://fortune.com/global500/2019/search/?profits=desc&sector=Technology.

33. Foxconn Technology Group, "2017 Social and Environmental Responsibility Report" (2018), 13, http://ser.foxconn.com/javascript/pdfjs/web/viewer.html ?file=/upload/CserReports/2e4ecfaa-df6f-429a-88cd-cf257828b0a7

_.pdf&page=1. In 2013, Google purchased a number of Hon Hai patents for "head-mounted displays that enable virtual images to be superimposed over real-world view, often used for aviation, engineering and gaming." See Global Patent Solutions, "Google Purchases Foxconn Patents for Wearable Tech," August 27, 2013, https://www.globalpatentsolutions .com/blog/google-purchases-foxconn-patents-wearable-tech/. For a wide-ranging 2014 discussion of Foxconn patents in diverse fields, see Steve Brachmann, "Foxconn Innovation: Cleaning Robots, Fool-Proofing Manufacturing and Rotating Notebook Screens," IPWatchdog, October 13, 2014, https://www.ipwatchdog.com/2014/10/13/foxconn-innovation -cleaning-robots-fool-proofing-manufacturing-and-rotating-notebook -screens/id=51670/.

34. Foxconn Technology Group, "2018 Social and Environmental Responsibility Report" (2019), 13, http://ser.foxconn.com/javascript/pdfjs /web/viewer.html?file=/upload/CserReports/5b75b277-d290-45f4-a9e1 -efe87475543b_.pdf&page=1.

35. Foxconn Industrial Internet Co., Ltd. (2017–present), http://www.fii-foxconn .com/en/Home/About.

36. Robin Kwong, "Terry Gou: Managing '1m Animals,'" *Financial Times*, January 20, 2012, https://www.ft.com/content/be3d2550-f9e6-34c0-91fb -afd639d3e750.

37. *Bloomberg*, "A Rare Look Inside Foxconn's Latest Facility," July 13, 2014, YouTube video, https://www.youtube.com/watch?v=ZJg707RDYUM.

38. He Huifeng, "Foxconn Hits Bumps in Road to Full Automation," *South China Morning Post*, July 29, 2016, http://www.scmp.com/business /companies/article/1996639/foxconn-hits-bumps-road-full-automation.

39. Foxconn's manufacturing and research centers are based in four municipalities with provincial status (Beijing, Tianjin, Shanghai, and Chongqing) and in nineteen provinces, including Anhui, Fujian, Gansu, Guangdong, Guangxi, Guizhou, Hainan, Hebei, Henan, Hubei, Hunan, Jiangsu, Jiangxi, Jilin, Liaoning, Shandong, Shanxi, Sichuan, and Zhejiang.

40. The nine municipalities include Guangzhou, Shenzhen, Zhuhai, Foshan, Huizhou, Dongguan, Zhongshan, Jiangmen, and Zhaoqing in Guangdong province. They are known as the nine Pearl River Delta municipalities.

41. He Huifeng, "Why America May Prove a Cheaper Option Than China for Foxconn," *South China Morning Post*, July 28, 2017, https://www .scmp.com/news/china/economy/article/2104480/why-america -may-prove-cheaper-option-china-foxconn.

42. Zhuhai Municipal Government, "Foxconn Selects Zhuhai for Greater Bay Opportunities," August 20, 2018, http://subsites.chinadaily.com.cn /zhuhai/2018-08/20/c_264431.htm.

43. Foxconn Technology Group's group profile (1974–2020) (in Chinese), http:// www.foxconn.com.cn/GroupProfile.html.

44. Foxconn Technology Group, "2018 Social and Environmental Responsibility Report" (2019), 25, http://ser.foxconn.com/javascript/pdfjs /web/viewer.html?file=/upload/CserReports/5b75b277-d290-45f4-a9e1 -efe87475543b_.pdf&page=1.

45. Lyu Chang, Li Jun, and Zhao Kai, "In Go-Ahead Guiyang, It All Figures," *China Daily*, September 20, 2013, http://europe.chinadaily.com.cn/epaper /2013-09/20/content_16981406.htm.

46. Belt and Road Portal, "Guiyang Transforms from 'an Unknown City' to 'China's Big Data Valley,'" May 15, 2019, https://eng.yidaiyilu.gov.cn /DigitalValley/AmazingGuiyang/90525.htm.

47. *China Daily*, "Guian New Area," February 27, 2015, http://www.eguizhou .gov.cn/2015-02/27/content_19670225.htm.

48. Guian New Area, Guizhou Province, "Apple Center to Inject New Energy into Guian's Big Data Development," June 8, 2018, http://en.gaxq.gov.cn /2018-06/08/c_241167.htm.

49. *Xinhua*, "Foxconn to Build Processing Base in Northwest China," November 20, 2015, http://www.chinadaily.com.cn/m/gansu/2015-11/20 /content_22505392.htm.

50. Foxconn Technology Group, "2012 Social and Environmental Responsibility Report" (2013), 4, http://ser.foxconn.com/javascript/pdfjs /web/viewer.html?file=/upload/CserReports/42470921-ed8f-4e16-8021 -81c8cb9a813b_.pdf&page=1.

Chapter 3: Apple Meets Foxconn

1. The worker's poem in the original Chinese, translated by Matthew A. Hale, is available at our book website.

2. Foxconn Technology Group's Company Milestones (1974–present), http://www.foxconn.com/GroupProfile_En/CompanyMilestones.html.

3. Walter Isaacson, *Steve Jobs* (London: Little, Brown, 2011).

4. Apple, "The Facts about Apple's Tax Payments" (November 6, 2017), https:// www.apple.com/newsroom/2017/11/the-facts-about-apple-tax-payments/.

5. Michael Moritz, *Return to the Little Kingdom: Steve Jobs, the Creation of Apple, and How It Changed the World* (New York: Overlook Press, [1984] 2009), 208–9.

6. City of Fremont, California, "Staff Report 1491: Report to Council on Referral of Former Apple Macintosh Factory History" (2012), http://fremontcityca.iqm2.com/Citizens/Detail_LegiFile.aspx?ID=1491 &highlightTerms=macintosh.

7. *Wired*, no. 506 (June 1997), https://www.wired.com/story/wired-cover -browser-1997/.

8. Steve Jobs, "Steve Jobs Hammers Michael Dell" (1997), YouTube video, https://www.youtube.com/watch?v=dXh8MPHKQl4.

9. Adam Lashinsky, *Inside Apple: The Secrets behind the Past and Future Success of Steve Jobs's Iconic Brand* (London: John Murray, 2012), 142.

10. Apple, "Think Different" (1997), YouTube video, https://www.youtube.com /watch?v=nVoIdConZys.

11. Malcolm Gladwell, "The Tweaker: The Real Genius of Steve Jobs," *New Yorker*, November 14, 2011, https://www.newyorker.com/magazine/2011 /11/14/the-tweaker.

12. *Dezeen Magazine*, "Steve Jobs Once Wanted to Hire Me—Richard Sapper," June 19, 2013, http://www.dezeen.com/2013/06/19/steve-jobs-once -wanted-to-hire-me-richard-sapper/.

13. Apple, "The First iMac Introduction" (1998), YouTube video, https://www .youtube.com/watch?v=0BHPtoTctDY.

14. Lashinsky, *Inside Apple*, 51.

15. *Fortune*, "What Makes Apple Golden?," March 3, 2008, http://money.cnn .com/2008/02/29/news/companies/amac_apple.fortune/index.htm.

16. Apple, "Apple Board of Directors Announces CEO Compensation" (January 19, 2000), https://www.apple.com/newsroom/2000/01/19Apple-Board-of -Directors-Announces-CEO-Compensation/.

17. David E. Sanger, "New Plants May Not Mean New Jobs," *New York Times*, March 25, 1984, http://www.nytimes.com/1984/03/25/jobs/new-plants-may -not-mean-new-jobs.html.

18. Jason Dean, "The Forbidden City of Terry Gou," *Wall Street Journal*, August 11, 2007, http://www.wsj.com/articles/SB118677584137994489.

19. Apple, "Apple Ships New Power Mac G5" (August 18, 2003), https://www .apple.com/newsroom/2003/08/18Apple-Ships-New-Power-Mac-G5/.

20. Thomas Dinges, "To Win, Focus on Speed, Not Just Cost," EBN (The Premier Online Community for Global Supply Chain Professionals), July 19, 2012, http://www.ebnonline.com/author.asp?section_id =1096&doc_id=247738.

21. CAFOD (Catholic Agency for Overseas Development), "Clean Up Your Computer: Working Conditions in the Electronics Sector" (2004), 3, http://www.peacelink.it/cybercultura/docs/176.pdf.

22. The Institute of Contemporary Observation, FinnWatch, and Finnish ECA (Export Credit Agency) Reform Campaign, "Day and Night at the Factory: Working Conditions of Temporary Workers in the Factories of Nokia and Its Suppliers in Southern China" (March 2005), 16. The report is archived by the authors and is uploaded to our book website.

23. *Macworld*, "Inside Apple's iPod Factories," June 12, 2006, http://www .macworld.co.uk/news/mac/inside-apples-ipod-factories-14915/.

24. BBC, "iPod 'Slave' Claims Investigated," June 14, 2006, http://news.bbc .co.uk/1/hi/5079590.stm.

25. Apple Computer adopted its supplier code of conduct on November 13, 2005. http://image2.sina.com.cn/IT/it/2006-06-18 /U58P2T1D995340F3647DT20060618165929.pdf.

26. Apple, "Report on iPod Manufacturing" (August 17, 2006), 3. Apple has removed the four-page factory audit report from its Supplier Responsibility web page. The report is archived by the authors and is uploaded to our book website.

27. Stephen Frost and Margaret Burnett, "Case Study: The Apple iPod in China," *Corporate Social Responsibility and Environmental Management* 14 (2007): 104.

28. Reporters Without Borders (Reporters Sans Frontières), founded in 1985, is a France-based nonprofit, nongovernmental organization that promotes and defends freedom of information and freedom of the press. See Reporters

Without Borders, "Foxconn Drops Lawsuit against Two *China Business News* Journalists," September 4, 2006, https://rsf.org/en/news /foxconn-drops-lawsuit-against-two-china-business-news-journalists.

29. Committee to Protect Journalists, "China: Apple Subcontractor Reduces Libel Damages Claim," August 31, 2006, https://cpj.org/2006/08/china -apple-subcontractor-reduces-libel-damages-cl.php.

30. The Responsible Business Alliance (RBA) publishes a code of conduct to set out social, environmental, and ethical industry standards in global electronics production chains. The RBA has grown to have more than 150 members around the world. http://www.responsiblebusiness.org/ code-of-conduct/.

31. Apple, "Apple Supplier Code of Conduct" (December 13, 2006), https://www .ilr.cornell.edu/sites/ilr.cornell.edu/files/apple-supplier-code-of-conduct.pdf.

32. Apple, "Macworld San Francisco 2007 Keynote Address" (January 9, 2007), https://podcasts.apple.com/lu/podcast/macworld-san-francisco-2007 -keynote-address/id275834665?i=1000026524322.

33. Apple, "Apple Reinvents the Phone with iPhone" (January 9, 2007), https://www.apple.com/newsroom/2007/01/09Apple-Reinvents-the-Phone -with-iPhone/.

34. Ian Parker, "The Shape of Things to Come: How an Industrial Designer Became Apple's Greatest Product," *New Yorker*, February 23, 2015, http://www.newyorker.com/magazine/2015/02/23/shape-things-come.

35. The tagline of an ad for Apple in Cork, "Why Work for Apple" (undated).

36. James B. Stewart, "How, and Why, Apple Overtook Microsoft," *New York Times*, January 29, 2015, http://www.nytimes.com/2015/01/30/business /how-and-why-apple-overtook-microsoft.html?_r=0.

37. Apple, "Apple Introduces the New iPhone 3G" (June 9, 2008), https://www .apple.com/newsroom/2008/06/09Apple-Introduces-the-New-iPhone-3G/.

38. Apple, "iPhone 3G on Sale Tomorrow" (July 10, 2008), https://www.apple .com/newsroom/2008/07/10iPhone-3G-on-Sale-Tomorrow/.

39. Apple, "Annual Report for the Fiscal Year Ended September 24, 2011" (2011), 30, http://d18rn0p25nwr6d.cloudfront.net/CIK-0000320193/64c7905f-0468 -48d9-8f25-e6ec8f3b5e32.pdf.

40. Apple's quarterly earnings reports (Form 10-Q), Q1 FY2010 – Q4 FY2018, https://investor.apple.com/sec-filings/default.aspx.

41. Apple's quarterly earnings reports (Form 10-Q).

42. Kenneth L. Kraemer, Greg Linden, and Jason Dedrick, "Capturing Value in Global Networks: Apple's iPad and iPhone" (2011), 5. http://econ.sciences -po.fr/sites/default/files/file/Value_iPad_iPhone.pdf.

43. Jason Dedrick and Kenneth L. Kraemer, "Market Making in the Personal Computer Industry," in *The Market Makers: How Retailers Are Reshaping the Global Economy*, ed. Gary G. Hamilton, Misha Petrovic, and Benjamin Senauer (Oxford: Oxford University Press, 2011), 303.

44. China Labor Watch, "Analyzing Labor Conditions of Pegatron and Foxconn: Apple's Low-Cost Reality," February 11, 2015, http://www.chinalaborwatch .org/report/107.

45. Jason Dedrick, Greg Linden, and Kenneth L. Kraemer, "We Estimate China Makes Only $8.46 from an iPhone—and That's Why Trump's Trade War Is Futile," *The Conversation*, July 7, 2018, https://theconversation.com/we-estimate-china-only-makes-8-46-from-an-iphone-and-thats-why-trumps-trade-war-is-futile-99258.

46. Apple, "Apple Celebrates One Billion iPhones" (July 27, 2016), https://www.apple.com/newsroom/2016/07/apple-celebrates-one-billion-iphones/.

47. Apple, "iPhone at Ten: The Revolution Continues" (January 8, 2017), https://www.apple.com/newsroom/2017/01/iphone-at-ten-the-revolution-continues/.

48. Tim Bajarin, "6 Reasons Why Apple Is So Successful," *Time*, May 7, 2012, http://techland.time.com/2012/05/07/six-reasons-why-apple-is-successful/.

49. Apple, "Annual Report for the Fiscal Year Ended September 28, 2013" (2013), 27, http://d1lge852tjjqow.cloudfront.net/CIK-0000320193/e3115d1d-4246-45ae-94f2-f8e3762d8e3e.pdf; Apple, "Annual Report for the Fiscal Year Ended September 28, 2019" (2019), 19, https://d18rn0p25nwr6d.cloudfront.net/CIK-0000320193/1a919118-a594-44f3-92f0-4ecca47b1a7d.pdf.

50. Apple, "The App Store Turns 10" (July 5, 2018), https://www.apple.com/newsroom/2018/07/app-store-turns-10/.

51. Apple, "App Store Shatters Records on New Year's Day" (January 5, 2017), https://www.apple.com/newsroom/2017/01/app-store-shatters-records-on-new-years-day/.

52. Apple, "App Store Caps Record-Breaking 2018 with Blockbuster Holiday Week" (January 3, 2019), https://www.apple.com/newsroom/2019/01/app-store-caps-record-breaking-2018-with-blockbuster-holiday-week/.

53. Apple, "Isabel Ge Mahe Named Apple's Managing Director of Greater China" (July 18, 2017), https://www.apple.com/newsroom/2017/07/isabel-ge-mahe-named-apple-managing-director-of-greater-china/.

54. Apple, "Annual Report for the Fiscal Year Ended September 24, 2016" (2016), 23, https://d18rn0p25nwr6d.cloudfront.net/CIK-0000320193/ffb58afc-aa5d-4b55-8d12-8e0937575a35.pdf; Apple, "Annual Report for the Fiscal Year Ended September 28, 2019" (2019), 20, https://d18rn0p25nwr6d.cloudfront.net/CIK-0000320193/1a919118-a594-44f3-92f0-4ecca47b1a7d.pdf.

55. Apple, "2016 10-K Report" and "2019 10-K Report."

56. National Bureau of Statistics of the People's Republic of China, "Statistical Communiqué of the People's Republic of China on the 2018 National Economic and Social Development," February 28, 2019, figure 1, http://www.stats.gov.cn/english/PressRelease/201902/t20190228_1651335.html. See also, Nick Leung, "China Brief: The State of the Economy," McKinsey & Company, March 2019, https://www.mckinsey.com/featured-insights/china/china-brief-the-state-of-the-economy.

57. *Xinhua*, "Vice Premier Li Keqiang Meets Apple's Tim Cook," March 28, 2012, http://en.people.cn/90883/7772779.html.

58. Apple, "Tim Cook: Chief Executive Officer," (2011–present), https://www.apple.com/leadership/tim-cook/.

59. Apple, "Tim Cook Named COO (Chief Operating Officer) of Apple" (October 14, 2005), https://www.apple.com/newsroom/2005/10/14Tim-Cook-Named-COO-of-Apple/.

60. Apple, "Apple Media Advisory" (October 5, 2011), https://www.apple.com/newsroom/2011/10/05Apple-Media-Advisory/.

61. Apple, "Apple's New Mac Pro to Be Made in Texas" (September 23, 2019), https://www.apple.com/newsroom/2019/09/apples-new-mac-pro-to-be-made-in-texas/.

62. John Lewis, "Tim Cook—A Courageous Innovator," *Time*, April 16, 2015, http://time.com/3822599/tim-cook-2015-time-100/.

63. Ryan Kailath and Alina Selyukh, "Apple Becomes World's 1st Private-Sector Company Worth $1 Trillion," NPR, August 2, 2018, https://www.npr.org/2018/08/02/632697978/apple-becomes-worlds-1st-private-sector-company-worth-1-trillion.

Chapter 4: Managing Foxconn

1. A selection of Gou's quotations can be found in Chang Dianwen's *Decoding Terry Gou's Quotations* (2008), published in Chinese by the Commonwealth Publishing Group in Taipei.

2. Chairman Mao sought to eliminate "capitalist roaders within the Party" by mobilizing the Red Guards to rebel during the Cultural Revolution. *Quotations from Chairman Mao Tse-tung* (Mao Zedong) is a collection of Mao's quotations, published from 1964 to 1976, https://en.wikisource.org/wiki/Quotations_from_Chairman_Mao_Tse-tung.

3. Jonathan Watts, "Foxconn Offers Pay Rises and Suicide Nets as Fears Grow over Wave of Deaths," *Guardian*, May 28, 2010, http://www.guardian.co.uk/world/2010/may/28/foxconn-plant-china-deaths-suicides.

4. C. W. Wang, C. L. Chan, and P. S. Yip, "Suicide Rates in China from 2002 to 2011: An Update," *Social Psychiatry and Psychiatric Epidemiology* 49 (2014): 929–41.

5. X. Y. Li, M. R. Phillips, Y. P. Zhang, D. Xu, and G. H. Yang, "Risk Factors for Suicide in China's Youth: A Case-Control Study," *Psychological Medicine* 38 (2008): 397–406.

6. Foxconn's Letter to Employees (May 2010), in the original Chinese, is on file with the authors and is available at our book website.

7. Apple, "Steve Jobs in 2010, at D8," (June 1, 2010), https://podcasts.apple.com/us/podcast/steve-jobs-in-2010-at-d8/id529997900?i=1000116189688.

8. Foxconn Technology Group, "2010 Social and Environmental Responsibility Report" (2011), 1, http://ser.foxconn.com/javascript/pdfjs/web/viewer.html?file=/upload/CserReports/d8604d35-877c-4cde-9e24-de891775b503_.pdf&page=1.

9. Apple, "Apple Supplier Responsibility: 2011 Progress Report," (2011), 19, https://www.apple.com/supplier-responsibility/pdf/Apple_SR_2011_Progress_Report.pdf.

10. Apple, "Apple Supplier Responsibility 2011," 18.

11. Apple, "Apple Supplier Responsibility 2011," 18–19.

12. Jason Dean, "The Forbidden City of Terry Gou," *Wall Street Journal*, August 11, 2007, http://www.wsj.com/articles/SB118677584137994489.

13. "Model workers" were hailed initially as the ideal citizens serving the people and the party-state in socialist China during the 1950s. The deployment of model workers has continued to present-day China, although with diminished political significance.

14. Henry Blodget, "CEO of Apple Partner Foxconn: Managing One Million Animals Gives Me a Headache," *Business Insider*, January 19, 2012, https://www.businessinsider.com/foxconn-animals-2012-1.

15. The blog post, dated January 17, 2012, has since been removed. Full text in the original Chinese is archived by the authors and is available at our book website.

16. John Biggs, "Foxconn Responds to CEO's 'Employees Are Animals' Comment," *TechCrunch*, January 20, 2012, https://techcrunch.com/2012/01/20 /foxconn-responds-to-ceos-employees-are-animals-comment/.

17. Frederick Winslow Taylor, *The Principles of Scientific Management* (New York: Dover Publications, [1911] 1998).

18. William M. Tsutsui, *Manufacturing Ideology: Scientific Management in Twentieth-Century Japan* (Princeton, NJ: Princeton University Press, 1998).

19. Rob Schmitz, "Foxconn's Newest Product: A College Degree," *Marketplace*, July 30, 2014, https://www.marketplace.org/2014/07/30/world /learning-curve/foxconns-newest-product-college-degree.

20. Foxconn Technology Group, "2018 Social and Environmental Responsibility Report" (2019), 23, http://ser.foxconn.com/javascript/pdfjs /web/viewer.html?file=/upload/CserReports/5b75b277-d290-45f4-a9e1 -efe87475543b_.pdf&page=1.

21. Foxconn Technology Group, "2015 Social and Environmental Responsibility Report" (2016), 9, http://ser.foxconn.com/javascript/pdfjs/web/viewer. html?file=/upload/CserReports/3a1ff599-f238-4fb0-824a-a6dc2b725fc0 _.pdf&page=1.

22. Foxconn Technology Group, "Foxconn Is Committed to a Safe and Positive Working Environment" (October 11, 2010), 1, http://regmedia.co.uk /2010/10/12/foxconn_media_statement.pdf.

23. Foxconn Technology Group, "2010 Social and Environmental Responsibility Report" (2011), 4, http://ser.foxconn.com/javascript/pdfjs/web/viewer.html ?file=/upload/CserReports/d8604d35-877c-4cde-9e24-de891775b503 _.pdf&page=1.

24. *Xinhua*, "Shenzhen Raises Minimum Wage to 1,320 Yuan a Month," March 4, 2011, http://www.chinadaily.com.cn/business/2011-03/04 /content_12114436.htm.

25. Fair Labor Association, "Fair Labor Association Secures Commitment to Limit Workers' Hours, Protect Pay at Apple's Largest Supplier," March 29, 2012, http://www.fairlabor.org/blog/entry/fair-labor-association-secures -commitment-limit-workers-hours-protect-pay-apples-largest.

26. The Fair Labor Association questionnaire surveys were conducted in Foxconn Guanlan (in total, 3.5 days between February 14 and February 17, 2012), Foxconn Longhua (4 days between March 5 and March 8, 2012), and

Foxconn Chengdu (4 days between March 6 and March 9, 2012). See Fair Labor Association, "Independent Investigation of Apple Supplier, Foxconn," (March 2012), 4, 6, 9, http://www.fairlabor.org/sites/default/files/documents /reports/foxconn_investigation_report.pdf.

27. National Bureau of Statistics of the People's Republic of China, "Investigative Report on the Monitoring of Chinese Rural Migrant Workers in 2012," section 5.1 and table 9 (in Chinese) (2013), http://www.stats.gov .cn/tjsj/zxfb/201305/t20130527_12978.html.

28. Fair Labor Association, "Independent Investigation of Apple Supplier, Foxconn," 9.

29. Foxconn workers' wage statements are on file with the authors, and they are available at our book website.

30. *Shenzhen Daily*, "Shenzhen's Minimum Wage Raised by 12%, Remains Highest in China," February 17, 2015, http://www.newsgd.com/gdnews /content/2015-02/17/content_118640191.htm.

Chapter 5: Voices of Student Interns

1. The school names are disclosed because internship programs are publicized on their websites and in student recruitment brochures. To protect the interviewed student interns and teachers, as well as managers and government officials, pseudonyms are used throughout.

2. Ministry of Education of the People's Republic of China, "Composition of Students in Senior Secondary Schools" (August 18, 2015), http://en.moe.gov .cn/documents/statistics/2014/national/201509/t20150902_205030.html.

3. State Council of the People's Republic of China, "Decision of the State Council on Accelerating the Development of Vocational Education" (in Chinese) (2005), http://www.gov.cn/zwgk/2005-11/09/content_94296.htm.

4. State Council of the People's Republic of China, "Decision of the State Council on Accelerating the Development of Modern Vocational Education" (in Chinese) (2014), http://www.gov.cn/zhengce/content/2014-06/22 /content_8901.htm; Ministry of Education, National Development and Reform Commission, Ministry of Finance, Ministry of Human Resources and Social Security, Ministry of Agriculture, and the State Council Office of Poverty Alleviation and Development, "Modern Vocational Education System Construction Plan (2014–2020)" (in Chinese) (2014), http://www.moe .gov.cn/publicfiles/business/htmlfiles/moe/moe_630/201406/170737.html.

5. Ministry of Education of the People's Republic of China, "Composition of Students in Senior Secondary Schools" (August 18, 2015).

6. Ministry of Education of the People's Republic of China, "National Medium and Long-Term Education Reform and Development Plan, 2010–2020," table 1 (in Chinese) (2010), http://www.gov.cn/jrzg/2010-07/29 /content_1667143.htm.

7. On February 13, 2019, for example, the State Council issued a circular to call for a national reform of China's vocational education system to better prepare its workforce for a market-oriented economy. See the State Council of the People's Republic of China, "Implementation Plan on National

Vocational Education Reform" (in Chinese) (2019), http://www.gov.cn
/zhengce/content/2019-02/13/content_5365341.htm.

8. Minhua Ling, "'Bad Students Go to Vocational Schools!': Education, Social
Reproduction, and Migrant Youth in Urban China," *China Journal* 73
(2015), 108–31.

9. Ministry of Education of the People's Republic of China, "Composition
of Students in Senior Secondary Schools" (August 18, 2015); Ministry of
Education of the People's Republic of China, "Composition of Students in
Senior Secondary Schools" (August 12, 2019), http://www.moe.gov.cn/s78
/A03/moe_560/jytjsj_2018/qg/201908/t20190812_394224.html.

10. Ministry of Education of the People's Republic of China, "Composition of
Students in Senior Secondary Schools" (August 18, 2015 and August 12,
2019).

11. Foxconn Technology Group, "Foxconn Response to Report Alleging Abuses
in Internship Program" (July 29, 2011), https://business-humanrights.org
/en/china-university-report-finds-abuses-in-foxconns-internship-program.

12. Foxconn Technology Group, "Foxconn Is Committed to a Safe and Positive
Working Environment" (October 11, 2010), 2, http://regmedia
.co.uk/2010/10/12/foxconn_media_statement.pdf.

13. Ross Perlin, *Intern Nation: How to Earn Nothing and Learn Little in the Brave
New Economy,* updated edition (London: Verso, 2012), p. 6.

14. Foxconn Technology Group, "'Win-Win Cooperation': iDPBG [integrated
Digital Product Business Group] Convenes the Intern Appraisal and
Awards Ceremony," *Foxconn Bridgeworkers*, no. 183 (2010): 23 (print edition)
(in Chinese).

15. The 2007 Administrative Measures for Internships at Secondary Vocational
Schools, jointly issued by the Ministries of Education and Finance, govern
the implementation of student internships under the framework of China's
Labor Law (effective January 1, 1995), Education Law (effective September
1, 1995), and Vocational Education Law (effective September 1, 1996) (in
Chinese), http://www.moe.gov.cn/publicfiles/business/htmlfiles/moe
/s3566/201001/xxgk_79114.html.

16. In March 2010, China's Ministry of Education issued a circular on "further
improving the work of secondary vocational school student internship
regarding skilled labor shortage of enterprises" (in Chinese), http://www
.moe.gov.cn/srcsite/A07/moe_950/201003/t20100324_87769.html.

17. The Law on the Protection of Minors of the People's Republic of Chinawas
amended in 2012 and came into force on January 1, 2013. Full text in Chinese:
http://www.npc.gov.cn/wxzl/gongbao/2013-02/25/content_1790872.htm.

18. In October 2010, the central government passed the Social Insurance
Law, which came into force in July 2011. In addition to the five types of
insurance, the law required a housing fund (previously optional). Employers
were responsible for calculating social insurance fees, withholding payments
for themselves and their employees, and making timely payments to the
Social Insurance Bureau and the Housing Fund Bureau.

19. As economic conditions and statutory minimum wages vary substantially across China, in 2011, we used the lower end of 200 yuan/month per person for illustration.

20. Huawei, "Huawei Named Chinese Investor of the Year at the 2014 British Business Awards" (January 7, 2015), https://connect-world.com/huawei -named-chinese-investor-of-the-year-at-the-2014-british-business-awards/.

21. Emily Honig, "The Contract Labor System and Women Workers: Pre-Liberation Cotton Mills of Shanghai," *Modern China* 9, no. 4 (1983): 421–54.

22. Ann-Margaret Esnard and Alka Sapat, *Displaced by Disaster: Recovery and Resilience in a Globalizing World* (New York: Routledge, 2014), 170.

23. Sichuan Provincial People's Government, "Sichuan: Top Choice of Taiwan Enterprises" (May 5, 2011), http://www.sc.gov.cn/10462/10758/10760/10765 /2011/5/5/10160504.shtml.

24. Andrew Ross, *Fast Boat to China: Corporate Flight and the Consequences of Free Trade—Lessons from Shanghai* (New York: Pantheon Books, 2006), 218.

25. Fair Labor Association, "Second Foxconn Verification Status Report" (2013), 5, http://www.fairlabor.org/sites/default/files/documents/reports/second _foxconn_verification_status_report_0.pdf#overlay-context=.

26. Zhengzhou Municipal Education Bureau (Henan), "Notification to Mobilize Secondary Vocational School Students for Employment (Internship) at Foxconn Shenzhen," June 12, 2010 (print edition) (in Chinese).

27. Henan Provincial Poverty Alleviation Office, "Announcement Regarding Foxconn Technology Group Worker Recruitment and Training in Impoverished Areas," July 14, 2010 (print edition) (in Chinese).

28. Henan Provincial Education Department, "Emergency Announcement on Organizing Secondary Vocational School Students for Internships at Foxconn Technology Group," no. 89, September 4, 2010 (in Chinese), http:// acftu.people.com.cn/GB/197470/12932391.html.

29. *China Daily*, "Foxconn Plans New Plant to Produce iPhone 7 Touch-Screen," November 25, 2014, http://www.chinadaily.com.cn /regional/2014-11/25/content_18974896.htm.

30. Zhengzhou Airport Economic Comprehensive Experimental Zone (Henan) (2014), YouTube video, https://www.youtube.com /watch?v=ZDZRWaMBhfY.

31. David Barboza, "How China Built 'iPhone City' with Billions in Perks for Apple's Partner," *New York Times*, December 29, 2016, https://www.nytimes .com/2016/12/29/technology/apple-iphone-china-foxconn.html.

32. Chad Raphael and Ted Smith, "The Future of Activism for Electronics Workers," in *The Routledge Companion to Labor and Media*, ed. Richard Maxwell (New York: Routledge, 2016), 330.

33. China's Labor Contract Law, effective January 1, 2008, restricts the widespread use of short contracts to evade employer responsibility. It seeks to protect employees' right to an open-ended contract after signing two consecutive fixed-term contracts, or following ten years of service. The intent is to enhance job security and work stability for employees.

34. Ilya Repin's (1844–1930) painting *Barge Haulers on the Volga*, accompanied by "Song of the Volga Boatmen," YouTube video, https://www.youtube.

com/watch?v=KfsWoNpHg2s; "The Song of the Volga Boatmen (English subtitles)," September 12, 2011, YouTube video, https://www.youtube.com /watch?v=JMYsrZQjlf0.

35. Guy Standing, *The Precariat: The New Dangerous Class* (London: Bloomsbury Academic, 2011), 16.

36. Ross Perlin, *Intern Nation: How to Earn Nothing and Learn Little in the Brave New Economy*, updated edition (London: Verso, 2012), 23.

Chapter 6: Fire and Brimstone

1. Lyrics translated from Chinese by Greg Fay, Kyoko Selden, and Mark Selden. "A Worker's Requiem" music video, featuring singing in Cantonese by Mininoise (Hong Kong grassroots folk band), is available online: https:// www.youtube.com/watch?v=INoyDhMlsto.

2. The impact of the Level 7 Fukushima disaster (the maximum classification of nuclear energy accidents on the International Nuclear Event Scale) extended beyond Japan's northeast, and indeed, beyond Japan. See Koide Hiroaki and Norma Field, "The Fukushima Nuclear Disaster and the Tokyo Olympics," *Asia-Pacific Journal* 17, issue 5, no. 3 (March 1, 2019), https://apjjf.org/2019/05/Koide-Field.html; see also the *Asia-Pacific Journal* archive, "Japan's 3.11 Earthquake, Tsunami, Atomic Meltdown": https:// apjjf.org/3-11.html.

3. Adam Satariano and Peter Burrows, "Apple's Supply-Chain Secret? Hoard Lasers," *Bloomberg Businessweek*, November 3, 2011, http://www. businessweek.com/magazine/apples-supplychain-secret-hoard -lasers-11032011.html.

4. Adam Lashinsky, *Inside Apple: The Secrets behind the Past and Future Success of Steve Jobs's Iconic Brand* (London: John Murray, 2012), 95.

5. Jena McGregor, "Tim Cook, the Interview: Running Apple 'Is Sort of a Lonely Job,'" *Washington Post*, August 13, 2016, http://www.washingtonpost. com/sf/business/2016/08/13/tim-cook-the-interview-running-apple-is-sort -of-a-lonely-job/?tid=a_inl&utm_term=.823cdf32f8c5.

6. Harry McCracken, "The 50 Best Inventions of 2010," *Time*, November 11, 2010, http://content.time.com/time/specials/packages/article /0,28804,2029497_2030652_2029804,00.html.

7. CBS News, "Bill Gates on Steve Jobs: We Grew Up Together," March 27, 2015, http://www.cbsnews.com/videos/bill-gates-on-steve-jobs-we-grew-up -together/.

8. Apple, "Apple Launches iPad 2" (March 2, 2011), https://www.apple.com /newsroom/2011/03/02Apple-Launches-iPad-2/.

9. Quoted in *Daily Mail*, "We Can't Make Them Fast Enough! Apple Claims to Have Sold EVERY iPad Ever Made (All 19.5 Million of Them)," April 22, 2011, https://www.dailymail.co.uk/sciencetech/article-1379227/Apple-admits-sold-EVERY-iPad-made.html?ITO%3D1490.

10. Agam Shah, "Watchdog Group Cites Continued Foxconn Abuses," *IDG News Service*, May 6, 2011, http://www.pcworld.com/businesscenter /article/227306/watchdog_group_cites_continued_foxconn_abuses.html.

11. The *Guardian* provided exclusive coverage of the investigative report compiled by SACOM (Students and Scholars Against Corporate Misbehavior). See Gethin Chamberlain, "Apple Factories Accused of Exploiting Chinese Workers" and "Apple's Chinese Workers Treated Inhumanely, Like Machines," *Guardian*, April 30, 2011, http://www.guardian.co.uk/technology/2011/apr/30/apple-chinese-factory-workers-suicides-humiliation; http://www.guardian.co.uk/technology/2011/apr/30/apple-chinese-workers-treated-inhumanely.

12. Jesus Diaz, "Foxconn Explosion Kills Two, iPad Production Line Halted," Gizmodo, May 20, 2011, http://gizmodo.com/5803963/would-the-foxconn-factory-explosion-further-delay-ipad-shipments.

13. Tania Branigan, "Workers Killed in Blast at China Plant of iPad Maker Foxconn," *Guardian*, May 20, 2011, http://www.guardian.co.uk/technology/2011/may/20/foxconn-apple-blast-china.

14. *China Digital Times,* "Directives from the Ministry of Truth: May 1–31, 2011," June 4, 2011, https://chinadigitaltimes.net/2011/06/directives-from-the-ministry-of-truth-may-1-31-2011/.

15. Charles Duhigg and David Barboza, "In China, Human Costs Are Built into an iPad," *New York Times*, January 25, 2012, http://www.nytimes.com/2012/01/26/business/ieconomy-apples-ipad-and-the-human-costs-for-workers-in-china.html.

16. Brid-Aine Parnell, "Blast at Apple Gear Factory Hurts 61," *Register*, December 19, 2011, http://www.theregister.co.uk/2011/12/19/apple_supplier_factory_explosion/.

Chapter 7: Wandering the City

1. "Shenzhen, Shenzhen," a Chinese migrant worker's song, with music composed by Xu Duo and lyrics (excerpts) translated by Jenny Chan and Mark Selden. Performed by Power Bass D Worker Band (2014), in Mandarin, available at: https://powerbassdworkerband.bandcamp.com/track/shenzhen-shenzhen.

2. Richard Sennett and Jonathan Cobb, *The Hidden Injuries of Class* (New York: W. W. Norton & Company, [1972] 1993).

3. Foxconn Technology Group, "2018 Social and Environmental Responsibility Report" (2019), 29, http://ser.foxconn.com/javascript/pdfjs/web/viewer.html?file=/upload/CserReports/5b75b277-d290-45f4-a9e1-efe87475543b_.pdf&page=1.

4. The disaster at the Zhili toy factory, partially owned by Hong Kong investors, occurred in Kuiyong Town, Shenzhen. In January 1993, the municipal authorities found that the three-story Zhili factory had obstructed passageways and locked windows and fire exits. Government inspectors called for thirteen modifications, and a deadline for corrections was set. However, to minimize the cost and prevent disruption of production, the manager bribed the fire prevention authority and obtained a certificate of safety without implementing the recommendations. On November 19, the "accident" took place, killing eighty-seven rural migrant workers, all but two of them women. It was China's deadliest fire death toll

since the initiation of foreign investment following the reform and opening during the late 1970s. See Anita Chan, *China's Workers under Assault: The Exploitation of Labor in a Globalizing Economy* (New York: M. E. Sharpe, 2001), 106–36.

5. In both Shanghai (24.2 million people) and Beijing (21.7 million people), rural migrants make up about 40 percent of those residing in the city. The pattern is repeated, with variations, in other megacities. See William Hurst and Christian Sorace, "Urban China: Changes and Challenges," in *Politics in China*, ed. William A. Joseph, 3rd ed. (Oxford: Oxford University Press, 2019), 349.

6. Foxconn Technology Group, "2014 Social and Environmental Responsibility Report" (2015), 11, http://ser.foxconn.com/javascript/pdfjs/web/viewer.html ?file=/upload/CserReports/1fdbd912-c592-4a56-b23f-ccfcabd60e83 _.pdf&page=1.

7. Three years of preschool education is *not* included in China's compulsory, free education program. As of 2018, only 63 percent of "mobile children" (children who moved with their parents in rural-to-urban labor migration) had access to public or private kindergartens in big cities with a population of five million people or above. Further statistical breakdown by types of kindergartens is not available. See National Bureau of Statistics of the People's Republic of China, "Investigative Report on the Monitoring of Chinese Rural Migrant Workers in 2018," section 5.1 (2019) (in Chinese), http://www.stats.gov.cn/tjsj/zxfb/201904/t20190429_1662268.html. On the difference between early education for rural and urban residents and the life consequences of the differences, see Sarah-Eve Dill, Yue Ma, Andrew Sun, and Scott Rozelle, "The Landscape of Early Childhood Development in Rural China," *Asia-Pacific Journal* 17, issue 16, no. 3 (August 15, 2019), https://apjjf.org/2019/16/Dill-Yue-Sun-Rozelle.html.

8. Austin Ramzy, "Person of the Year 2009, Runners-Up: The Chinese Worker," *Time*, December 16, 2009, http://content.time.com/time/specials /packages/article/0,28804,1946375_1947252_1947256,00.html.

9. Fang Cai, John Giles, Philip O'Keefe, and Dewen Wang, *The Elderly and Old Age Support in Rural China: Challenges and Prospects* (Washington, DC: The World Bank, 2012), 3, https://openknowledge.worldbank.org /bitstream/handle/10986/2249/675220PUB0EPI0067882B09780821386859 .pdf?sequence=1.

10. "Embrace Life" is included in the New Workers Art Troupe's 2007 album. English translation by Jack Qiu. Lyrics in the original Chinese: https:// emumo.xiami.com/song/bqvdQND3ae18?spm=a1z1s.6659513.0.0.GbtbsE.

Chapter 8: Chasing Dreams

1. Leslie T. Chang, *Factory Girls: From Village to City in a Changing China* (New York: Spiegel & Grau, 2008).

2. Foxconn Technology Group, "2011 Social and Environmental Responsibility Report" (2012), 12, http://ser.foxconn.com/javascript/pdfjs/web/viewer.html ?file=/upload/CserReports/8a6fb59c-e3c3-495e-abb0-35e727328912 _.pdf&page=1.

3. Foxconn Technology Group, "2017 Social and Environmental Responsibility Report" (2018), 24, http://ser.foxconn.com/javascript/pdfjs/web/viewer .html?file=/upload/CserReports/2e4ecfaa-df6f-429a-88cd-cf257828b0a7 _.pdf&page=1.

4. Foxconn Technology Group, "2018 Social and Environmental Responsibility Report" (2019), 25, http://ser.foxconn.com/javascript/pdfjs /web/viewer.html?file=/upload/CserReports/5b75b277-d290-45f4-a9e1 -efe87475543b_.pdf&page=1.

5. A female worker lamented "the systemic nature" of workplace harassment, tying it to a lack of effective redress mechanisms at Foxconn. She charged the company with cultivating a victim-blaming culture and noted the deep-seated problem of a lack of gender rights awareness among managers and workers. See also, Jiayun Feng, "'I Am a Woman Worker at Foxconn, and I Demand a System That Opposes Sexual Harassment': A Translated Essay," SupChina, January 26, 2018, https://supchina.com/2018/01/26/i-am -a-woman-worker-at-foxconn-demand-system-opposes-sexual-harassment/.

6. See Foxconn Technology Group's social and environmental responsibility reports. The 2008 report is on file with the authors. The other ten reports, published in 2010 and thereafter, are available online. Foxconn Technology Group (2009, p. 22; 2010, p. 19; 2011, p. 14; 2012, p. 12; 2013, p. 12; 2014, p. 12; 2015, p. 26; 2016, p. 27; 2017, p. 29; 2018, p. 25; 2019, p. 24), http:// ser.foxconn.com/viewCserReport_listYearReport.action.

7. Foxconn Technology Group, "Foxconn Code of Conduct Policy—Social and Environmental Responsibility" (2019), 6, http://ser.foxconn.com /javascript/pdfjs/web/viewer.html?file=/upload/policyAttachments /%0D979c9ad3-a8e3-4eb6-9779-86ce2e51c8a3_.pdf&page=1.

8. Dexter Roberts, "China's Young Men Act Out in Factories," *Bloomberg*, May 2, 2014, http://www.bloomberg.com/news/articles/2014-05-01 /chinas-young-male-factory-workers-change-the-assembly-line.

9. China's sex ratio at birth approached 120 boys per 100 girls during the 1990s and 2000s, reflecting the lasting impact of the "one-child policy" on family and the labor market. By international reference the normal range is 103 to 106 boys to every 100 girls. Today, with the relaxation of the one-child limit, some couples wish to have a son *and* a daughter, rather than accepting a one-daughter-only family, thereby preserving more or less the distorted sex ratios. See Deborah S. Davis, "Demographic Challenges for a Rising China," *Daedalus: The Journal of the American Academy of Arts and Sciences* 143, no. 2 (2014): 30–31.

10. Weimei Sun and Brian Creech, "Celebratory Consumerism on China's Singles' Day: From Grass-Roots Holiday to Commercial Festival," *Global Media and Communication* 15, no. 2 (2019): 248.

11. Arjun Kharpal, "Apple Was the Top-Selling Mobile Phone Brand on Alibaba Platforms during Singles Day, Beating Chinese Rivals," *CNBC*, November 12, 2018, https://www.cnbc.com/2018/11/12/alibaba-singles-day -2018-apple-was-the-top-selling-mobile-phone-brand.html.

12. Stephanie Clifford and Miguel Helft, "Apple Stores Chief to Take the Helm at J. C. Penney," *New York Times*, June 14, 2011, http://www.nytimes .com/2011/06/15/business/economy/15shop.html?_r=0.

13. Apple Retail Stores, China (as of March 2020): the forty-two stores are located in four provincial-level municipalities (Beijing, Shanghai, Tianjin, and Chongqing) and ten provinces (Fujian, Guangdong, Guangxi, Henan, Jiangsu, Liaoning, Shandong, Sichuan, Yunnan, and Zhejiang), http://www.apple.com/cn/retail/storelist/.

14. *Economist,* "Apple in China," February 16, 2012, http://www.economist.com/node/21547884.

15. Apple, "The Song" (also known as "The Old Record") (2015), http://v.qq.com/page/h/f/9/h00153ascf9.html.

16. Apple, "The City" (2017), https://www.facebook.com/watch/?v=1547851685234355.

17. The Huawei music video "Dream It Possible" (2015), composed by Andy Love and performed by Delacey, is available online at: https://www.youtube.com/watch?v=o9F1wq-k7dk.

18. "Wo de Meng" is the Chinese rendition of "Dream It Possible," with lyrics written by Wang Haitao and Jane Zhang, performed by Jane Zhang: https://www.youtube.com/watch?v=70qyvaQLLZQ&list=RD70qyvaQLLZQ&start_radio=1&t=79.

19. *Dreamwork China* (2011), an independent multimedia project that focuses on the "dreams and rights of a new generation of Chinese migrant workers in the world's factory," was initiated by Ivan Franceschini, Tommaso Facchin, and Tommaso Bonaventura. A thirteen-minute excerpt (narrated in Mandarin with English subtitles) from the hour-long documentary is available online at: http://www.dreamworkchina.com/en/portraits/.

20. Karen Eggleston, Jean C. Oi, Scott Rozelle, Ang Sun, Andrew Walder, and Xueguang Zhou, "Will Demographic Change Slow China's Rise?" *Journal of Asian Studies* 72, no. 3 (2013): 506.

21. Quoted in Quan Gao and Junxi Qian, "Migrant Workers in an Era of Religious Revival: Industrial Capitalism, Labour, and Christianity in Shenzhen," *China Quarterly* 241 (March 2020): 77.

Chapter 9: Confronting Environmental Crisis

1. Friends of Nature, Green Stone Environmental Action Network, Green Beagle, EnviroFriends, and Institute of Public and Environmental Affairs, "The Other Side of Apple II: Pollution Spreads through China's Water Supply Chain" (2011), a five-minute documentary, YouTube video, https://www.youtube.com/watch?v=rpFz9VAX8zM.

2. Ted Smith, David A. Sonnenfeld, and David N. Pellow, eds., *Challenging the Chip: Labor Rights and Environmental Justice in the Global Electronics Industry*, (Philadelphia: Temple University Press, 2006).

3. Greenpeace, "Green My Apple Bears Fruit," May 31, 2007, http://www.greenpeace.org/international/en/news/features/greening-of-apple-310507/.

4. Friends of Nature, Institute of Public and Environmental Affairs, Green Beagle, EnviroFriends, and Green Stone, Environmental Action Network, "The Other Side of Apple II: Pollution Spreads through Apple's Supply

China" (August 31, 2011), http://wwwoa.ipe.org.cn//Upload/Report-IT-V-Apple-II-EN.pdf.

5. Rob Schmitz, "In China, Concerns Grow over Environmental Costs of Apple Products," *Marketplace*, November 28, 2011, https://www .marketplace.org/2011/11/28/tech/apple-economy/china-concerns-grow -over-environmental-costs-apple-products.

6. Paul Mozur, "China Scrutinizes 2 Apple Suppliers in Pollution Probe," *Wall Street Journal*, August 4, 2013, http://online.wsj.com/news/articles /SB10001424127887323420604578648002283373528.

7. Lv Se Jiang Nan [Greening Southern Jiangsu], Institute of Public and Environmental Affairs, Friends of Nature, EnviroFriends, and Nature University, "Who is Polluting the Taihu Basin? Green Choice Alliance, IT Industry Supply Chain Investigative Report—Phase VII" (August 1, 2013), 3, http://wwwoa.ipe.org.cn//Upload/20131112123538SWY.pdf.

8. Zhang Houfei is a former Foxconn team leader. This is his real name. He attended media interviews and participated in our research project.

9. Ted Smith and Chad Raphael, "Health and Safety Policies for Electronics Workers," in *The Routledge Companion to Labor and Media*, ed. Richard Maxwell (New York: Routledge, 2016), 83.

10. Apple, "Apple Supplier Responsibility: 2011 Progress Report" (2011), 20, https://www.apple.com/supplier-responsibility/pdf/Apple_SR_2011 _Progress_Report.pdf.

11. *Shanghai Daily*, "Poisoned Workers in Apple Plea," February 23, 2011, https:// archive.shine.cn/nation/Poisoned-workers-in-Apple-plea/shdaily.shtml.

12. Kathleen E. McLaughlin, "Silicon Sweatshops: An Illness in Suzhou," *GlobalPost*, May 30, 2010, https://www.pri.org/stories/2010-03-17/silicon -sweatshops-illness-suzhou; Kathleen E. McLaughlin, "Silicon Sweatshops: More Workers Fall Ill in China," *GlobalPost*, June 25, 2010, https://www.pri .org/stories/2010-06-25/silicon-sweatshops-more-workers-fall-ill-china.

13. David Barboza, "Workers Sickened at Apple Supplier in China," *New York Times*, February 22, 2011, https://www.nytimes.com/2011/02/23 /technology/23apple.html.

14. Apple, "Apple Supplier Responsibility: 2012 Progress Report" (2012), 16, https://www.apple.com/supplier-responsibility/pdf/Apple_SR_2012 _Progress_Report.pdf.

15. Apple, "Apple Supplier Responsibility: 2013 Progress Report," (2013), 16, https://www.apple.com/supplier-responsibility/pdf/Apple_SR_2013 _Progress_Report.pdf.

16. Ma Jun is the 2015 Skoll Awardee. The Skoll Foundation presents awards to those who have demonstrated impact on solving some of the world's most pressing problems. http://skoll.org/contributor/ma-jun/.

17. Liu Jianqiang, "Apple Has Made No Progress at All," chinadialogue, August 31, 2011, https://www.chinadialogue.net/article/show/single /en/4500--Apple-has-made-no-progress-at-all-.

18. Apple, "Apple Supplier Responsibility: 2012 Progress Report," 3; Apple, "Apple Suppliers 2011" (2012), 1, http://files.rassegna.it/userdata/sites /rassegnait/attach/2012/01/applesupplierlist2011_247409.pdf.

19. Apple, "Focus on Toxins: Safe Products and Healthy Work Environments," (August 2014), http://www.apple.com/uk/environment/our-progress /posts/201408-focus-on-toxins.html.

20. Apple, "Environmental Responsibility Report: 2014 Progress Report, Covering FY2013" (2014), 15, https://www.apple.com/environment/reports /docs/Apple_Environmental_Responsibility_Report_2014.pdf.

21. Gethin Chamberlain, "'Metal Particles Splash into Eyes': Study Claims iPhone Workers Face Toxic Risks," *Guardian*, January 16, 2018, https:// www.theguardian.com/global-development/2018/jan/16/workers-making -iphones-in-china-exposed-to-toxic-hazards-report-says-apple-catcher -technology.

22. China Labor Watch, "Apple's Failed CSR [Corporate Social Responsibility] Audit: A Report on Catcher Technology Polluting the Environment and Harming the Health of Workers" (January 16, 2018), http://www .chinalaborwatch.org/report/131.

23. Smith, Sonnenfeld, and Pellow, *Challenging the Chip*, 11.

24. "Phone Story," an educational game created by Molleindustria in 2011, provokes a critical reflection on a smartphone's own technological platform: http://www.phonestory.org/.

25. Stuart Dredge, "Apple Bans Satirical iPhone Game Phone Story from Its App Store," *Guardian*, September 14, 2011, https://www.theguardian.com /technology/appsblog/2011/sep/14/apple-phone-story-rejection.

26. *Panorama*, "Apple's Broken Promises," on BBC One and iPlayer, December 18, 2014, http://www.bbc.co.uk/iplayer/episode/b04vs348 /panorama-apples-broken-promises.

27. Sean McGrath, "BBC Was Wrong to Single Out Apple in Panorama Investigation," *MicroScope*, December 19, 2014, https://www.computerweekly .com/microscope/opinion/BBC-was-wrong-to-single-out-Apple-in -Panorama-investigation.

28. Jeff Williams, "Email to Staff from Apple Senior Vice President of Operations Jeff Williams," December 19, 2014, http://www.bbc.co.uk/news /technology-30548468.

29. Apple, "Annual Green Bond Impact Report—2018 Update" (2019), 2, https://s2.q4cdn.com/470004039/files/doc_downloads/additional_reports /Apple_GreenBond_Report_2018.pdf.

30. Apple, "Supplier Clean Energy—Program Update" (April 2017), https:// images.apple.com/environment/pdf/Apple_Supplier_Clean_Energy _Program_Update_April_2017.pdf.

31. Apple, "Apple Launches New Clean Energy Programs in China to Promote Low-Carbon Manufacturing and Green Growth" (October 22, 2015), https://www.apple.com/newsroom/2015/10/22Apple-Launches-New-Clean -Energy-Programs-in-China-To-Promote-Low-Carbon-Manufacturing-and -Green-Growth/.

32. Dexter Roberts, "Apple Manufacturer Foxconn Goes Green in China's Guizhou," *Bloomberg*, July 12, 2014, https://www.bloomberg.com/news /articles/2014-07-11/apple-manufacturer-foxconn-goes-green-in-chinas -guizhou.

33. Apple, "Environmental Responsibility Report—2017 Progress Report, Covering Fiscal Year 2016" (2017), 3, https://images.apple.com/environment /pdf/Apple_Environmental_Responsibility_Report_2017.pdf.

34. Romain Dillet, "Apple's Lisa Jackson Says the EPA [Environmental Protection Agency] Hasn't Changed, Leadership Has Changed," *TechCrunch*, September 19, 2017, https://techcrunch.com/2017/09/19/apples-lisa-jackson -says-the-epa-hasnt-changed-leadership-has-changed/.

35. Elizabeth Jardim, "What 10 Years of Smartphone Use Means for the Planet," Greenpeace, February 27, 2017, https://www.greenpeace.org/international /story/6913/what-10-years-of-smartphone-use-means-for-the-planet/.

36. Heather White and Lynn Zhang codirected the documentary film *Complicit* (2017): http://www.complicitfilm.org/.

37. Hsin-Hsing Chen, "Professionals, Students, and Activists in Taiwan Mobilize for an Unprecedented Collective-Action Lawsuit against a Former Top American Electronics Company," *East Asian Science, Technology and Society* 5, no. 4 (2011): 563.

38. *Taipei Times*, "Former RCA Employees Win Decade-Long Legal Battle," April 18, 2015, https://www.taipeitimes.com/News/front/archives/2015 /04/18/2003616192.

39. Green America, "200,000 Petitions & Counting: Health, Labor & Environment Groups Say 'Clean Up Samsung': Global Day of Action Against Samsung," May 1, 2018, https://www.greenamerica.org/press- release/200000-petitions-counting-health-labor-environment-groups-say- clean-samsung-global-day-action-against-samsung.

40. Stop Samsung—No More Deaths! International Campaign for Health and Labor Rights of Samsung Electronics Workers, "Two Legal Wins," July 10, 2017, https://stopsamsung.wordpress.com/2017/07/10/two-legal-wins -sharps-achieves-new-momentum/.

Chapter 10: Dead Man Walking

1. Zhang Guangde, and his son Tingzhen, are real names. The Zhang family has received media and our interviews regarding the industrial accident at Foxconn Longhua in Shenzhen.

2. Ching Kwan Lee, "Pathways of Labor Activism," in *Chinese Society: Change, Conflict, and Resistance*, ed. Elizabeth J. Perry and Mark Selden, 3rd ed. (London: Routledge, [2000] 2010), 76.

3. Mary E. Gallagher and Baohua Dong, "Legislating Harmony: Labor Law Reform in Contemporary China," in *From Iron Rice Bowl to Informalization: Markets, Workers, and the State in a Changing China*, ed. Sarosh Kuruvilla, Ching Kwan Lee, and Mary E. Gallagher (Ithaca, NY: Cornell University Press, 2011), 59.

4. *China Labour Statistical Yearbook 2018*, "Labor Disputes Accepted and Settled," table 8-1 (Beijing: China Statistics Press, 2019).

5. *China Labour Statistical Yearbook 2018* (2019).

6. Aaron Halegua, "Who Will Represent China's Workers? Lawyers, Legal Aid, and the Enforcement of Labor Rights" (U.S.-Asia Law Institute, New

York University School of Law, 2016), 1, https://www.aaronhalegua.com/chinasworkers/.

7. Ching Kwan Lee, *Against the Law: Labor Protests in China's Rustbelt and Sunbelt* (Berkeley: University of California Press, 2007), 260.

8. Patricia Chen and Mary Gallagher, "Mobilization without Movement: How the Chinese State 'Fixed' Labor Insurgency," *ILR Review* 71, no. 5, (2018): 1033.

9. Feng Chen and Xin Xu, "'Active Judiciary': Judicial Dismantling of Workers' Collective Action in China," *China Journal* 67 (2012): 91.

Chapter 11: Strikes and Protests

1. Huw Beynon, *Working for Ford,* 2nd ed. (Harmondsworth, UK: Penguin, [1973] 1984).

2. In *Modern Times,* Charlie Chaplin's 1936 film masterpiece, his iconic Little Tramp character struggles to survive in a harsh industrial world.

3. Mark Selden and Elizabeth J. Perry, "Introduction: Reform, Conflict, and Resistance in Contemporary China," in *Chinese Society: Change, Conflict, and Resistance,* ed. Elizabeth J. Perry and Mark Selden, 3rd ed. (London: Routledge, [2000] 2010), 1–30.

4. Murray Scot Tanner, "China Rethinks Unrest," *Washington Quarterly* 27, no. (2004): 138.

5. Murray Scot Tanner, "Chinese Government Responses to Rising Social Unrest" (Santa Monica, CA: The RAND Corporation, 2005), 5.

6. Dan Weihua, "A Multilevel, Multicausal Analysis of Mass Incidents Related to Police during the Period of Social Transformation," *Policing Studies* 8 (2010): 25 (in Chinese).

7. Kai Chang and Fang Lee Cooke, "Legislating the Right to Strike in China: Historical Development and Prospects," *Journal of Industrial Relations* 57, no. 3 (2015): 44–55.

8. Hong Kong–based China Labour Bulletin interactive Strike Map, with reference to reports of Chinese labor strikes collected from news archives and other digital sources (effective January 2011): https://maps.clb.org.hk/strikes/en.

9. Geoffrey Crothall, "China's Labour Movement in Transition," *Made in China* 3, no. 2 (April–June, 2018): 28, http://www.chinoiresie.info/PDF/Made-in-China-02-2018.pdf.

10. Beverly J. Silver, *Forces of Labor: Workers' Movements and Globalization since 1870* (Cambridge: Cambridge University Press, 2003), 13.

11. Yang Su and Xin He, "Street as Courtroom: State Accommodation of Labor Protest in South China," *Law and Society Review* 44, no. 1 (2010): 157–84.

12. Ching Kwan Lee and Yonghong Zhang, "The Power of Instability: Unraveling the Microfoundations of Bargained Authoritarianism in China," *American Journal of Sociology* 118, no. 6 (2013): 1475–508.

13. Reuters, "Workers Protest at Foxconn Plant in China," April 27, 2012, https://www.reuters.com/article/us-china-foxconn/workers-protest-at-foxconn-plant-in-china-idusbre83q0jv20120427.

14. Our translation of the 2012 Foxconn Wuhan management directive (an excerpt).

15. That year, in early 2012, Apple had faced bad press of Foxconn suicides, explosions, injuries, and deaths. The company paid the Fair Labor Association (FLA) to conduct investigations at three selected Foxconn factories to devise a series of remedial action plans. See Auret van Heerden, "FLA Investigation of Foxconn in China," *Global Labour Journal* 3, no. 2 (2012): 278–81.

16. Yu Zhonghong is a pen name.

17. Yu Zhonghong's open letter to Terry Gou. The open letter is translated from Chinese into English by Kyoko Selden and Mark Selden. It is on file with the authors and is available at our book website.

18. Apple, "iPhone 5 First Weekend Sales Top Five Million" (September 24, 2012), https://www.apple.com/newsroom/2012/09/24iPhone-5-First -Weekend-Sales-Top-Five-Million/.

19. AP, "China Apple Factory Riot: Foxconn Workers Riot Suspends Work at Facility," September 24, 2012, http://www.wjla.com/articles/2012/09/china -apple-factory-riot-foxconn-workers-riot-suspends-work-at-facility-80213 .html.

20. AppleInsider, "Riot Reported at Apple Partner Manufacturer Foxconn's iPhone 5 Plant," September 23, 2012, http://appleinsider.com/articles /12/09/23/riot_reported_at_apple_partner_manufacturer_foxconns _iphone_5_plant.

21. Apple, "Apple Announces Changes to Increase Collaboration across Hardware, Software, and Services" (October 29, 2012), https://www.apple .com/newsroom/2012/10/29Apple-Announces-Changes-to-Increase- Collaboration-Across-Hardware-Software-Services/.

22. CBS News, "What's Next for Apple?," December 20, 2015, http://www .cbsnews.com/news/60-minutes-apple-tim-cook-charlie-rose/.

23. Foxconn Technology Group, "2012 Social and Environmental Responsibility Report" (2013), 14, http://ser.foxconn.com/javascript/pdfjs /web/viewer.html?file=/upload/CserReports/42470921-ed8f-4e16-8021 -81c8cb9a813b_.pdf&page=1.

24. All-China Federation of Trade Unions (ACFTU), "ACFTU Marks 80th Anniversary" (2005) (print edition).

25. Zhan Lisheng, "Guangzhou: Hotbed for Rise of Trade Unions," *China Daily*, August 29, 2006, http://www.newsgd.com/business/zones /200608290055.htm.

26. Mingwei Liu, "'Where There Are Workers, There Should Be Trade Unions': Union Organizing in the Era of Growing Informal Employment," in *From Iron Rice Bowl to Informalization: Markets, Workers, and the State in a Changing China*, ed. Sarosh Kuruvilla, Ching Kwan Lee, and Mary E. Gallagher (Ithaca, NY: Cornell University Press, 2011), 157.

27. Kong Xianghong, "Capacity-Building and Reform of Chinese Trade Unions: Using Legal and Democratic Means to Resolve the Conflict of Roles of Trade Union Chairs," in *Industrial Democracy in China: With*

Additional Studies on Germany, South-Korea, and Vietnam, ed. Rudolf Traub-Merz and Kinglun Ngok (Beijing: China Social Sciences Press, 2012), 80.

28. Foxconn Technology Group, "2014 Social and Environmental Responsibility Report" (2015), http://ser.foxconn.com/javascript/pdfjs/web/viewer.html ?file=/upload/CserReports/1fdbd912-c592-4a56-b23f-ccfcabd60e83 _.pdf&page=1.

29. "Apple's Statement on Factory Conditions in China," December 26, 2012, http://www.nytimes.com/2012/12/27/business/apples-statement-on-factory -conditions-in-china.html?ref=business.

30. Beverly J. Silver, "Theorising the Working Class in Twenty-First-Century Global Capitalism," in *Workers and Labour in a Globalised Capitalism: Contemporary Themes and Theoretical Issues,* ed. Maurizio Atzeni (Houndmills, Basingstoke, UK: Palgrave Macmillan, 2014), 52.

31. Tim Pringle and Quan Meng, "Taming Labor: Workers' Struggles, Workplace Unionism, and Collective Bargaining on a Chinese Waterfront," *ILR Review* 71, no. 5 (2018): 1073.

32. *China Labour Statistical Yearbook 2017,* "Number of Grassroots Trade Union by Region (2016)"; and, "Trade Union Members in Grassroots Trade Union by Region (2016)" (Beijing: China Statistics Press, 2018), 410–13.

33. The International Trade Union Confederation's (ITUC) primary mission is the promotion and defense of workers' rights and interests, through international cooperation between trade unions, campaigning, and advocacy within the major global institutions. China is *not* affiliated with the ITUC.

34. Economic Rights Institute and Electronics Watch, "The Link between Employment Conditions and Suicide: A Study of the Electronics Sector in China" (November 2018), http://electronicswatch.org/the-link-between -employment-conditions-and-suicide-a-study-of-the-electronics-sector-in -china-november-2018_2549396.pdf.

Chapter 12: Apple, Foxconn, and the Lives of China's Workers

1. Yan Jun's poem in the original Chinese, translated by Greg Fay and Jeffery Hermanson, is available at our book website.

2. National Bureau of Statistics of the People's Republic of China, "Investigative Report on the Monitoring of Chinese Rural Migrant Workers in 2018," figure 2 (2019) (in Chinese), http://www.stats.gov.cn/tjsj /zxfb/201904/t20190429_1662268.html.

3. The research office of the All-China Federation of Trade Unions conducted the questionnaire survey at one thousand enterprises during May and June of 2010 and collected a valid sample of 4,453 respondents, including "new" and "old" generations of Chinese rural migrant workers (2,711 in the former group and 1,742 in the latter). The new generation is defined as those who were born after 1980. See the All-China Federation of Trade Unions, "Survey Into and Some Proposals Regarding the Conditions of the New Generation of Rural Migrant Workers at Enterprises in 2010" (2011) (in Chinese), http://acftu.people.com.cn/GB/67582/13966631.html.

4. National Bureau of Statistics of the People's Republic of China, "Investigative Report on the Monitoring of Chinese Rural Migrant Workers

in 2016," table 1 (in Chinese), April 28, 2017, http://www.stats.gov.cn/tjsj /zxfb/201704/t20170428_1489334.html; National Bureau of Statistics of the People's Republic of China, "Investigative Report on the Monitoring of Chinese Rural Migrant Workers in 2018," table 2 (in Chinese), April 29, 2019, http://www.stats.gov.cn/tjsj/zxfb/201904/t20190429_1662268.html.

5. Yujeong Yang and Mary Gallagher, "Moving In and Moving Up? Labor Conditions and China's Changing Development Model," *Public Administration and Development* 37 (2017): 173.

6. National Bureau of Statistics of the People's Republic of China, "Investigative Report on the Monitoring of Chinese Rural Migrant Workers in 2013," table 1 (2014) (in Chinese), http://www.stats.gov.cn /tjsj/zxfb/201405/t20140512_551585.html; National Bureau of Statistics of the People's Republic of China, "Investigative Report on the Monitoring of Chinese Rural Migrant Workers in 2018," figure 1 (2019) (in Chinese), http://www.stats.gov.cn/tjsj/zxfb/201904/t20190429_1662268.html.

7. National Bureau of Statistics of the People's Republic of China, "Investigative Report on the Monitoring of Chinese Rural Migrant Workers in 2012," table 4 (2013) (in Chinese), http://www.stats.gov.cn/tjsj /zxfb/201305/t20130527_12978.html; National Bureau of Statistics of the People's Republic of China, "Investigative Report on the Monitoring of Chinese Rural Migrant Workers in 2018," table 3 (2019) (in Chinese), http://www.stats.gov.cn/tjsj/zxfb/201904/t20190429_1662268.html.

8. Apple, "Apple Supplier Responsibility: 2014 Progress Report" (2014), 13, https://www.apple.com/supplier-responsibility/pdf/Apple_SR_2014 _Progress_Report.pdf.

9. In October 2017 the Electronic Industry Citizenship Coalition became the Responsible Business Alliance to reflect its expanded reach to "electronics, retail, auto and toy companies committed to supporting the rights and well-being of workers and communities worldwide affected by the global supply chain." http://www.responsiblebusiness.org/about/rba/.

10. Electronic Industry Citizenship Coalition (EICC), "Electronics Industry Supports Student Workers: EICC and Stanford University's REAP (Rural Education Action Program) Develop Vocational School Credentialing System in China" (December 15, 2015), http://www.responsiblebusiness.org /news/student-workers/.

11. Electronic Industry Citizenship Coalition and Stanford University's Rural Education Action Program, "Electronics Industry Recognizes Vocational Schools in China for Excellence" (June 29, 2016), http://www .responsiblebusiness.org/news/credentialed-schools-china/.

12. Scott Rozelle, Prashant Loyalka, and James Chu, "China's Human Capital Challenge and What Can Be Done about It," presentation with slides on "Responsible Electronics 2013: Student Workers" (October 2, 2013), http://www.slideshare.net/EICCoalition/responsible-electronics-2013 -student-workers.

13. BBC, "Foxconn Admits Employing Under-Age Interns," October 16, 2012, http://www.bbc.com/news/technology-19965641.

14. For example, in May 2010, at Honda's auto-parts factory in Foshan city in central Guangdong, approximately 70 percent of the 1,800-person

workforce was composed of student interns. See Florian Butollo and Tobias ten Brink, "Challenging the Atomization of Discontent: Patterns of Migrant-Worker Protest in China during the Series of Strikes in 2010," *Critical Asian Studies* 44, no. 3, (2012): 426.

15. Earl V. Brown Jr. and Kyle A. deCant, "Exploiting Chinese Interns as Unprotected Industrial Labor," *Asian-Pacific Law and Policy Journal* 15, no. 2, (2014): 195.

16. The regulations superseded the 2007 Administrative Measures and came into force on April 11, 2016. The full text of the "Regulations on the Management of Vocational School Student Internships" is available online (in Chinese): http://www.moe.gov.cn/srcsite/A07/moe_950/201604 /t20160426_240252.html.

17. "Regulations on the Management of Vocational School Student Internships" (2016).

18. China Labor Watch, "Amazon's Supplier Factory Foxconn Recruits Illegally: Interns Forced to Work Overtime" (August 8, 2019), http://www .chinalaborwatch.org/report/143.

19. See, for example, Nectar Gan, "Chinese Student 'Interns' Spend 10-hour Days Sorting Packages after Single's Day Shopping Spree," *South China Morning Post*, November 20, 2016, https://www.scmp.com/news /china/society/article/2047684/chinese-student-interns-spend-10-hour -days-sorting-packages-after; Tom Hancock, Yuan Yang, and Nian Liu, "Illegal Student Labour Fuels JD.com 'Singles Day' Sale," *Financial Times*, November 21, 2018, http://polyucrdn.eksx.com/userfiles/file/Jenny %20Chan%20Illegal%20student%20labour%20FT%2021%20NOV %202018.pdf.

20. Tim Pringle, *Trade Unions in China: The Challenge of Labour Unrest* (Abingdon, Oxon, UK: Routledge, 2011), 162.

21. Jenny Chan, "Jasic Workers Fight for Union Rights," *New Politics* (An Independent Socialist Journal) 17, no. 2, whole number 66 (Winter 2019): 84–89; Jenny Chan, "A Precarious Worker-Student Alliance in Xi's China," *China Review* 20, no. 1 (February 2020): 165–90.

22. Au Loong Yu, "The Jasic Struggle in China's Political Context," *New Politics* (An Independent Socialist Journal) 17, no. 2, whole number 66 (Winter 2019): 91.

23. Christian Shepherd, "At a Top Chinese University, Activist 'Confessions' Strike Fear into Students," Reuters, January 21, 2019, https://www.reuters .com/article/us-china-rights-confessions/at-a-top-chinese-university-activist -confessions-strike-fear-into-students-idUSKCN1PF0RR; Pak Yiu, "Student Labour Activists Say Chinese Police Stepping Up Use of Video 'Confessions,'" AFP, March 3, 2019, https://www.hongkongfp.com/2019/03/03/student -labour-activists-say-chinese-police-stepping-use-video-confessions/.

24. Mary E. Gallagher, *Authoritarian Legality in China: Law, Workers, and the State* (New York: Cambridge University Press, 2017).

25. Kim Hyojoung, "Micromobilization and Suicide Protest in South Korea, 1970–2004," *Social Research* 75, no. 2, (2008): 549.

26. Jude Howell and Tim Pringle, "Shades of Authoritarianism and State-Labour Relations in China," *British Journal of Industrial Relations* 57, no. 2 (2019): 223–46.

27. *Xinhua*, "Full Text of Resolution on CPC Central Committee Report," October 24, 2017, http://news.xinhuanet.com/english/2017-10/24/c_136702625.htm.

28. Xiaoxiao's poem in the original Chinese, translated by Greg Fay, is available at our book website.

29. The selected poems written by Xu Lizhi were translated into English by Matthew A. Hale and colleagues, and published online on Nao's blog (https://libcom.org/blog/xulizhi-foxconn-suicide-poetry). Xu Lizhi's poems in the original Chinese were edited by Qin Xiaoyu, *Xin de Yi Tian* (A New Day), published posthumously in 2015 by the Writers Publishing House. See also, *La machine est ton seigneur et ton maître* (The Machine Is Your Lord and Master), a collection of short writings and poems about the Foxconn experience, translated into French by Celia Izoard and published by Agone in 2015. Three years later, when Foxconn broke the ground for its new facility in Mount Pleasant, Wisconsin, Adjunct Press (Milwaukee, WI) published *Selected Poems of Xu Lizhi (1990–2014)*.

30. *Xinhua*, "Xi Urges Breaking New Ground in Workers' Movement, Trade Unions' Work," October 29, 2018, http://www.xinhuanet.com/english/2018-10/29/c_137567374.htm.

31. Feng Chen and Xuehui Yang, "Movement-Oriented Labour NGOs in South China: Exit with Voice and Displaced Unionism," *China Information* 31, no. 2, (2017): 155–75.

32. One of the notable examples was the forced closure of the Qinghu Community Center (2012–2019) based in Shenzhen, outside of the north gate of Foxconn Longhua, in May 2019. The community service center had provided a wide range of social and educational activities for workers from Foxconn and other factories, as well as local residents in the neighborhood.

Epilogue

1. Apple, "Apple Supplier Responsibility: 2016 Progress Report" (2016), 2, https://www.apple.com/supplier-responsibility/pdf/Apple_SR_2016_Progress_Report.pdf.

2. Apple, "Apple Supplier Responsibility: 2017 Progress Report" (2017), 15, https://www.apple.com/supplier-responsibility/pdf/Apple_SR_2017_Progress_Report.pdf.

3. Apple, "Apple Special Event: Apple WWDC [Worldwide Developers Conference] 2016 Keynote Address," (June 13, 2016), https://podcasts.apple.com/us/podcast/apple-wwdc-2016-keynote-address-1080p/id509310064?i=1000430685297.

4. Tim Cook, "Tim Cook's MIT Commencement Address 2017," June 9, 2017, YouTube video, https://www.youtube.com/watch?v=ckjkz8zuMMs.

5. Apple, "Apple Supplier Responsibility: 2019 Progress Report" (2019), 2, https://www.apple.com/supplier-responsibility/pdf/Apple_SR_2019_Progress_Report.pdf.

6. Frederick Mayer and Gary Gereffi, "Regulation and Economic Globalization: Prospects and Limits of Private Governance," *Business and Politics* 12, no. 3 (2010): 8.

7. Mary Catt, "Apple Inc. Names ILR Professor to Advisory Board," *Cornell Chronicle*, August 6, 2013, http://news.cornell.edu/stories/2013/08/apple-inc-names-ilr-professor-advisory-board.

8. Apple, "Apple Supplier Responsibility: 2013 Progress Report" (2013), 24, https://www.apple.com/supplier-responsibility/pdf/Apple_SR_2013_Progress_Report.pdf.

9. Brown University's Watson Institute for International Studies, "Locke to Chair Apple's Academic Advisory Board," June 26, 2013, http://watson.brown.edu/news/2013/locke-chair-apples-academic-advisory-board.

10. Richard M. Locke, "Can Global Brands Create Just Supply Chains? A Forum on Corporate Responsibility for Factory Workers," *Boston Review*, May 21, 2013, http://bostonreview.net/forum/can-global-brands-create-just-supply-chains-richard-locke.

11. Richard M. Locke, *The Promise and Limits of Private Power: Promoting Labor Standards in a Global Economy* (Cambridge: Cambridge University Press, 2013).

12. David Weil, *The Fissured Workplace: Why Work Became So Bad for So Many and What Can Be Done to Improve It* (Cambridge, MA: Harvard University Press, 2014), 8.

13. Lin Thung-hong and Yang You-ren, "The Foxconn Employees and to Call to the Attention," June 13, 2010, http://sites.google.com/site/laborgogo2010eng.

14. "Protesta contra suicidios en Foxconn" (Protest against Suicides in Foxconn), Guadalajara, Mexico, June 10, 2010, YouTube video, narrated in Spanish, https://www.youtube.com/watch?v=4ikF9vD3R_A.

15. Worker rights supporters in New York City held a memorial service for Foxconn workers outside Apple's Fifth Avenue store on June 7, 2010.

16. San Francisco Chinese Progressive Association, "Apple's First Ever Store Overwhelmed with 'Death Pad' Protesters in San Francisco," June 17, 2010, http://sfcitizen.com/blog/2010/06/18/apples-first-ever-store-overwhelmed-with-deathpad-protesters-in-san-francisco/.

17. United Students Against Sweatshops, "Open Letter to Apple CEO Steve Jobs," June 14, 2010. The letter is on file with the authors and is available at our book website.

18. Jack Linchuan Qiu, *Goodbye iSlave: A Manifesto for Digital Abolition* (Urbana: University of Illinois Press, 2016).

19. Apple, "Apple Launches App Development Curriculum for High School and Community College Students" (May 24, 2017), https://www.apple.com/newsroom/2017/05/apple-launches-app-development-curriculum-for-high-school-community-college-students/.

20. Apple, "Apple Announces Updates to iTunes U" (June 30, 2014), https://www.apple.com/newsroom/2014/06/30Apple-Announces-Updates-to-iTunes-U/.

21. See, for example, Asia Monitor Resource Center, *Labour Rights in High Tech Electronics: Case Studies of Workers' Struggles in Samsung Electronics and Its Asian Suppliers* (Hong Kong: Asia Monitor Resource Center, 2013).

22. Rutvica Andrijasevic and Devi Sacchetto, "'Disappearing Workers': Foxconn in Europe and the Changing Role of Temporary Work Agencies," *Work, Employment, and Society* 31, no. 1 (2017): 54–70.

23. Devi Sacchetto and Martin Cecchi, "On the Border: Foxconn in Mexico," openDemocracy, January 16, 2015, https://www.opendemocracy.net /devi-sacchetto-mart%C3%ACn-cecchi/on-border-foxconn-in-mexico.

24. André Campos, Marcel Gomes, and Irene Schipper, "Labour Conditions at Foreign Electronics Manufacturing Companies in Brazil: Case Studies of Samsung, LGE, and Foxconn," Reporter Brasil and SOMO (Centre for Research on Multinational Corporations)/GoodElectronics, (December, 2017), 43. https://goodelectronics.org/wp-content/uploads/sites/3/2018/01 /Labour-conditions-at-foreign-electronics-manufacturing-companies -in-Brazil.pdf.

25. David Barboza, "Before Wisconsin, Foxconn Vowed Big Spending in Brazil; Few Jobs Have Come," *New York Times*, September 20, 2017, https:// www.nytimes.com/2017/09/20/business/foxconn-trump-wisconsin.html; Simon Romero, "Dilma Rousseff Is Ousted as Brazil's President in Impeachment Vote," *New York Times*, September 1, 2016, https://www.nytimes.com/2016/09/01/world/americas/brazil-dilma-rousseff -impeached-removed-president.html; Tina Lu,"Foxconn Leaving Brazil?," *Counterpoint Research*, September 2, 2017, https://www.counterpointresearch .com/foxconn-leaving-brazil/.

26. *News18.com*, "Xiaomi Unveils Second Manufacturing Unit in India in Partnership with Foxconn," March 20, 2017, https://www.news18.com/news /tech/xiaomi-unveils-second-manufacturing-unit-in-india-in-partnership -with-foxconn-1362152.html.

27. Pankaj Doval, "Foxconn Plans to Invest Up to Rs 32,000 Crore," *Times of India*, July 4, 2017, https://timesofindia.indiatimes.com/business/india-business /foxconn-plans-to-invest-up-to-rs-32000-crore/articleshow/59433253.cms.

28. Sujata Anandan, "The Overconfidence of Devendra Fadnavis," *The Wire*, November 22, 2019, https://thewire.in/politics/the-overconfidence-of -devendra-fadnavis.

29. Hsiao-Wen Wang, "Hon Hai: The Yogyakarta Move," *CommonWealth Magazine*, January 9, 2014, https://english.cw.com.tw/article/article .action?id=450.

30. *Jakarta Post*, "Apple's First R&D Center to Operate in Second Quarter," March 30, 2017, http://www.thejakartapost.com/news/2017/03/30/apples -first-rd-center-to-operate-in-second-quarter.html.

31. Jess Macy Yu and J. R. Wu, "Foxconn Plans U.S. Display Making Plant for Over $10 Billion, Scouting for Location," Reuters, June 22, 2017, https:// www.reuters.com/article/us-foxconn-strategy-idUSKBN19D0AH.

32. Dan Kaufman, "Did Scott Walker and Donald Trump Deal Away the Wisconsin Governor's Race to Foxconn?," *New Yorker*, November 3, 2018,

https://www.newyorker.com/news/dispatch/did-scott-walker-and-donald
-trump-deal-away-the-governors-race-to-foxconn.

33. Wisconn Valley: Foxconn in Wisconsin, https://wisconnvalley.wi.gov/Pages
/Home.aspx; Foxconn Technology Group, "Foxconn to Break Ground on
Advanced Manufacturing Campus Phase of Wisconn Valley Science &
Technology Park," March 18, 2019, https://urbanmilwaukee.com
/pressrelease/foxconn-to-break-ground-on-advanced-manufacturing-campus
-phase-of-wisconn-valley-science-technology-park/.

34. Austin Carr, "Inside Wisconsin's Disastrous $4.5 Billion Deal with Foxconn,"
Bloomberg Businessweek, February 9, 2019, https://www.bloomberg.com/news
/features/2019-02-06/inside-wisconsin-s-disastrous-4-5-billion-deal
-with-foxconn.

35. Scott Gordon, "When Great Lakes Water Is 'Public' and When It Isn't,"
WisContext, April 19, 2018, https://www.wiscontext.org
/when-great-lakes-water-public-and-when-it-isnt.

36. Foxconn's three-page letter to Mark R. Hogan, secretary and CEO of the
Wisconsin Economic Development Corporation, was shared with Wisconsin
Governor Tony Evers, January 17, 2019, https://www
.wisconnvalleycenter.com/wp-content/uploads/2019/01/Letter-to-WEDC.pdf.

37. Josh Dzieza, "Foxconn Releases and Cancels Plans for a Giant Dome in
Wisconsin," *The Verge*, October 3, 2019, https://www.theverge.com
/2019/10/3/20896815/foxconn-wisconsin-fii-giant-dome-plans-release-cancel.

Appendix 3: Fieldwork in China

1. SACOM (Students and Scholars Against Corporate Misbehavior), "The
Truth of the Apple iPad: Behind Foxconn's Lies" (2011), YouTube video,
https://www.youtube.com/watch?v=V3YFGixp9Jw.

2. WhatsApp (founded in 2009), owned by Facebook, provides end-to-end
encryption. By contrast, WeChat (founded in 2011 by the Chinese internet
company Tencent) is relatively less secure. The Chinese government has
steered internet users toward online communication sites that it can reliably
monitor.

Appendix 4: Foxconn Facilities around the World

1. A partial list of six Foxconn's websites: Hon Hai / Foxconn Technology
Group: http://www.foxconn.com; Foxconn Technology Group: http://www
.foxconn.com.cn/; Foxconn Czech Republic: http://www.foxconn.cz/;
Foxconn Slovakia: http://www.foxconnslovakia.sk/; Foxconn Brazil: http://
foxconn.com.br/; Foxconn Australia: http://foxconnaustralia.com.au/.

Selected Bibliography

Al, Stefan, ed. *Factory Towns of South China: An Illustrated Guidebook.* Hong Kong: Hong Kong University Press, 2012.

————, ed. *Villages in the City: A Guide to South China's Informal Settlements.* Hong Kong: Hong Kong University Press, and Honolulu, Hawaii: University of Hawaii Press, 2014.

Althusser, Louis, and Étienne Balibar. *Reading Capital.* Translated by Ben Brewster. Later printing ed. London: Verso, 2009.

Andors, Phyllis. "Women and Work in Shenzhen." *Bulletin of Concerned Asian Scholars* 20, no. 3 (1988): 22–41.

Andors, Stephen. *China's Industrial Revolution: Politics, Planning, and Management, 1949 to the Present.* New York: Pantheon Books, 1977.

Andreas, Joel. *Disenfranchised: The Rise and Fall of Industrial Citizenship in China.* Oxford: Oxford University Press, 2019.

————. "Reconfiguring China's Class Order after the 1949 Revolution." In *Handbook on Class and Social Stratification in China*, edited by Yingjie Guo, 21–43. Cheltenham, UK: Edward Elgar, 2016.

Anner, Mark. "Workers' Power in Global Value Chains: Fighting Sweatshop Practices at Russell, Nike, and Knights Apparel." In *Transnational Trade Unionism: Building Union Power*, edited by Peter Fairbrother, Marc-Antonin Hennebert, and Christian Lévesque, 23–41. New York: Routledge, 2013.

Appelbaum, Richard, and Nelson Lichtenstein, eds. *Achieving Workers' Rights in the Global Economy.* Ithaca, NY: Cornell University Press, 2016.

Appelbaum, Richard P., Cong Cao, Xueying Han, Rachel Parker, and Denis Simon. *Innovation in China.* Cambridge, UK: Polity Press, 2018.

Arrighi, Giovanni. "China's Market Economy in the Long Run." In *China and the Transformation of Global Capitalism*, edited by Ho-fung Hung, 22–49. Baltimore: Johns Hopkins University Press, 2009.

Atzeni, Maurizio, ed. *Workers and Labour in a Globalised Capitalism: Contemporary Themes and Theoretical Issues.* Basingstoke, UK: Palgrave MacMillan, 2014.

Atzeni, Maurizio, and Immanuel Ness, eds. *Global Perspectives on Workers' and Labour Organisations.* Singapore: Springer Nature, 2018.

Bair, Jennifer. "Global Capitalism and Commodity Chains: Looking Back, Going Forward." *Competition & Change* 9, no. 2 (2005): 153–80.

Baldoz, Rick, Charles Koeber, and Philip Kraft, eds. *The Critical Study of Work: Labor, Technology, and Global Production*. Philadelphia: Temple University Press, 2001.

Beynon, Huw. *Working for Ford*. 2nd ed. Harmondsworth, UK: Penguin, 1984.

Blauner, Robert. *Alienation and Freedom: The Factory Worker and His Industry*. Chicago: University of Chicago Press, 1964.

Blecher, Marc. *China against the Tides: Restructuring through Revolution, Radicalism, and Reform*. 3rd ed. New York: Continuum, 2010.

Braverman, Harry. *Labor and Monopoly Capital: The Degradation of Work in the Twentieth Century*. 25th anniversary ed. New York: Monthly Review Press, 1998.

Brown, William, and Chang Kai, eds. *The Emerging Industrial Relations of China*. Cambridge: Cambridge University Press, 2017.

Burawoy, Michael. "The Functions and Reproduction of Migrant Labor: Comparative Material from Southern Africa and the United States." *American Journal of Sociology* 81, no. 5 (1976): 1050–87.

———. *The Politics of Production: Factory Regimes under Capitalism and Socialism*. London: Verso, 1985.

———, ed. "Precarious Engagements: Combat in the Realm of Public Sociology." *Current Sociology* 62, no. 2 (2014).

Candland, Christopher, and Rudra Sil, eds. *The Politics of Labor in a Global Age: Continuity and Change in Late-Industrializing and Post-Socialist Economies*. Oxford: Oxford University Press, 2001.

Cartier, Carolyn. "From 'Special Zones' to Cities and City-Regions in China." In *Developmentalist Cities? Interrogating Urban Developmentalism in East Asia*, edited by Jamie Doucette and Bae-Gyoon Park, 196–218. Leiden, The Netherlands: Brill, 2019.

Chan, Anita, ed. *Chinese Workers in Comparative Perspective*. Ithaca, NY: Cornell University Press, 2015.

Chan, Chris King-chi. *The Challenge of Labor in China: Strikes and the Changing Labour Regime in Global Factories*. London: Routledge, 2010.

Chan, Jenny. "State and Labor in China, 1978–2018." *Journal of Labor and Society* 22, no. 2 (June 2019): 461–75.

Chan, Kam Wing. "The Global Financial Crisis and Migrant Workers in China: 'There Is No Future as a Laborer; Returning to the Village Has No Meaning.'" *International Journal of Urban and Regional Research* 34, no. 3 (July 2010): 1–19.

Chan, Ming K. *Historiography of the Chinese Labor Movement, 1895–1949: A Critical Survey and Bibliography*. Stanford, CA: Hoover Institution Press, 1981.

———. "Labor in Modern and Contemporary China." *International Labor and Working-Class History* 11 (May 1977): 13–18.

———. "A Turning Point in the Modern Chinese Revolution: The Historical Significance of the Canton Decade, 1917–27." In *Remapping China: Fissures in Historical Terrain*, edited by Gail Hershatter, Emily Honig, Jonathan N. Lipman, and Randall Stross, 224–42. Stanford, CA: Stanford University Press, 1996.

Chang, Leslie T. *Factory Girls: From Village to City in a Changing China*. New York: Spiegel & Grau, 2008.

Chen, Feng. "Against the State: Labor Protests in China in the 1950s." *Modern China* 40, no. 5 (2014): 488–518.

———. "Union Power in China: Source, Operation, and Constraints." *Modern China* 35, no. 6 (2009): 662–89.

Chen, Feng, and Xin Xu. "'Active Judiciary': Judicial Dismantling of Workers' Collective Action in China." *China Journal* 67 (2012): 87–107.

Chen, Hsin-Hsing. "Professionals, Students, and Activists in Taiwan Mobilize for an Unprecedented Collective-Action Lawsuit against a Former Top American Electronics Company." *East Asian Science, Technology, and Society* 5, no. 4 (2011): 555–65.

Chen, Patricia, and Mary Gallagher. "Mobilization without Movement: How the Chinese State 'Fixed' Labor Insurgency." *ILR Review* 71, no. 5 (2018): 1029–52.

Chen, Xi. *Social Protest and Contentious Authoritarianism in China*. New York: Cambridge University Press, 2012.

Cheng, Tiejun, and Mark Selden. "The Origins and Social Consequences of China's Hukou System." *China Quarterly* 139 (1994): 644–68.

Chesneaux, Jean. *The Chinese Labor Movement, 1919–1927*. Translated by H. M. Wright. Stanford, CA: Stanford University Press, 1968.

Choi, Susanne Y. P., and Yinni Peng. *Masculine Compromise: Migration, Family, and Gender in China*. Oakland: University of California Press, 2016.

Chomsky, Noam. *Profit over People: Neoliberalism and Global Order*. New York: Seven Stories Press, 1999.

Chu, Yin-wah, ed. *Chinese Capitalisms: Historical Emergence and Political Implications*. Basingstoke, UK: Palgrave Macmillan, 2010.

Chuang, Julia. *Beneath the China Boom: Labor, Citizenship, and the Making of a Rural Land Market*. Oakland: University of California Press, 2020.

Chun, Jennifer Jihye. *Organizing at the Margins: The Symbolic Politics of Labor in South Korea and the United States*. Ithaca, NY: Cornell University Press, 2009.

Clawson, Dan. *The Next Upsurge: Labor and the New Social Movements*. Ithaca, NY: Cornell University Press, 2003.

Cooney, Sean, Sarah Biddulph, and Ying Zhu. *Law and Fair Work in China*. Abingdon, Oxon, UK: Routledge, 2013.

Cowie, Jefferson. *Capital Move: RCA's Seventy-Year Quest for Cheap Labor*. New York: The New Press, 2001.

Davis, Deborah S., and Wang Feng, eds. *Creating Wealth and Poverty in Postsocialist China*. Stanford, CA: Stanford University Press, 2009.

Davis, Deborah S., and Sara L. Friedman, eds. *Wives, Husbands, and Lovers: Marriage and Sexuality in Hong Kong, Taiwan, and Urban China*. Stanford, CA: Stanford University Press, 2014.

de Peuter, Greig, Nicole S. Cohen, and Enda Brophy, eds. "Interrogating Internships: Unpaid Work, Creative Industries, and Higher Education." Special Issue. *tripleC: Communication, Capitalism, and Critique* 13, no. 2 (2015): 329–602.

Deyo, Frederic C. *Beneath the Miracle: Labor Subordination in the New Asian Industrialism*. Berkeley: University of California Press, 1989.

Diamant, Neil J., Stanley B. Lubman, and Kevin J. O'Brien, eds. *Engaging the Law in China: State, Society, and Possibilities for Justice*. Stanford, CA: Stanford University Press, 2005.

Dirlik, Arif, and Maurice Meisner, eds. *Marxism and the Chinese Experience*. Armonk, NY: M. E. Sharpe, 1989.

Distelhorst, Greg, and Richard M. Locke. "Does Compliance Pay? Social Standards and Firm-level Trade." *American Journal of Political Science* 62, no. 3 (2018): 695–711.

Distelhorst, Greg, Richard M. Locke, Timea Pal, and Hiram Samel. "Production Goes Global, Compliance Stays Local: Private Regulation in the Global Electronics Industry." *Regulation & Governance* 9, no. 3 (2015): 224–42.

Doucette, Jamie. "Minjung Tactics in a Post-Minjung Era? The Survival of Self-Immolation and Traumatic Forms of Labour Protest in South Korea." In *New Forms and Expressions of Conflict in the Workplace*, edited by Gregor Gall, 212–32. London: Palgrave Macmillan, 2013.

Drahokoupil, Jan, Rutvica Andrijasevic, and Devi Sacchetto, eds. *Flexible Workforces and Low Profit Margins: Electronics Assembly between Europe and China*. Brussels, Belgium: ETUI (European Trade Union Institute), 2016.

Economic Rights Institute, and Electronics Watch. "The Link between Employment Conditions and Suicide: A Study of the Electronics Sector in China." November 2018. http://electronicswatch.org/the-link-between-employment-conditions-and-suicide-a-study-of-the-electronics-sector-in-china-november-2018_2549396.pdf.

Edwards, Richard. *Contested Terrain: The Transformation of the Workplace in the Twentieth Century*. New York: Basic Books, 1979.

Elfstrom, Manfred. "Counting Contention." *Made in China* 2, no. 4 (2017): 16–19.

Elfstrom, Manfred, and Sarosh Kuruvilla. "The Changing Nature of Labor Unrest in China." *ILR Review* 67, no. 2 (2014): 453–80.

Engels, Friedrich. *The Condition of the Working Class in England*. Oxford: Oxford University Press, 2009.

Ernst, Dieter, and Barry Naughton. "China's Emerging Industrial Economy: Insights from the IT Industry." In *China's Emergent Political Economy: Capitalism in the Dragon's Lair*, edited by Christopher A. McNally, 39–59. London: Routledge, 2008.

Evans, Peter. *Embedded Autonomy: States and Industrial Transformation*. Princeton, NJ: Princeton University Press, 1995.

Fantasia, Rick. *Cultures of Solidarity: Consciousness, Action, and Contemporary American Workers*. Berkeley: University of California Press, 1988.

Featherstone, Lisa, and United Students Against Sweatshops. *Students Against Sweatshops*. London: Verso, 2002.

Florence, Eric. "How to Be a Shenzhener: Representations of Migrant Labor in Shenzhen's Second Decade." In *Learning from Shenzhen: China's Post-Mao Experiment from Special Zone to Model City*, edited by Mary Ann O'Donnell, Winnie Wong, and Jonathan Bach, 86–103. Chicago: The Chicago University Press, 2017.

Franceschini, Ivan, and Elisa Nesossi. "State Repression of Chinese Labor NGOs: A Chilling Effect?" *China Journal* 80 (2018): 111-29.

Franceschini, Ivan, and Kevin Lin. "Labour NGOs in China: From Legal Mobilisation to Collective Struggle (and Back?)." *China Perspectives* no. 2019/1 (2019): 75-84.

Frazier, Mark W. *The Making of the Chinese Industrial Workplace: State, Revolution, and Labor Management.* Cambridge: Cambridge University Press, 2002.

Freeman, Joshua B. *Behemoth: A History of the Factory and the Making of the Modern World.* New York: W. W. Norton & Company, 2018.

Friedman, Eli. *Insurgency Trap: Labor Politics in Postsocialist China.* Ithaca, NY: Cornell University Press, 2014.

Friends of the Nao Project. "The Poetry and Brief Life of a Foxconn Worker: Xu Lizhi (1990–2014)." Nao's blog. 2014. https://libcom.org/blog/xulizhi-foxconn-suicide-poetry.

Froissart, Chloé. "Negotiating Authoritarianism and Its Limits: Worker-Led Collective Bargaining in Guangdong Province." *China Information* 32, no. 1 (2017): 23–45.

Fu, Diana. *Mobilizing without the Masses: Control and Contention in China.* Cambridge: Cambridge University Press, 2018.

Fuchs, Christian. *Digital Labour and Karl Marx.* New York: Routledge, 2014.

Fuchs, Daniel, Patricia Fuk-Ying Tse, and Xiaojun Feng. "Labour Research under Coercive Authoritarianism: Comparative Reflections on Fieldwork Challenges in China." *Economic and Industrial Democracy* 40, no. 1 (2019): 132–55.

Fung, Archon, Dara O'Rourke, and Charles Sabel. *Can We Put an End to Sweatshops?* Boston, MA: Beacon Press, 2001.

Fürst, Juliane, Silvio Pons, and Mark Selden, eds. *The Cambridge History of Communism,* vol. 3, *Endgames? Late Communism in Global Perspective, 1968 to the Present.* Cambridge: Cambridge University Press, 2017.

Gallagher, Mary E. *Authoritarian Legality in China: Law, Workers, and the State.* Cambridge: Cambridge University Press, 2017.

———. *Contagious Capitalism: Globalization and the Politics of Labor in China.* Princeton, NJ: Princeton University Press, 2005.

Gereffi, Gary. "The Organization of Buyer-Driven Global Commodity Chains: How U.S. Retailers Shape Overseas Production Networks." In *Commodity Chains and Global Capitalism,* edited by Gary Gereffi and Miguel Korzeniewicz, 95–122. Westport, CT: Praeger, 1994.

Gereffi, Gary, John Humphrey, and Timothy Sturgeon. "The Governance of Global Value Chains." *Review of International Political Economy* 12, no. 1 (2005): 78–104.

Goodman, David S. G. *Class in Contemporary China.* Cambridge, UK: Polity Press, 2014.

———, ed. *The New Rich in China: Future Rulers, Present Lives.* Abingdon, Oxon, UK: Routledge, 2008.

Göbel, Christian. "Social Unrest in China: A Bird's-Eye View." In *Handbook of Protest and Resistance in China*, edited by Teresa Wright, 27-45. Cheltenham, UK: Edward Elgar Publishing, 2019.

Greene, Julie. "The Condition of the Working Class in Shenzhen." *Dissent* 65, no. 4 (2018): 78–85.

————. *The Canal Builders: Making America's Empire at the Panama Canal*. New York: Penguin Press, 2009.

Greenpeace. "From Smart to Senseless: The Global Impact of 10 Years of Smartphones." Washington, DC, 2017. https://www.greenpeace.org/usa/wp-content/uploads/2017/03/FINAL-10YearsSmartphones-Report-Design-230217-Digital.pdf.

Grimes, Seamus, and Yutao Sun. "China's Evolving Role in Apple's Global Value Chain." *Area Development and Policy* 1, no. 1 (2016): 94–112.

Guo, Yingjie, ed. *Handbook on Class and Social Stratification in China*. Cheltenham, UK: Edward Elgar, 2016.

Hamilton, Gary G., Misha Petrovic, and Benjamin Senauer, eds. *The Market Makers: How Retailers Are Reshaping the Global Economy*. Oxford: Oxford University Press, 2011.

Harney, Alexandra. *The China Price: The True Cost of Chinese Competitive Advantage*. New York: Penguin Press, 2008.

Harrison, Bennett. *Lean and Mean: The Changing Landscape of Corporate Power in the Age of Flexibility*. New York: Guilford Press, 1997.

Harvey, David. *The Enigma of Capital and the Crises of Capitalism*. New York: Oxford University Press, 2010.

————. *The Limits to Capital*. 1982. Updated ed. London: Verso, 2006.

He, Xin, Lungang Wang, and Yang Su. "Above the Roof, Beneath the Law: Perceived Justice behind Disruptive Tactics of Migrant Wage Claimants in China." *Law & Society Review* 47, no. 4 (2013): 702–38.

Heilmann, Sebastian, and Elizabeth J. Perry, eds. *Mao's Invisible Hand: The Political Foundations of Adaptive Governance in China*. Harvard Contemporary China Series 17. Cambridge, MA: Harvard University Asia Center, 2011.

Henderson, Jeffrey. *The Globalization of High-Technology Production*. London: Routledge, 1989.

Herod, Andrew. *Labour Geographies: Workers and the Landscapes of Capitalism*. New York: Guilford Press, 2001.

Hershatter, Gail. *The Workers of Tianjin, 1900–1949*. Stanford, CA: Stanford University Press, 1986.

Ho, Ming-sho. *Working Class Formation in Taiwan: Fractured Solidarity in State-Owned Enterprises, 1945–2012*. New York: Palgrave Macmillan, 2014.

Honig, Emily. *Sisters and Strangers: Women in the Shanghai Cotton Mills, 1919–1949*. Stanford, CA: Stanford University Press, 1986.

Honig, Emily, and Gail Hershatter. *Personal Voices: Chinese Women in the 1980s*. Stanford, CA: Stanford University Press, 1988.

Hopkins, Terence K., and Immanuel Wallerstein. "Commodity Chains in the World-Economy prior to 1800." *Review* (Fernand Braudel Center) 10, no. 1 (1986): 157–70.

Howell, Jude. "Adaptation under Scrutiny: Peering through the Lens of Community Governance in China." *Journal of Social Policy* 45, no. 3 (2016): 487–506.

———. "Trade Unionism in China: Sinking or Swimming?" *Journal of Communist Studies and Transition Politics* 19, no. 1 (2003): 102–22.

———. "All-China Federation of Trade Unions beyond Reform? The Slow March of Direct Elections." *China Quarterly* 196 (December 2008): 845–63.

Hsing, You-tien. *Making Capitalism in China: The Taiwan Connection*. New York: Oxford University Press, 1998.

Hsing, You-tien, and Ching Kwan Lee, eds. *Reclaiming Chinese Society: The New Social Activism*. London: Routledge, 2010.

Huang, Philip C. C. "China's Informal Economy, Reconsidered: An Introduction in Light of Social-Economic and Legal History." *Rural China: An International Journal of History and Social Science* 14, no. 1 (2017): 1–17.

Hui, Elaine Sio-ieng. *Hegemonic Transformation: The State, Laws, and Labour Relations in Post-Socialist China*. New York: Palgrave Macmillan, 2018.

Hung, Ho-fung, ed. *China and the Transformation of Global Capitalism*. Baltimore, MD: Johns Hopkins University Press, 2009.

Hung, Ho-fung, and Mark Selden. "China's Postsocialist Transformation and Global Resurgence: Political Economy and Geopolitics." In *The Cambridge History of Communism*, vol. 3, *Endgames? Late Communism in Global Perspective, 1968 to the Present*, edited by Juliane Fürst, Silvio Pons, and Mark Selden, 502–28. Cambridge: Cambridge University Press, 2017.

Hurst, William. *The Chinese Worker after Socialism*. Cambridge: Cambridge University Press, 2009.

Hutchison, Jane, and Andrew Brown, eds. *Organizing Labour in Globalizing Asia*. London: Routledge, 2001.

Jiang, Bin, Huaqing Wang, Linda Larsen, Fengyu Bao, Zhigang Li, and Mathew Pryor. "Quality of Sweatshop Factory Outdoor Environments Matters for Workers' Stress and Anxiety: A Participatory Smartphone-Photography Survey." *Journal of Environmental Psychology* 65 (October 2019), 1–17.

Katznelson, Ira, and Aristide R. Zolberg, eds. *Working-Class Formation: Nineteenth-Century Patterns in Western Europe and the United States*. Princeton, NJ: Princeton University Press, 1986.

Kim, Hyojoung. "Micromobilization and Suicide Protest in South Korea, 1970–2004." *Social Research* 75, no. 2 (2008): 543–78.

Kim, Jaesok. *Chinese Labor in a Korean Factory: Class, Ethnicity, and Productivity on the Shop Floor in Globalizing China*. Stanford, CA: Stanford University Press, 2013.

Klein, Naomi. *No Logo*. 10th anniversary ed. London: Fourth Estate, 2010.

Koo, Hagen. *Korean Workers: The Culture and Politics of Class Formation*. Ithaca, NY: Cornell University Press, 2001.

Kraemer, Kenneth L., Jason Dedrick, and Sandra Yamashiro. "Refining and Extending the Business Model with Information Technology: Dell Computer Corporation." *Information Society* 16, no. 1 (2000): 5–21.

Kuczera, Malgorzata, and Simon Field. "Learning for Jobs: OECD Reviews of Vocational Education and Training—Options for China." OECD (Organization for Economic Co-operation and Development), 2010.

Kuruvilla, Sarosh. "Editorial Essay—From Cautious Optimism to Renewed Pessimism: Labor Voice and Labor Scholarship in China." *ILR Review* 71, no. 5 (2018): 1013–28.

Kuruvilla, Sarosh, Ching Kwan Lee, and Mary E. Gallagher, eds. *From Iron Rice Bowl to Informalization: Markets, Workers, and the State in a Changing China.* Ithaca, NY: Cornell University Press, 2011.

Kuruvilla, Sarosh, and Hao Zhang. "Labor Unrest and Incipient Collective Bargaining in China." *Management and Organization Review* 12, no. 1 (2016): 159–87.

LaBaron, Genevieve, ed. *Researching Forced Labour in the Global Economy: Methodological Challenges and Advances.* Oxford: Oxford University Press, 2019.

Lamas, Andrew, Todd Wolfson, and Peter Funke, eds. *The Great Refusal: Herbert Marcuse and Contemporary Social Movements.* Philadelphia: Temple University Press, 2017.

Lardy, Nicholas R. *Markets over Mao: The Rise of Private Business in China.* Washington, DC: Peterson Institute for International Economics, 2014.

Lee, Ching Kwan. *Against the Law: Labor Protests in China's Rustbelt and Sunbelt.* Berkeley: University of California Press, 2007.

———. *Gender and the South China Miracle: Two Worlds of Factory Women.* Berkeley: University of California Press, 1998.

———. "Pathways of Labor Activism." In *Chinese Society: Change, Conflict and Resistance*, edited by Elizabeth J. Perry and Mark Selden, 57–79. 3rd ed. London: Routledge, 2010.

———. "Precarization or Empowerment? Reflections on Recent Labor Unrest in China." *Journal of Asian Studies* 75, no. 2 (2016): 317–33.

Lee, Ching Kwan, and Mark Selden. "Inequality and Its Enemies in Revolutionary and Reform China." *Economic and Political Weekly* 43, no. 52 (2008): 27–36.

Lee, Ching Kwan, and Yonghong Zhang. "The Power of Instability: Unraveling the Microfoundations of Bargained Authoritarianism in China." *American Journal of Sociology* 118, no. 6 (2013): 1475–508.

Lee, Joonkoo, and Hyun-Chin Lim. *Mobile Asia: Capitalisms, Value Chains and Mobile Telecommunication in Asia.* Seoul: Seoul National University Press, 2018.

Leung, Parry P. *Labor Activists and the New Working Class in China.* New York: Palgrave Macmillan, 2015.

Li, Minqi. *China and the 21st Century Crisis.* London: Pluto Press, 2016.

Lichtenstein, Nelson. *State of the Union: A Century of American Labor.* Revised and expanded ed. Princeton, NJ: Princeton University Press, 2013.

Liebman, Benjamin L., and Curtis J. Milhaupt, eds. *Regulating the Visible Hand? The Institutional Implications of Chinese State Capitalism.* Oxford: Oxford University Press, 2016.

Lin, Chun. *China and Global Capitalism: Reflections on Marxism, History, and Contemporary Politics.* New York: Palgrave Macmillan, 2013.

———. *The Transformation of Chinese Socialism.* Durham, NC: Duke University Press, 2006.

Lin, Kevin, Liana Foxvog, Olga Martin-Ortega, and Opi Outhwaite. "Time for a Reboot: Monitoring in China's Electronics Industry." International Labor Rights Forum (ILRF) and Business, Human Rights and the Environment (BHRE) Research Group, School of Law, University of Greenwich, September 2018.

Ling, Minhua. *The Inconvenient Generation: Migrant Youth Coming of Age on Shanghai's Edge.* Stanford: Stanford University Press, 2020.

Litzinger, Ralph A. "The Labor Question in China: Apple and Beyond." *South Atlantic Quarterly* 112, no. 1 (2013): 172–78.

Liu, Hwa-Jen. *Leverage of the Weak: Labor and Environmental Movements in Taiwan and South Korea.* Minneapolis: University of Minnesota Press, 2015.

Liu, Mingwei. "Union Organizing in China: Still a Monolithic Labor Movement?" *ILR Review* 64, no. 1 (2010): 30–52.

———. "'Where There Are Workers, There Should Be Trade Unions': Union Organizing in the Era of Growing Informal Employment." In *From Iron Rice Bowl to Informalization: Markets, Workers, and the State in a Changing China,* edited by Sarosh Kuruvilla, Ching Kwan Lee, and Mary E. Gallagher, 157–72. Ithaca, NY: Cornell University Press, 2011.

Liu, Mingwei, and Chris Smith, eds. *China at Work: A Labour Process Perspective on the Transformation of Work and Employment in China.* London: Palgrave, 2016.

Locke, Richard M. *The Promise and Limits of Private Power: Promoting Labor Standards in a Global Economy.* Cambridge: Cambridge University Press, 2013.

Lora-Wainwright, Anna. *Fighting for Breath: Living Morally and Dying of Cancer in a Chinese Village.* Honolulu: University of Hawaii Press, 2013.

———. *Resigned Activism: Living with Pollution in Rural China.* Cambridge, MA: MIT Press, 2017.

Lüthje, Boy, and Florian Butollo. "Why the Foxconn Model Does Not Die: Production Networks and Labour Relations in the IT Industry in South China." *Globalizations* 14, no. 2 (2017): 216–31.

Lüthje, Boy, Stefanie Hürtgen, Peter Pawlicki, and Martina Sproll. *From Silicon Valley to Shenzhen: Global Production and Work in the IT Industry.* Lanham, MD: Rowman and Littlefield, 2013.

Luxemburg, Rosa. *The Accumulation of Capital.* Translated by Agnes Schwarzschild. London: Routledge Classics, 2003.

Mak, Karin. "Until Our Last Breath: Voices of Poisoned Workers in China." In *Listening on the Edge: Oral History in the Aftermath of Crisis,* edited by Mark Cave and Stephen M. Sloan, 166–82. New York: Oxford University Press, 2014.

Marx, Karl. *Capital: A Critique of Political Economy.* Vol. 1. Translated by Ben Fowkes. London: Penguin Classics, 1990.

Marx, Karl, and Friedrich Engels. *The Communist Manifesto.* London: Penguin Classics, 2002.

Maxwell, Richard, ed. *The Routledge Companion to Labor and Media.* New York: Routledge, 2016.

McKay, Steven C. *Satanic Mills or Silicon Islands? The Politics of High-Tech Production in the Philippines.* Ithaca, NY: Cornell University Press, 2006.

McNally, Christopher A. "Sichuan: Driving Capitalist Development Westward." *China Quarterly* 178 (June 2004): 426–47.

Meisner, Maurice. *Mao's China and After: A History of the People's Republic.* 3rd ed. New York: Free Press, 1999.

Milkman, Ruth, and Kim Voss. *Rebuilding Labor: Organizing and Organizers in the New Union Movement.* Ithaca, NY: Cornell University Press, 2004.

Montgomerie, Johnna, and Samuel Roscoe. "Owning the Consumer: Getting to the Core of the Apple Business Model." *Accounting Forum* 37 (2013): 290–99.

Moore, Phoebe, Martin Upchurch, and Xanthe Whittaker, eds. *Humans and Machines at Work: Monitoring, Surveillance, and Automation in Contemporary Capitalism.* London: Palgrave Macmillan, 2018.

Nathan, Dev, Meenu Tewari, and Sandip Sarkar, eds. *Labour in Global Value Chains in Asia.* Cambridge: Cambridge University Press, 2016.

Naughton, Barry. *The Chinese Economy: Adaptation and Growth.* 2nd ed. Cambridge, MA: MIT Press, 2018.

Naughton, Barry, and Kellee S. Tsai, eds. *State Capitalism, Institutional Adaptation, and the Chinese Miracle.* New York: Cambridge University Press, 2015.

Nee, Victor, and Sonja Opper. *Capitalism from Below: Markets and Institutional Change in China.* Cambridge, MA: Harvard University Press, 2012.

Neilson, Brett and Ned Rossiter. "Precarity as a Political Concept, or Fordism as Exception." *Theory, Culture and Society* 25, nos. 7-8 (2008): 51-72.

Ness, Immanuel. *Southern Insurgency: The Coming of the Global Working Class.* London: Pluto Press, 2016.

Nowak, Jörg. *Mass Strikes and Social Movements in Brazil and India: Popular Mobilisation in the Long Depression.* Cham, Switzerland: Palgrave Macmillan, 2019.

Ovetz, Robert, ed. *Workers' Inquiry and Global Class Struggle: Strategies, Tactics, Objectives.* London: Pluto Press, 2020.

Pei, Min-Xin. "Labour's Battle for Political Space: The Role of Worker Associations in Contemporary China." In *Urban Spaces in Contemporary China: The Potential for Autonomy and Community in Post-Mao China,* edited by Deborah S. Davis, Richard Kraus, Barry Naughton, and Elizabeth J. Perry, 302–25. Washington, DC: Woodrow Wilson Centre Press and Cambridge: Cambridge University Press, 1995.

Pena, Devon G. *The Terror of the Machine: Technology, Work, Gender, and Ecology on the U.S.-Mexico Border.* Austin: CMAS Books, the Center for Mexican American Studies, the University of Texas at Austin, 1997.

Perlin, Ross. *Intern Nation: How to Earn Nothing and Learn Little in the Brave New Economy.* Updated ed. London: Verso, 2012.

Perry, Elizabeth J. *Challenging the Mandate of Heaven: Social Protest and State Power in China.* Armonk, NY: M. E. Sharpe, 2002.

———. *Shanghai on Strike: The Politics of Chinese Labor.* Stanford, CA: Stanford University Press, 1993.

Perry, Elizabeth J., and Mark Selden, eds. *Chinese Society: Change, Conflict and Resistance.* 3rd ed. London: Routledge, 2010.

Piven, Frances Fox, and Richard Cloward. "Collective Protest: A Critique of Resource Mobilization Theory." *International Journal of Politics, Culture, and Society* 4, no. 4 (1991): 435–58.

———. *Poor People's Movements: Why They Succeed and How They Fail.* New York: Pantheon Books, 1977.

Polanyi, Karl. *The Great Transformation: The Political and Economic Origins of Our Time.* Boston: Beacon Press, 2001.

Pringle, Tim. *Trade Unions in China: The Challenge of Labour Unrest.* Abingdon, Oxon, UK: Routledge, 2011.

Pun, Ngai. *Made in China: Women Factory Workers in a Global Workplace.* Durham, NC: Duke University Press, 2005.

Pun, Ngai, Rutvica Andrijasevic, and Devi Sacchetto. 2020. "Transgressing North-South Divide: Foxconn Production Regimes in China and the Czech Republic." *Critical Sociology* 46. no. 2 (2020): 307–22.

Qiu, Jack Linchuan. *Goodbye iSlave: A Manifesto for Digital Abolition.* Urbana: University of Illinois Press, 2016.

Quentin, David, and Liam Campling. "Global Inequality Chains: Integrating Mechanisms of Value Distribution into Analyses of Global Production." *Global Networks* 18, no. 1 (2018): 33–56.

Raphael, Chad, and Ted Smith. "The Future of Activism for Electronics Workers." In *The Routledge Companion to Labor and Media,* edited by Richard Maxwell, 327–42. New York: Routledge, 2016.

Riskin, Carl, "China's Human Development after Socialism." In *The Cambridge History of Communism,* vol. 3, edited by Juliane Fürst, Silvio Pons, and Mark Selden, 474–501. Cambridge: Cambridge University Press, 2017.

Roediger, David R., and Elizabeth D. Esch. *The Production of Difference: Race and the Management of Labor in U.S. History.* Oxford: Oxford University Press, 2012.

Ross, Andrew. *Low Pay, High Profile: The Global Push for Fair Labor.* New York: The New Press, 2004.

Roth, Karl Heinz, ed. *On the Road to Global Labor History: A Festschrift for Marcel van der Linden.* Leiden, The Netherlands: Koninklijke Brill NV, 2017.

Rozelle, Scott, and Natalie Johnson. *China's Invisible Crisis: How a Growing Urban-Rural Divide Could Sink the World's Second-Largest Economy.* New York: Basic Books, 2019.

Sargeson, Sally. *Reworking China's Proletariat.* Houndmills, UK: Macmillan Press, 1999.

Seidman, Gay W. *Beyond the Boycott: Labor Rights, Human Rights, and Transnational Activism.* New York: Russell Sage Foundation, 2007.

———. *Manufacturing Militance: Workers' Movements in Brazil and South Africa, 1970–1985.* Berkeley: University of California Press, 1994.

Selden, Mark. "China, Japan, and the Regional Political Economy of East Asia, 1945–1995." In *Network Power: Japan and Asia*, edited by Peter J. Katzenstein and Takashi Shiraishi, 306–40. Ithaca, NY: Cornell University Press, 1997.

———. *The Political Economy of Chinese Development.* Armonk, NY: M. E. Sharpe, 1993.

———. "The Proletariat, Revolutionary Change, and the State in China and Japan." In *Labor in the World Social Structure*, edited by Immanuel Wallerstein, 58–120. Beverly Hills, CA: Sage, 1983.

Selwyn, Benjamin. "Poverty Chains and Global Capitalism." *Competition & Change* 23, no. 1 (2019): 71–97.

———. *The Struggle for Development.* Cambridge, UK: Polity Press, 2017.

Sennett, Richard, and Jonathan Cobb. *The Hidden Injuries of Class.* Reprint ed. New York: W. W. Norton & Company, 1993.

Shaffer, Lynda Norene. *Mao and the Workers: The Hunan Labor Movement, 1920–23.* Armonk, NY: M. E. Sharpe, 1982.

Sharif, Naubahar, and Yu Huang. "Industrial Automation in China's 'Workshop of the World.'" *China Journal* 81 (January 2019): 1–22.

Shirk, Susan L. *The Political Logic of Economic Reform in China.* Berkeley: University of California Press, 1993.

Silver, Beverly J. *Forces of Labor: Workers' Movements and Globalization since 1870.* Cambridge: Cambridge University Press, 2003.

Sklair, Leslie. *Assembling for Development: The Maquila Industry in Mexico and the United States.* Boston: Unwin Hyman, 1989.

———. "Social Movements and Global Capitalism." In *The Cultures of Globalization,* edited by Frederic Jameson and Masao Miyoshi, 291–311. Durham, NC: Duke University Press, 1998.

Smith, Richard. *Green Capitalism: The God That Failed.* Bristol, UK: World Economics Association, 2016.

Smith, Steve A. *Like Cattle and Horses: Nationalism and Labor in Shanghai, 1895–1927.* Durham, NC: Duke University Press, 2002.

Smith, Ted, David A. Sonnenfeld, and David Naguib Pellow, eds. *Challenging the Chip: Labor Rights and Environmental Justice in the Global Electronics Industry.* Philadelphia: Temple University Press, 2006.

Smith, Ted, and Chad Raphael. "Health and Safety Policies for Electronics Workers." In *The Routledge Companion to Labor and Media*, edited by Richard Maxwell, 78–90. New York: Routledge, 2016.

Smith, Vicki. *Crossing the Great Divide: Worker Risk and Opportunities in the New Economy.* Ithaca, NY: Cornell University Press, 2001.

So, Alvin Y., and Yin-wah Chu. *The Global Rise of China.* Cambridge, UK: Polity Press, 2016.

Solinger, Dorothy J. *Contesting Citizenship in Urban China: Peasant Migrants, the State, and the Logic of the Market.* Berkeley: University of California Press, 1999.

———. *States' Gains, Labor's Losses: China, France, and Mexico Choose Global Liaisons, 1980–2000.* Ithaca, NY: Cornell University Press, 2009.

———, ed. *Polarized Cities: Portraits of Rich and Poor in Urban China.* Lanham, MD: Rowman and Littlefield, 2019.

Sorace, Christian, Ivan Franceschini, and Nicholas Loubere, eds. *Afterlives of Chinese Communism: Political Concepts from Mao to Xi.* Canberra, AU: Australian National University Press, and London: Verso, 2019.

Standing, Guy. *The Precariat: The New Dangerous Class.* London: Bloomsbury Academic, 2011.

Starosta, Guido. "The Outsourcing of Manufacturing and the Rise of Giant Global Contractors: A Marxian Approach to Some Recent Transformations of Global Value Chains." *New Political Economy* 15, no. 4 (2010): 543–63.

Stewart, Paul, Mike Richardson, Andy Danford, Ken Murphy, Tony Richardson, and Vicki Wass. *We Sell Our Time No More: Workers' Struggles against Lean Production in the British Car Industry.* London: Pluto Press, 2009.

Su, Yang, and Xin He. "Street as Courtroom: State Accommodation of Labor Protest in South China." *Law and Society Review* 44, no. 1 (2010): 157–84.

Sun, Wanning, and Ling Yang, eds. *Love Stories in China: The Politics of Intimacy in the Twenty-First Century.* Abingdon, Oxon, UK: Routledge, 2020.

Swider, Sarah. *Building China: Informal Work and the New Precariat.* Ithaca, NY: Cornell University Press, 2015.

Tanner, Murray Scot. "China Rethinks Unrest." *Washington Quarterly* 27, no. 3 (2004): 137–56.

Tarrow, Sidney. *Power in Movement: Social Movements and Contentious Politics.* Revised and updated 3rd ed. Cambridge: Cambridge University Press, 2011.

Taylor, Bill, and Qi Li. "Is the ACFTU a Union and Does It Matter?" *Journal of Industrial Relations* 49, no. 5 (2007): 701–15.

Taylor, Frederick Winslow. *The Principles of Scientific Management.* Unabridged republication. Mineola, NY: Dover Publications, 1998.

Taylor, Phil, Kirsty Newsome, and Al Rainnie. "'Putting Labour in Its Place': Global Value Chains and Labour Process Analysis." *Competition & Change* 17, no. 1 (2013): 1–5.

Thompson, E. P. *The Making of the English Working Class.* New York: Vintage, 1963.

Tilly, Charles. "Globalization Threatens Labor's Rights." *International Labor and Working-Class History* 47 (1995): 1–23.

———. "Models and Realities of Popular Collective Action." *Social Research* 52, no. 4 (1985): 717–47.

Tsutsui, William M. *Manufacturing Ideology: Scientific Management in Twentieth-Century Japan.* Princeton, NJ: Princeton University Press, 1998.

van der Pijl, Kees, ed. *Handbook of the International Political Economy of Production.* Cheltenham, UK: Edward Elgar, 2015.

Walder, Andrew G. *Communist Neo-Traditionalism: Work and Authority in Chinese Industry.* Berkeley: University of California Press, 1986.

Walder, Andrew G., and Gong Xiaoxia. "Workers in the Tiananmen Protests: The Politics of the Beijing Workers' Autonomous Federation." *Australian Journal of Chinese Affairs* (now known as *The China Journal*) 29 (January 1993): 1–29.

Wallerstein, Immanuel. "Upsurge in Movements around the Globe." In *We Are Many: Reflections on Movement Strategy from Occupation to Liberation*, edited by Kate Khatib, Margaret Killjoy, and Mike McGuire, 104–14. California: AK Press, 2012.

Walter, Andrew, and Xiaoke Zhang, eds. *East Asian Capitalism: Diversity, Continuity, and Change.* Oxford: Oxford University Press, 2012.

Waters, Sarah. "A Capitalism That Kills: Workplace Suicides at France Telecom." *French Politics, Culture & Society* 32, no. 3 (2014): 121–41.

Webster, Edward, Rob Lambert, and Andries Bezuidenhout. *Grounding Globalization: Labour in the Age of Insecurity.* Malden, MA: Blackwell, 2008.

Wedeman, Andrew. "Unrest and Regime Survival." In *Handbook of Protest and Resistance in China*, edited by Teresa Wright, 12–26. Cheltenham, UK: Edward Elgar Publishing, 2019.

White, Gordon. "Restructuring the Working Class: Labor Reform in Post-Mao China." In *Marxism and the Chinese Experience*, edited by Arif Dirlik and Maurice Meisner, 152–68. Armonk, NY: M. E. Sharpe, 1989.

Whyte, Martin King. "The Changing Role of Workers." In *The Paradox of China's Post-Mao Reforms*, edited by Merle Goldman and Roderick MacFarquhar, 173–96. Cambridge, MA: Harvard University Press, 1999.

Woronov, T. E. *Class Work: Vocational Schools and China's Urban Youth.* Stanford, CA: Stanford University Press, 2016.

Wright, Erik Olin. "Working-Class Power, Capitalist-Class Interests, and Class Compromise." *American Journal of Sociology* 105, no. 4 (2000): 957–1002.

Wright, Teresa, ed. *Handbook of Resistance and Protest in China.* Cheltenham, UK: Edward Elgar Publishing, 2019.

Wu, Weiping, and Mark Frazier, eds. *The SAGE Handbook on Contemporary China.* Thousand Oaks, CA: Sage, 2018.

Yeung, Henry Wai-chung. *Strategic Coupling: East Asian Industrial Transformation in the New Global Economy.* Ithaca, NY: Cornell University Press, 2016.

———, ed. *Globalizing Regional Development in East Asia: Production Networks, Clusters, and Entrepreneurship.* London: Routledge, 2010.

Zhan, Shaohua. "What Determines Migrant Workers' Life Chances in Contemporary China? Hukou, Social Exclusion, and the Market." *Modern China* 37, no. 3 (2011): 243–85.

Zhang, Lu. *Inside China's Automobile Factories: The Politics of Labor and Worker Resistance.* New York: Cambridge University Press, 2015.

Index

About the Authors

JENNY CHAN (PhD, 2014) is an Assistant Professor of Sociology at the Hong Kong Polytechnic University. Prior to joining the university, she was a Lecturer of Sociology and Contemporary China Studies, and a Junior Research Fellow of Kellogg College, University of Oxford. She serves as the Vice President of the International Sociological Association's Research Committee on Labour Movements (2018–2022). Her articles have been published in *Critical Sociology, Current Sociology, Modern China, Rural China,* the *China Review, Critical Asian Studies, Globalizations, Human Relations,* the *South Atlantic Quarterly, Inter-Asia Cultural Studies, Journal of Labor and Society,* the *Asia-Pacific Journal, Global Labour Journal, New Labor Forum, New Politics, New Technology, Work and Employment (NTWE),* and other edited volumes.

MARK SELDEN is a Research Associate at Cornell University and Columbia University. He is Editor of the *Asia-Pacific Journal.* His research encompasses the modern and contemporary geopolitics, political economy, and history of China, Japan, and the Asia Pacific, ranging broadly across themes of war and revolution,

inequality, development, environment, precarity, social move-
ments, regional and world social change, and historical memory.
He is the author or editor of more than thirty books, including
China in Revolution: The Yenan Way Revisited; *The Political Economy
of Chinese Development*; *Chinese Village, Socialist State*; *Chinese Society:
Change, Conflict and Resistance*; *The Resurgence of East Asia: 500, 150
and 50 Year Perspectives*; and *The Cambridge History of Communism*.
His homepage is www.markselden.info.

 PUN NGAI is a Professor of Sociology
at the University of Hong Kong. She
is the author of *Made in China: Women
Factory Workers in a Global Workplace*
(2005), which received the C. W. Mills
Award and was translated into French,
German, Italian, Polish, and Chinese.
Her second book is *Migrant Labor in
China: Post-Socialist Transformations*
(2016). She has published numerous articles in *Modern China,* the
China Journal, the *China Quarterly*, *China Perspectives,* the *Global La-
bour Journal*, *Cultural Anthropology*, *Positions*, *Feminist Economics*, *Cur-
rent Sociology*, *Inter-Asia Cultural Studies*, the *South Atlantic Quarterly*,
the *Third World Quarterly*, the *British Journal of Sociology of Education*,
Information, Communication & Society (ICS), and *Work, Employment and
Society (WES)*, among others.

About Haymarket Books

Haymarket Books is a radical, independent, nonprofit book publisher based in Chicago. Our mission is to publish books that contribute to struggles for social and economic justice. We strive to make our books a vibrant and organic part of social movements and the education and development of a critical, engaged, international left.

We take inspiration and courage from our namesakes, the Haymarket martyrs, who gave their lives fighting for a better world. Their 1886 struggle for the eight-hour day—which gave us May Day, the international workers' holiday—reminds workers around the world that ordinary people can organize and struggle for their own liberation. These struggles continue today across the globe—struggles against oppression, exploitation, poverty, and war.

Since our founding in 2001, Haymarket Books has published more than five hundred titles. Radically independent, we seek to drive a wedge into the risk-averse world of corporate book publishing. Our authors include Noam Chomsky, Arundhati Roy, Rebecca Solnit, Angela Y. Davis, Howard Zinn, Amy Goodman, Wallace Shawn, Mike Davis, Winona LaDuke, Ilan Pappé, Richard Wolff, Dave Zirin, Keeanga-Yamahtta Taylor, Nick Turse, Dahr Jamail, David Barsamian, Elizabeth Laird, Amira Hass, Mark Steel, Avi Lewis, Naomi Klein, and Neil Davidson. We are also the trade publishers of the acclaimed Historical Materialism Book Series and of Dispatch Books.

Also Available from Haymarket Books

Bit Tyrants: The Political Economy of Silicon Valley
Rob Larson

Building Global Labor Solidarity in a Time of Accelerating Globalization
Edited by Kim Scipes

China on Strike: Narratives of Workers' Resistance
Edited by Hao Ren
English edition edited by Zhongjin Li and Eli Friedman

Extracting Profit: Imperialism, Neoliberalism,
and the New Scramble for Africa
Lee Wengraf

Live Working or Die Fighting: How the Working Class Went Global
Paul Mason

On New Terrain: How Capital Is Reshaping the Battleground of Class War
Kim Moody

Striving to Survive: Workers' Resistance to Factory Relocations in China
Fan Shigang, introduction by Sam Austin and Pun Ngai